T0051643

PRAISE FOR
REHEARSALS FOR LIVING

"Lyrical, visionary, and transcendent . . . While chronicling the continuing unfolding calamities of settler colonialism and racial capitalism with care and razor-sharp clarity, Simpson and Maynard point readers to portals for different futures through the infinite possibilities of Black-Indigenous resistance."
—Andrea J. Ritchie, author of *Invisible No More: Police Violence Against Black Women and Women of Color*

"Simpson and Maynard draw out a political vision that emerges from epistolary connections—letters, animated by stories, that seek out, engage, imagine, and narrate different kinds and types of liberation. Accentuated by entangled Black-Indigenous histories and geographies, *Rehearsals for Living* actualizes friendship as correspondence, modeling a mode of togetherness that we can practice, learn from, and revise."
—Katherine McKittrick, author of *Demonic Grounds* and *Dear Science and Other Stories*

"A profound and sublime work of memory, witnessing, refusal, dreaming. In the trenchant tradition of Black and Indigenous feminisms, this brilliant book moves us away from the language of crisis or victimhood to the precise and intimate encounters of kinship and liberation. The letters between Maynard and Simpson magnificently shapeshift and engage on multiple levels, and in doing so, rigorously demand an accounting for horrific violences while illuminating lives and worlds anew. A masterclass in literary form, ethical orientations, and collective futures."
—Harsha Walia, author of *Border and Rule: Global Migration, Capitalism, and the Rise of Racist Nationalism*

"The beautifully named *Rehearsals for Living* is a gift conjured by a pair of brilliant scholars during the dark days and months of the pandemic, lit by a powerful resistance movement, fueled and rendered magical by a profound and challenging dialogue that offers ways to collectively think and be and act in a chaotic world."
—Roxanne Dunbar-Ortiz, author of *An Indigenous Peoples' History of the United States*

ROBYN MAYNARD

Rehearsals for living

LEANNE BETASAMOSAKE SIMPSON

HAYMARKET BOOKS
CHICAGO, ILLINOIS

Published simultaneously in Canada by Knopf Canada / Penguin Random House Canada

Published in 2022 by
Haymarket Books
P.O. Box 180165
Chicago, IL 60618
773-583-7884
www.haymarketbooks.org
info@haymarketbooks.org

ISBN: 978-1-64259-689-2

Distributed to the trade in the US through Consortium Book Sales and Distribution (www.cbsd.com) and internationally through Ingram Publisher Services International (www.ingramcontent.com).

This book was published with the generous support of Lannan Foundation and Wallace Action Fund.

Special discounts are available for bulk purchases by organizations and institutions. Please email info@haymarketbooks.org for more information.

Cover artwork courtesy of Howardena Pindell and Garth Greenan Gallery, New York.
Cover and text design by Kate Sinclair.

Printed in Canada by union labor.

Library of Congress Cataloging-in-Publication data is available.

10 9 8 7 6 5 4 3 2 1

To Lamar, Minowewebeneshiinh and Nishna.

THE ABOLITIONIST PAPERS SERIES

Edited by Naomi Murakawa

Also in this series:

Change Everything:
Racial Capitalism and the Case for Abolition
Ruth Wilson Gilmore

Abolition. Feminism. Now.
Angela Y. Davis, Gina Dent,
Erica R. Meiners, and Beth E. Richie

We Do This 'Til We Free Us:
Abolitionist Organizing and Transforming Justice
Mariame Kaba

CONTENTS

FOREWORD

Ruth Wilson Gilmore

Spectacles

Robyn Maynard and Leanne Betasamosake Simpson's beautiful book helped me see something I had not quite seen before. For some years now I've offered a lecture called "Meanwhile: Making Abolition Geographies." The lecture's basic principle goes something like this: abolition is life in rehearsal because freedom is a place. Sometimes the lecture stretches out into several talks, and other times it's a one off. The content changes but the structure is consistent. On most occasions I'll invoke issues specific to where my hosts are located to help listeners "see" what I'm talking about with some immediacy. So, lectures have referenced the Chicago Teachers' Strike, Brazil's Landless Workers' Movement (MST), solidarity with South African self-built communities, Water Protectors at Standing Rock, nurses' unions building a global movement hospital-by-hospital and country-by-country, and so on.

Although most of the content in "Meanwhile" is about relatively recent occurrences, it is a historical geography of the future. In other words, the purpose isn't to document that a specific thing happened, but rather to offer thickly analytical, detailed descriptions of many different ways people arrive at arranging themselves into a social force—whether in California, or Portugal, or the Black Atlantic, or North America, or South Asia. The social-spatial fights, connecting past to present, are waged by farmworkers or public sector unions, environmental justice activists or schoolchildren, long distance migrants, care workers, households and communities, transport workers, people in prison, detention, and jail, students, sex workers, formerly and currently incarcerated people and their loved ones, Indigenous peoples fighting for true decolonization, and people who claim space by occupying land in urban and rural areas of the global south (wherever in the world that may be). Any of those places, and more, can figure in the historical geographies of the future, by making abolition geographies as we go.

In short, the purpose of "Making Abolition Geographies" is to say: See? Abolition is presence, and also process. Therefore, by moving our attention from place to place it's possible to sketch out the shape and vitality of an internationalist movement in process of becoming itself. Each segment, then, consists of patiently explaining the conditions under which people who might have set out to do one thing to improve a situation persisted by also, often unexpectedly, doing something else along the way. Each segment lays out a plot of time and space with narrative detail, in which people become excited by the possibility of change and surprised by where the dramatic incidents of change-in-motion might have sent them. They bend courses, because practice makes different. Any of the stories can therefore become a model for others. We know that people use elements and provocations from many aspects of life—material and symbolic—to make sense of specific challenges, and to assemble impulses into patterns that help, short term or longer, to bend our course through constellations of forces, toward eventually becoming constellations ourselves.

The *Rehearsals for Living* you hold in your hands helped me better to see what I've been trying to do with my lectures. Let me explain. While some of the episodes in "Meanwhile" are big, and even noisy, they tend not to be spectacles of the type that, widespread, gripped so much planetary attention in the wake of George Floyd's murder in 2020. Those spectacles matter: we revolt because we cannot breathe, and people take to the streets in the effort to clear up the organized abandonment and organized violence that condense the weight of centuries. All true. And yet, because I've been nearsighted my entire life, I also think of spectacles as eyeglasses—lenses that sharpen focus onto small or blurry or distant details. In combination, these two kinds of spectacles support practical remedy, as instruments that help with vision—with the ability to see things we would miss without them. When I read *Rehearsals for Living*, spectacles in this double sense charted my course as I bent over the expansive meditations gracing every page. And there's a third spectacle I can see here: a constantly unfolding drama, whose lines and characters and spaces remain thrillingly unfixed, underlying "life in rehearsal." Robyn Maynard and

Leanne Betasamosake Simpson embody and express how practice makes different. Nobody has to become them as we become us. This necessary book is a model—through the shared process of two brilliant thinkers it gifts us clarity to see rehearsals otherwise and elsewhere.

Lisbon, November 15, 2021

PART ONE

On Letter Writing, Commune,
and the End of (This) World

Dear Leanne,

About five years ago now, I sat down with a copy of your book, *As We Have Always Done*. I'd planned to flip through the first few pages over my morning coffee. In the end, though, I stayed put, reading almost the whole text in one go, and was suddenly overcome with a strong feeling that I wanted to know you. Your words beckoned me to join you in what you called "constellations of co-resistance": constellations that affirmed life and world-making in a time of acute racial violence. We spoke on the phone shortly after. I remember that I was in a Subway restaurant in downtown Montreal, squatting the free Wi-Fi to do a final fact-check of some op-ed I'd written. I could barely make out your voice over the very loud—and very bad—music. I don't recall the details of what we talked about, but I know that I have wanted to chart old and new constellations with you ever since.

I've been meaning to write you for a long time, and yet it's hard to know where to begin. So I guess I will start where I'm at: I can't stop doom-scrolling the multiple crises of our time.

At this moment, I'm preoccupied and filled with dread by the reports of rising temperatures, the just-about-last chances regularly announced by climate scientists, the continually shelved fact that things must be drastically and immediately shifted if we are to avoid "untold suffering." I'm preoccupied with what goes unwritten in so many reports, but what I know in my bones: some communities' "untold suffering" will vastly exceed that experienced by others. Some communities have been facing "untold suffering" for multiple generations.

I don't want to live in this preoccupation, in this dread that sometimes comes to visit me and threatens to immobilize. So I suppose this is me reaching out, simply, for a levelling of the grounds beneath my feet. For communion. To help transform the source of this dread into a place from which we can, instead, plot, conspire, dream, and attend to life, *otherwise*. To attend to the celebration, the preservation of life, without eliding our own communities' intimate proximity to death and loss. Talking and thinking with you has always helped me focus on the vitality, the livingness of the traditions that our work emerges from, regardless of what the last several centuries of European atrocities have wreaked on our peoples. Our conversations are a salve against the sharp edges of everyday life. But I don't see you as much as I would like, and the phone is not my medium. So I've decided to write you this letter. I'm writing you a letter even though it feels cringey because I'm shy. I'm writing you a letter even though I may never send it, even though you may never write me back.

I am writing to you a letter at the end of (this) world.

From Cyclone Idai in Malawi, Mozambique and Zimbabwe to Hurricane Dorian in the Bahamas, the devastating forest fires displacing Indigenous communities from the Amazon rainforest through to the Mishkeegogamang Ojibway Nation in Northwest Ontario, our respective communities—that is, Black and Indigenous communities—are collectively positioned on the very forefront of the unfolding catastrophe.

It would require a deliberate obfuscation to view the racially uneven distribution of harms that the climate collapse engenders as accidental. Even if we didn't take into account the melting of Arctic ice caps, rising sea waters, and eroded shorelines, desertification, and species extinction that are now nearly, if not totally, inevitable, the reality is that not only are an array of world-endings already before us: *they have already arrived.* Our respective communities have borne, already, multiple apocalypses that were inflicted upon us, if un-identically, from the "barbarity time" of genocide/slavery/settler colonialism. The apocalypse is imagined, after all, in most classic Euro-Western settler tropes, in terms of the lack of clean drinking water, the destruction of the places "we" (they) live, the poisoning of the earth, inhumane and restrictive responses to people left hungry, displaced, in desperation: this is a condition that is already deeply familiar to our kin across Turtle Island and globally. You wrote about this in *Dancing On Our Turtle's Back:* "By 1822—when many Nishnaabeg in the north and the west were still living as they always had—we were facing the complete political, cultural, and social collapse of everything we had ever known. My ancestors resisted and survived what must have seemed like an apocalyptic reality of occupation and subjugation in a context where they had few choices." To remix Public Enemy, "Armageddon-been-in-effect": it is the apocalypses of slavery and settler colonialism that bind our collective pasts and presents together in the calamity at hand.

Today, the racially uneven environmental catastrophes of the present are inextricably connected to the unfinished catastrophes of 1492—the two genocides at the heart of the Americas, to paraphrase M. NourbeSe Philip, when a death-making commitment to extraction and dispossession took hold on a global scale. In this burgeoning global logic and political economy, our ancestors became, through distinct but interrelated processes, what Cedric J. Robinson once described as "a collection of things of convenience for use and/or eradication." The factory of post-apocalyptic life that has unfolded its dramas over the last half millennium means that our collective histories are mapped out, too, onto the racially and geographically differentiated vulnerabilities amidst the present-future disaster.

As we are confronted with the crisis of the earth's viability, then, amidst so many crises, I am writing you so we can think together about what it means for us to build livable lives together in the wreckage.

AS I WRITE YOU FROM THE end of this world, I'm also very aware both of our respective, if unidentical, subject positions as domestic enemies of and inside the settler-state, and of our presence within one of the main arteries of Western empire. I am writing to you from the belly of the beast. Despite its pretensions of being a "benevolent" nation-state, Canada plays an important role in the massive carbon unloading, and the ecological and human devastation wrought by extractive industries. These industries produce over 50 percent of the world's carbon emissions, not to mention the cataclysmic environmental devastation of the tar sands pipelines that run through more than 350 Indigenous nations in so-called Canada alone. Much of the unmaking of Black and Indigenous lives and the ecosystems that have historically sustained our lives, spanning Turtle Island, the Caribbean, Africa, and South and Central America, can be traced right back here.

In fact, while I am haunted by the spectre of the pending crises, there is something about our sheer physical proximity to the authors of these monstrosities that is weighing heavily on me. Out of a mix of curiosity and compulsion, I created a Google Maps itinerary to figure out how long it would take me to travel from my house to some of the places where our collective apocalypses are being drawn up. A kind of a walking tour that maps out some of the contemporary architects of the warfare against human and non-human life. As it turns out, it would take one hour and twelve minutes to walk (twenty-eight minutes on the TTC) from my home to the main office of James Bay Resources Limited. While this is not a household name, James Bay is a Canadian company that is based in the Niger Delta region that is the homelands of the Ogoni people. In the Delta and across the region, gas flares resulting from oil extraction burn off CO_2 emissions comparable to the annual output of Sweden. It is a site of both racial and ecological destruction: mutated food crops, toxic drinking water, rainwater that melts through the tin roofs of people's homes, and a wide assortment of permanent human and non-human health crises. Of course, even as this site of transnational anti-Black violence produces flares that are visible from space, there is no discernable trace of this at its company headquarters in Toronto (that would be "uncivilized"). Enabling Google Street View, it is clear that little evidence links the decisions made in this metropolitan office to the crimes enacted "over there": we see a medium-rise grey building, flanked by two Starbucks cafés and underground parking.

Anyways. Leaving this office on foot, it would only take me eight minutes to walk to the headquarters of Barrick Gold, another Toronto-based company. The headquarters lack grandeur, at least from the outside—the building is a sprawling high-rise with a face of green-tinted glass windows—but Barrick is a Big Deal for the Canadian economy. In 2018, they made a profit of $7.24 billion, and were prepared to pay their new CEO $18-million US in 2019. They are also a Big Deal as the bringers of premature death, a Big Deal in the *thieffing* of Black lives, their executives' annual bonuses siphoned from the poisoned bodies and lands of those globally marked as *surplus*. While in the headlines less than in the past, Barrick Gold, of course, is the majority owner of Acacia Mining, its sites marked by an array of environmental and human atrocities against the local Tanzanian population, largely of the Indigenous Kuria community, where human rights organizations have attested to an array of sexual and physical abuses by company-run security, as well as a body count that continues to rise, reaching, according to state officials, several hundred extrajudicial murders since the late 1990s. The heavy metals and toxins produced at the site seep into the river, soil, and nearby air of the 70,000 people who live nearby. Yet the transnational links between this Toronto office and the world-endings, the unceasing onslaught of Black dispossession, elsewhere, escape my field of vision.

Nine minutes after leaving this office-front, where I would see nothing and feel everything, I would arrive at the headquarters of Belo Sun Mining Corporation. Here my Street View seems to glitch, only showing me the front of a seemingly closed dollar store called "Rainbow Jade" inside of what appears to be a mini-mall. But honestly, this does not matter, I know that I am not likely missing much, even as this company is set to build Brazil's largest open-pit gold mine, the Volta Grande mine, in the heart of the still-burning Amazon rainforest (you can see these fires, too, from NASA cameras in space). This mine, this future abomination that is orchestrated from somewhere probably close to "Rainbow Jade," will leach toxins into the lands and waters of the Indigenous Juruna and Arara peoples, who have opposed the mine and are labouring for the ongoing survival of their peoples. But bad news for Indigenous peoples is good news for colonizers everywhere: following the election of white-supremacist president Jair Bolsonaro, a

CBC News tweet declared that "Critics have lambasted the former paratrooper for his homophobic, racist and misogynist statements, but his government could open new investment opportunities" for Canadian investors.

(colonizer meet colonizer.)

It does not take great imagination to say that if I can't, virtually, see this building, it is probably either grey or brownish or whiteish, probably tall, and it wouldn't take much time to take it in. And only one (!) minute after leaving this building—whatever it really looks like—even as I've crossed a *hemisphere* in terms of impact, I will find myself at the last stop: the headquarters of Copper One (yet another high-rise). Currently undertaking a legal battle against the Algonquins of Barrière Lake to mine the resources on their traditional hunting grounds, Copper One is not yet dissuaded, despite years of community resistance in the form of blockades and legal challenges. Anyways.

You might note that this tour starts and ends somewhat arbitrarily. It could go on all day, what with more than one thousand mining companies based in Canada (with more than 50 percent of the world's mining companies traded through the Toronto Stock Exchange, to be precise). This tour of invisible carnage shows us that Toronto really *is* the global hub that it is so widely celebrated to be. It is on and around Bay Street that we find the direct lines between capitalist accumulation and those racial subjects whose lands and labours are *being* accumulated and poisoned. It also shows us that the climate crisis is not "coming"—for some, its arrival began long ago.

All of this in ninety minutes—likely less, because I am a fast walker. I am drawn to this walk that links Toronto and the settler nation-state to the global flows of capital accumulation emerging from racial and ecological assaults, largely—but not exclusively—on Black and Indigenous lives, both here and a multitude of elsewheres. Maybe we will walk this route together, sometime. I think I would like to. But I am not sure why I keep refreshing the browser expecting for something more to reveal itself to me, as I look for some trace or hint of the barbarism behind the veneer. Of course this is fruitless: Toronto, like the Canadian society it encapsulates, keeps the violence on which it relies firmly out of view, a perfectly modern society that tidily keeps its atrocities out of plain sight. This absent and absented violence is what it is to look upon the house of "the modern barbarian," walking in and amongst their streets, while, to use the words of Aimé Césaire, "the hour of the barbarian is at hand." Even if I were to enter these unremarkable buildings, they would probably just be filled with the dead-eyed graduates of schools like the U of T Peter Munk School of Global Affairs (named after Barrick Gold's former CEO), who likely spend their lunch breaks stalking their ex-girlfriends' Instagram accounts, posting on 4chan, and sending unsolicited dick pics: the modern technocrats of empire. I know that I will make this pilgrimage on my own at some point, possibly before I send you this letter. I also know that I will be disappointed, and then irritated with myself for being disappointed, and then devastated at the state of the world that white supremacy built.

I suppose that part of my frustration, and why I continue to return to these (e-)locations looking for something, fucking *anything*, is that it is hard to believe that this—THIS—is what is to show for the accumulated catastrophes of our past-presents, our ancestors' lives and bodies and dreams of otherwise being funnelled—accumulated—toward these undifferentiated grey masses of rock, brick, steel and glass filled with undifferentiated living (just barely) pink-grey masses of human-shaped greed. It is difficult to let it sink in—that it is for this that so many of us are dead and are dying. That should we make it through this, our great-grandkids will have to look at pictures of this unremarkable landscape, these boring and unimaginative tributes to stolen wealth and stolen lives, to make sense of the who, why, and where of it all.

I am acutely aware that it is our collective destruction as Black subjects, as Indigenous subjects, along with the rest of the global *wretched of the earth*, that is being drawn up in these boardrooms of global finance (and theirs and their grandchildren's too, though they are too arrogant to see this).

The IPCC reports bring to light what is to come: previously unknown levels of fires, floods, droughts, famines, and shortages of all kinds. A planetary crisis on multiple frequencies, the state and corporate ruling classes working together to commit and recommit the planet, anew, to death or near-death.

And for some this has long been clear. In the words of Nigerian activist and scholar Oladosu Adenike, "the crisis is already here": in Nigeria, on the continent. The major famine that struck Somalia in 2011 was in part a result, climate scientists suggest, of global warming. Several African island nations—Mauritius, Cape Verde, and Seychelles—are slated to face flooding, to eventually disappear entirely underwater, as sea levels rise a result of climate change. Audre Lorde wrote several decades ago, now, that "[w]e are Black people living in a time when the consciousness of our intended slaughter is all around us." To be aware of the ongoing possibility of imminent world-endings is part of what constitutes and has constituted Black (and Indigenous) life globally for five centuries. Her words take on a renewed urgency in the calamity at hand.

And yet even as the final assault on the viability of the earth is being authored on the many Bay Streets of the global north, this is being called the Anthropocene: a crisis caused by *human* activity that puts *human* life at risk. This is an affront! Because it is not "humans," is it? The Human has never been a politically neutral category. In this anthropocentric framing of the climate crisis it is important to ask: Who, exactly, is imagined as a human?

I'm not immune from this slippage, of course. I sometimes bring my son L. to the Leslie Spit, a beach, ish, in Toronto. I don't know if you've been there; I visit it semifrequently because it's not too far and I'm afraid of driving, but I like to spend as much time outdoors as I can. While he and I meander near the water collecting "treasure" (rocks) for him to bring home, I often muse that perhaps this is what this city would look like after humans, that this is how the earth might begin to recover itself. The brown-grey sand is lined with rebar, large chunks of concrete. I have let L. go barefoot here, but warily, me carefully scrutinizing the ground beneath his feet as his lean brown legs propel him freely in and out of the shallow water. The beach pebbles are mixed in with ground-up bricks and chunks of glass, most but not all of their hard edges softened over time. Broken tiles mixed throughout the sand and rocks have re-emerged to look, almost but not quite, like the stones that they were forged from. It's beautiful somehow, despite feeling somewhat post-apocalyptic: like the ghost of an abandoned city that the environment is slowly taking back. It has a hopeful feel, to me: like if we ruined this earth through greed and gross irresponsibility, it would find a way to recover itself without people in the way. As I point this out to my son, trying to use language that makes sense to a four-year-old, I always need to catch myself; I do not want to teach us the wrong lesson. It's an easy slippage, and one with deadly implications. Because "We," "people," did not do this, I tell L., correcting myself as I tell him about how the earth is sick and we have to make sure we do what we can to fix it. It is not "humanity" that poisoned so much earthly human and non-human life, but a small and highly powerful minority of humanity, and the order they have imposed on all earthly life.

I am exhausted by the notion that the "age of humans"—and all the violent universality that the term presumes and disguises—is responsible for what is threatening our communities today. It voids the current catastrophe of its politics, of its history. Put otherwise, it is a way of "All Lives Matter"-ing the climate crisis by erasing both the real authors and the first victims of the crimes enacted on planetary life. That is to say, if "we" are responsible, who is presumed to be included within the parameters of the pronoun here? After all, you and I, and our respective communities, are not the same "we" that are included when Canadian legislators and pundits talk about keeping "us" safe with increased police budgets, or expanded powers to tighten "our" border. The currency of the concept of a universal "we"—Sylvia Wynter calls this the "referent *we*"—has always been a violent exclusion relying on who is a historical subject, who is considered a full human, a national citizen, with Black and Indigenous communities, of course, written out of the very boundaries of the concept. It's perhaps the final insult that you and I, our respective communities, only enter, exceedingly belatedly, and only abstractly and contingently, into the universal "we" once it is time to identify the architects of the climate disaster, only to disappear from it again in the next headline, thought, etc.

I FEEL THAT I NEED TO go backward in order to go forward. If we are going to find a way to make livable lives in these times, it is necessary to move beyond "human-related activities": the climate crisis is tethered to its origins in slavery and colonialism, genocide and capitalism. Most recently, I've been drawn to some of the generative political and intellectual work that is re-conceiving the framework of the Anthropocene by disturbing the very grounds on which IPCC reports stand. Because climate scientists frequently, still, describe global warming and its attendant horrors as the result of "anthropogenic" activities (i.e. originating in *human*-centred actions). It is necessary to write the catastrophe of the climate crisis into its rightful historical context. Some of re-framings that I find especially compelling allow us to supplement, expand, and work beyond the Anthropocene are the *Plantationocene*, the *racial Capitalocene*, the *interminable catastrophe*. I'll admit that I'm less concerned with the particular naming that we settle on than with what these give us, the possibilities that they invoke, and where they allow us to go, or maybe, to put it differently, what it is that is at stake in these re-framings. Beyond the necessary questioning of the "referent *we*," of the absences created when we call the climate catastrophe "human-made," I am drawn to the temporal reframing that they provide us, the alternative "origin stories"—to think alongside Kathryn Yussof's *A Billion Black Anthropocenes or None*—of the crisis that now threatens the possibility for a habitable earth.

Because as Black and Indigenous communities have long understood and insisted, the Industrial Revolution—which the IPCC regards as the moment when "anthropogenic activities" began to increase the world's carbon production massively—was not forged by *humans* in any even sense of the word. It was forged, in fact, by the violent *ejection* of some, most, of the world's inhabitants from the conception of who is considered to be a human. The Industrial Revolution emerged from Europe and its settler outposts. It was quite literally fuelled by the violently coerced labour of kidnapped Africans, on lands from which Indigenous populations had been murdered and forcibly removed. The origins of the current climate devastation originated with the wealth and labour produced by "New World" slave plantations, producing, further, goods made out of the stolen resources of colonized people everywhere. South African climate activist and scholar Vishwas Satgar refers to this as "imperial ecocide" as a way of insisting that an *ecocide* accompanied the racial violence of genocide and slavery. He uses the term to capture the fact that the economic systems of slavery and colonialism and capitalism were accompanied by the planned and unplanned destruction of the earth and of previous ways it had been cared for and tended to. If "we," as Audre Lorde writes, were "never meant to survive" slavery and colonialism (not, she clarifies, as *human beings*), neither were many of the discardable places on which kidnapped Africans laboured—those Indigenous lands, cleared via the largest-known genocide in human history, upon which the Industrial Revolution was built.

Trinidadian anti-colonial freedom-fighter turned postcolonial prime minister Eric Williams described, in his 1944 text *Capitalism and Slavery*, how, by the eighteenth century, Barbados was "already suffering from the inevitable consequences of slave labor and quick extraction of profit from the soil." The slave plantations of the colony, across the entire island, were geared toward the production of a monoculture crop of sugarcane. By 1663, the physical environment of the slave colony was *already* described as "decaying fast" due to soil exhaustion. This was known by planters at the time to have devastating environmental impacts, but it was understood to be the most profitable method. As

Thomas Jefferson wrote of the state of Virginia, "we can buy an acre of new land cheaper than we can manure an old one." Black *people* were treated, of course, with the same disregard as the soil they were forced to labour on, worked literally to death while positioned as an "exploitable source of energy," with Indigenous communities, when considered at all, understood only as a barrier to access to the land.

Also, it is no side note to say that absented, so frequently, from the master narrative of the climate crisis as "human-made" are the West's crimes against Africa! African social justice activists and writers like Nigerian eco-socialist activist Nnimmo Bassey have been resoundingly clear that this continually goes missing from most discussions on the so-called Anthropocene. The devastation of the continent caused by the mass kidnapping and theft of twenty million Africans (seven million of whom died en route to the coast before reaching the ships); the 1885 "scramble for Africa" and its afterlives—the parcelling out of nearly the entire continent and its resources—these histories are also the history of the climate emergency. This massive human and environmental pillaging *developed* the riches of Europe and its settler outposts by devastating existing African societies and economies, as Walter Rodney details in his 1972 magnum opus, *How Europe Underdeveloped Africa*. On the human end, Europe's globalized barbarism resulted, of course, in the massive human atrocities of the Nama and Ovaherero genocide in Namibia and the violent suppression of the so-called "Mau Mau Rebellion," to name only a couple. But just as crucially, *it also put into place the eco-logic crisis at hand*: the desertification of the Sahara, the salinization of the Niger Delta region, and the deforestation and the soil degradation caused by monocrops, which were imposed most harshly on lands that were not intended for white settlement. (Africans were considered "capable of no development or culture" and the vast majority of lands set up, outside of those set to be settler colonies—South Africa, Rhodesia, Kenya—were set up *only* for colonial extraction, a practice which has left ongoing environmental devastation).

There is more than something, then, of slavery's afterlife in the fact that the parts of the world predicted to face the most acute and early devastation of the climate crisis are, now, the Caribbean and the continent of Africa.

Of course, our histories are intertwined with one another's. If we read these (unfinished) histories alongside the works of Glen Coulthard, Patrick Wolfe, and Jodi Byrd on genocide, settler colonialism, and the dispossession of Indigenous peoples from their lands in the service of capital and white settlement, it is clear that Black and Indigenous peoples, to the Europeans and their settler societies, existed along a spectrum of non- or hardly-human entities, utilized, alongside minerals, monocrops and livestock, as racialized and gendered assemblages to be funnelled toward building a white (settler) vision of a future society in which our peoples' respective survival was an afterthought. Put otherwise, the massive destruction, gendered and murderous, of (Indigenous) human life and land dispossession; the commodification, exploitation and fungibility of (Black) human life; and the relentless expropriation and destruction of non-human nature are inextricably linked: a disregard for all living things *except for their value as property to be accumulated.*

All of this to say is that Europe's Industrial Revolution was accomplished by thieffing our ancestors' collective lives, labour, and lands and transforming them into capital. A crisis put in place by a worldview that set up the world, its resources and peoples, as things to be collected and conquered. And now, those who have suffered the most from that barbarism stand to die first.

The climate catastrophe was born not from "mankind" but from the slave plantation, the settler town, the prison, the reservation. It is unsurprising, then, that the solutions being forwarded by those in power are more of the same— the border wall, the immigration detention centre, the refugee camp, the open-pit mine. For us to live in anything that I hope we can one day call freedom, it is necessary to put a swift end to the death-drive-disguised-as-worldview—the murderous episteme that is being imposed on us by the master/settler/CEO.

———

IN A RECENT CONVERSATION THAT YOU had with Dionne Brand, she said something that resonated strongly with me, referring to the election of Donald Trump: "The morning when we realized that Trump was elected I thought, *So the real monster has arrived.* The one we've been staving off and making concessions to." And I suppose it should come as no surprise that in the wake of apocalyptic climactic predictions, we are seeing, too, the rise of Bolsonaro, Ford, Kenney—the *real monsters*, to put Brand's words in the plural. They are staking their final claims to the world-on-fire their predecessors have put into place, building up their riches on a tiny platform overlooking the ruins, and surrounded by barricades as they wring every last bit of remaining life-force out of the earth's surface. But here is what is at stake: *we do not want to get on that platform!* Because what we would find behind those barricades would be nothing akin to freedom. The logic that requires the platform and the barricades (and the high-rise offices funded by our dead) is precisely the logic that got us into this calamity, and it will not, cannot, lead us out.

We are, already, living and organizing on entirely different terms than those laid out by the monsters, however imperfectly, and these terms have long-standing historical traditions. We are engaged, I believe, with asking one another: What does it mean to try to build worlds that affirm, rather than destroy, life, and to do so from outside the barricades?

All world-endings are not tragic. There are some world-endings that I am comfortable with. I frame the present epoch as "late capitalism" as a kind of aspirational descriptor more than as a strictly Marxist category. In order to make earthly planetary survival possible, some versions of this world *need* to end (and indeed, should never have begun in the first instance). Some worlds, after all, depended on the ongoing violent, always racial- and gender-differentiated foreclosures of other worlds. While I am devastated and terrified by the IPCC predictions for the living things on this earth, to avoid the worst-case scenarios now predicted by global scientific consensus, it is necessary to have the courage to envision the end of *this* world, that is, the world that white supremacy built, to move toward futures that are premised on life rather than (human, ecological, animal, microbial) waste. This disruption is what Frantz Fanon was getting at when he wrote, in *The Wretched of the Earth*, that "decolonization, which sets out to change the order of the world, is, obviously, a program of complete disorder." Disorder is not the same as chaos. It implies, instead, a radical rupture from the dominant order, which is, after all, murderous. A program of disorder implies, here, that we radically alter—and indeed breach entirely with—the current order of things and the global violences upon which this order relies.

I believe that world-ending and world-making can occur, are occurring, have always occurred, simultaneously. Given that racial and ecological violence are interwoven and inextricable from one another, more now than ever, Black and Indigenous communities—who are globally positioned as "first to die" within the climate crisis—are also on the front lines of world-making practices that threaten to overthrow the current (death-making) order of things. Put otherwise, our communities, quite literally the post-apocalyptic survivors of world-endings already, are best positioned to imagine what this may be. This, after all, is the radical promise (if as of yet unachieved) that was and is extended to us by the world-making projects of *abolition* and *decolonization*. (More on this, between us, soon.)

If our histories are intimately intertwined with one another's, so too are our futures. Your work has helped me enormously, in thinking through how to collectively survive—and co-resist!—in the ongoing apocalypse. And I think that understanding the contemporary catastrophe as the *longue durée* of slavery, colonialism, and (ongoing) settler colonialism *also* has the ability to shape, and re-shape, our world-making, and our interlocking justice struggles, in the face of the climate crisis. So this is what I am wondering with you: how do our respective political traditions inform old/new ways of knowing that are, by necessity, outside of the barricades, beyond and against the death-drive of white supremacy, racial capitalism, and constant and unceasing extraction? What kind of world-making, what kind of livingness do we see emerging, as always-already in the works, from the past-present Black and Indigenous traditions of radicalism, resistance, and co-resistance? How do you see, as you've put it, an "ethical Michi Saagiig Nishnaabeg response to colonially induced climate change"?

These are some of the questions I am thinking of with and alongside you at the end of the world. If you feel inclined to write me back, please feel free to answer them. Or ignore them entirely. The future feels daunting. Maybe writing together, walking together, witnessing these times together in this way will help us to forge ahead differently. At the very least, it might help us to limit our doom-scrolling. And maybe it will help us to anchor ourselves and one another as we try to find a way to map out liberated futures for our children, and theirs, in a time where any notion of *future* feels unnavigable. I'm hoping, mostly, in writing you, that maybe this grounding, together, will help remind me, remind us, that we and ours have been building livable worlds all along, despite and against forces aligned to steal our light, and that we will continue to do so no matter what comes our way.

Robyn,

The first thing I underlined in my now worn-out copy of *Policing Black Lives: State Violence in Canada from Slavery to the Present*, was the very first line of the acknowledgements section: "Writing *Policing Black Lives* was a community affair—born out of movement work, it is geared toward nourishing those same movements that have given me life over the last years." I knew after reading that first line that this book was going to be different. *Policing Black Lives* was written for different reasons than most books published in Canada. Reasons that I had profound respect for—knowledge, research, analysis, and writing born out of movement work and geared towards nourishing, sustaining, and propelling movements for Black life—robust intellectual work in service of radical Black futurities. *Policing Black Lives* holds up community, and shines a light on the generations of freedom fighters whose individual and collective sacrifices have brought us to this moment. As I read on, I underlined your careful and gentle insistence that Black and Indigenous struggles, while distinct, were also linked. This was significant to me because it gestured towards a more rigorous and nuanced relationality between Black and Indigenous communities, reminiscent of radical Black feminist traditions embodied in so many: writers like Makeda Silvera, NourbeSe Philip, Dionne Brand, and Afua Cooper. In *Policing Black Lives* you were the first one to gather together the work of Black feminists and organizers and provide us with a volcano of meticulously researched evidence that destroyed Canadian innocence and exceptionalism with regard to transatlantic slavery and anti-Blackness. In *Policing Black Lives*, you taught me abolition on stolen land is the practice of caring.

My book *As We Have Always Done: Indigenous Freedom Through Radical Resistance* came out in the same year as your *Policing Black Lives*. I remember wishing your book had come out first, because it would have made *As We Have Always Done* more complete and rigorous. I would have brought *Policing Black Lives* into conversation with the chapters in *As We Have Always Done*, and from an Indigenous perspective pointed towards the same robust and nuanced relationality between Indigenous and Black communities you had done in *Policing Black Lives*, albeit from my own Nishnaabeg perspective. When an occasion presented itself to launch *As We Have Always Done* in in Kanien'kehá:ka (Mohawk) territory in Tio'tia:ke (Montreal), where you were living at the time, I wanted to invite you into a conversation, a thinking-through, between ourselves and our books.

You graciously accepted the invitation and our conversation took place on April 14, 2018. This was the very first time we had met in person. I remember the Black community of Montreal showing up in power at the event. I remember being very nervous, as one should be when their first encounter with someone is on a stage with a mic in front of a beautiful, intelligent audience. I remember your pink lipstick. I remember my Blistex. I remember being painfully aware I was dressed like I was from Ontario. I can't remember very much about what we talked about, but we obviously had the sense to record it, because there is an edited transcript of part of our conversation in *Until We Are Free: Reflections on Black Lives Matter in Canada*. This was our first visit.

Roughly a year later, in 2019, as part of my work at the Dechinta Centre for Research and Learning in Denendeh, I helped organize a solidarity gathering that took place in March, in the territory of the Yellowknives Dene First Nation (YKDFN). Our idea was simple—to invite a small group of Black, Brown and Indigenous activists, thinkers, writers, and organizers to spend time with us, in the spring, on an island in what the Yellowknives Dene known as Tı̨ndeè, or "big lake." Together we fished nets under the ice, travelled by snowmobile and sleigh across the frozen lake, shared moose ribs cooked over the fire, stories from YKDFN Elders, our own ideas, and time with each other. We wanted to invest in our relationship with each other and our affinities, outside of the institution, the internet, and crises, because we believed that the land would pull out a different set of conversations and gift us with a different way of relating. We wanted to sit together on the land, immersed in a Dene world, engage in a practice of Dene hospitality to see if we related to each other in a different way.

This is exactly what happened. The land nurtured a set of conversations and way of relating to each other outside of the institution and its formations. I remember you and I eating muskox around the fire, talking about how different eating muskox around a fire in the bush was from meeting in a hallway or bar at a conference, or interacting online. We were meeting, and there was no crisis or blockade or protest or agenda. We were coming together to nourish each other, to relate to each other, to listen and share, and to breathe together, to use NourbeSe Philip's thinking. I could intellectualize about the experience and speak in terms of relationality and relationship-building, something I think Black and Indigenous activists in the 1960s and 1970s understood far better than us. I could talk about this from an Indigenous methodological angle, with visiting and developing relationships of trust as foundational to any exchange of knowledge and experience. I could write about the spiritual dimension of this work from, again, Indigenous perspectives—being surrounded by trees, medicines, air, sky, and water. In a sense, though, none of that particularly matters, other than to say, I think land-based politics "grounded in a sustained and nurturing relationship with the natural world and in protecting nature as a means of protecting ourselves" can be one generative means of nourishing Black and Indigenous politics of solidarity.

Our starting point was simple: land and place-making,

although perhaps different, were and remain important to both Black and Indigenous peoples.

Our starting point was a refusal of the nation-state and racial capitalism, colonialism and heteropatriarchy embodied in those structures.

Our starting point was a recognition that transatlantic slavery and, as Saidiya Hartman says, "its afterlives" and colonialism, mean we have distinctive and intertwined histories, presences, theory and world-building practices.

We imagined the synergistic potential of Black land politics and Indigenous land politics towards liberated lands and bodies.

After that gathering, the possibilities to continue this work seemed endless: trips to the sugar bush, hikes in downtown Toronto, exchanges between Freedom Schools, gatherings in the Caribbean . . . and then the pandemic hit.

Our lives shrunk into our homespaces during stay-at-home orders. There was an urgency in addressing the pandemic under white supremacy because we knew that Black, Brown and Indigenous peoples are always the first to die, and that any state solutions will be made first to save white people's lives and livelihoods.

Zoom seemed like the very last place we wanted to continue this work. In fact, to me, it felt like virtual environments were antithetical to this work. And so, you and I decided to write each other letters because we couldn't see each other in person. As an honoured radical Black feminist methodology of scaffolding the intimate and personal within the global, letter writing made sense. We decided to not only write what we know, but to attempt to think through things together, to generate through this intentional relationship a sort of study of Black and Indigenous relationality through the study of our own responsive relationality. In hindsight, and after reading Katherine McKittrick's *Dear Science*, I realize that each of us drew on our distinct "rebellious methodologies" in this project—for you, Black theory, story, knowledge and methodologies of knowledge production; for me, Nishnaabeg story as theory, knowledge and methodologies of knowledge production. The intersection was friendship, collaboration, song, story, movement work, citations, analytics, and oral practice.

These interstitial spaces are this book.

We made a commitment to each other to think alongside each other, through the chaos of the global COVID-19 pandemic, through the ongoing pandemic of Black and Indigenous death and erasure, and through the beautiful revolutions of Black and Indigenous organizing and resistance. We agreed to be first and foremost empathetic, responsible, and gentle with each other, which required a trust and vulnerability that for me was new in intellectual work. We did not shy away from the issues and tensions between our two communities.

What began as a series of letters with footnotes between us has grown into something that has expanded outside of the two of us, and then grown again into *Rehearsals for Living*. This book is a chronicle of our thinking in a particular moment of time. It's messy. It's incomplete. It's gentle. It is, in its simplest form, a record of our relationality. The recording of this record required a divestment of the arrogance of the expert in favour of openness, intimacy, care and humility, and so these are also songs that chronicle our love and friendship. And like making a record, listening became perhaps the most important methodology. You are a fully formed thinker, writer, and researcher, not because of the credentials of the academy, but because of your practice, your ethics, and your bodies of work. You are steeped in an extensive network of movement and organizing experience, in Black systems of knowledge production, analysis and theory-making, in addition to the written work of Black and anti-colonial scholars. Robyn Maynard, I have learned so very much from you, and from those formations of young Black activists on our streets, bringing forth new worlds before our very eyes.

There are many Indigenous and Black peoples that have done and are doing the same kinds of thinking in the academy, and outside on the streets and in encampments, in prisons, around kitchen tables and in the bush. We are centring Indigenous and Black life and lives because we are Nishnaabeg and Black, not because we don't value our relationships and solidarity with anti-colonial racialized peoples in Canada and beyond.

Weweni. We will go carefully.

Here I am finally answering your first letter, four months late and now at the beginning of the global pandemic and under a stay-at-home order. The frequency of worry is vibrating through everything right now. You've been checking in on me. I've been worrying about you—in a big city, a single parent, a little one who requires more than anyone can give in a small space. And you've been busy. I've watched

BLM Toronto mobilizing and raising, as of this minute, $32,112 for the Black Lives Matter Emergency Fund, to support one-time stipends of $125–$250 to Black folks in the GTA who need greater support in this time of school closures, unemployment, isolation and caring for the sick. I am in complete awe of the organizing power of young Black activists.

That's not all you've (and I mean both you personally and your broader community) been up to, though. This is day six of a hunger strike by eight people at the Laval migrant prison (Laval Immigration Holding Centre) who are demanding the immediate release of everyone detained, as well as safe and decent housing during the COVID-19 pandemic. I know this because of your solidarity work.

You and your relations, my friend, are (still) busy building a different world at the end of this one. This is something I've emphasized over and over again in my own work. I cherish the belief and practice that it is never enough to just critique the system and name our oppression. We also have to create the alternative, on the ground and in real time. In part, for me, because Nishnaabeg ethics and theory demand no less. In part because in Nishnaabeg thinking, knowledge is mobilized, generated, and shared by collectively *doing*. It's more than that, though. There is an aspect of self-determination and ethical engagement in organizing to meet our peoples' material needs. There is a collective emotional lift in doing something worthwhile for our peoples' benefit, however short-lived that benefit might be. These spaces become intergenerational, diverse places of Indigenous joy, care and conversation, and these conversations can be affirming, naming, critiquing, as well as rejecting and pushing back against the current systems of oppression. This for me seems like the practice of movement-building that our respective radical practices have been engaged with for centuries. I see Black activists and organizers, scholars and artists theorizing and practising something similar and also different, coming from your practices of resistance, your rich, generous, brilliant intellectual traditions.

And so here Black and Indigenous communities are once again. Another crisis amongst a multitude of crises, from police and carceral violence to pipelines and global warming to the missing and murdered to opioids, and the list goes on and on.

Our struggles have placed us here in each other's presence, and on the shores of Chi'Nibish, or Lake Ontario, we have been in each other's presence for four centuries.

Black and Indigenous communities are, of course, big and gloriously diverse. Our lived experiences with the pandemic specific, entangled and sometimes overlapping. We have heard stories of Indigenous youth aging out of the child welfare system during the pandemic with no support systems in place; we've witnessed massive spikes in overdoses and deaths in Indigenous street communities; we've heard Elders and residential school survivors worry about their vulnerability to COVID-19 because of their experiences with tuberculosis and other infectious diseases in residential schools. I worry particularly about my Anishinaabeg, Cree and Dene relations in the north. Asabiinyashkosiwagong Nitam-Anishinaabeg (Grassy Narrows First Nation or Asubpeeschoseewagong Netum Anishinabek First Nation),

Wabaseemoong Independent Nation and Wabauskang First Nation in northern Ontario will endure this pandemic with all of the same challenges as other remote First Nations, but with community members who already have compromised health from mercury poisoning in the 1970s. Most communities in the northern parts of Canada don't have a doctor. In the Northwest Territories at the start of this there were only six critical care beds and just thirteen ventilators. The Assembly of Manitoba Chiefs was concerned about their ability to handle a health care crisis and reached out to Cuban doctors for support. We know the Canadian health care system is shaped by anti-Black and anti-Indigenous racism—84 percent of Indigenous peoples participating in a recent study in British Columbia report that they have experienced discrimination in the health care system. We know from the meticulous work of Samir Shaheen-Hussain in *Fighting for a Hand to Hold: Confronting Medical Colonialism Against Indigenous Children in Canada* that this is a foundation of Canada. We know that the killing of Joyce Echaquan from the community of Manawan, Atikamekw in Quebec was unfortunately not unusual; what was unusual was that she, in her last act of resistance, filmed it on Facebook Live. For prairie First Nations and Métis people, the death-making machine of white racism has already intensified during the pandemic with the brutal killing of two Métis men, Jake Sansom and Morris Cardinal, who were out hunting to feed their family; and with threats to intentionally spread COVID-19 to Indigenous peoples. In Somba'ke (Yellowknife), the women's shelter has adopted physical distancing measures to keep their clients safe—which means they can only house three women instead of the normal six, and they have stopped taking in homeless women altogether. This at a time when the World Health Organization reports that women and children are more vulnerable to intimate partner and family violence because of "stress, the disruption of social and protective networks, loss of income and decreased access to services."

In mid-March, Inuit residents of Kangiqliniq (Rankin Inlet) in Nunavut blockaded the road to the Meliadine mine owned by Agnico Eagles Mine Limited, a Canadian multinational gold mine, in a fight to protect their community by demanding the suspension of mining operations amid COVID-19. This is not an isolated case. The hydro and oil and gas industries have continued to endanger Indigenous peoples in Wet'suwet'en homelands, in the communities of Fort St. John and that of the Tiny House Warriors, by continuing work on the Site C dam and along pipeline routes (Coastal GasLink and Trans Mountain), housing hundreds of workers in mancamps, just as they are doing to Indigenous peoples on the African continent. So, while white, middle-class Canadians in the south isolate themselves in their houses with Netflix, grocery delivery, working their secure jobs from home with complete confidence that their governments have their best interests in mind, Indigenous communities must actively organize to protect their lives.

And it's not just remote and northern communities that are experiencing the pandemic under colonialism. Queer, Two-Spirit, and trans Indigenous peoples, who always have to navigate and cope with transphobia and heteronormativity in the health care system, now must do so under crisis conditions. People who call the Downtown Eastside (DTES) home in Vancouver don't have adequate housing, access to handwashing, a safe drug supply, or supportive health care. Organizers in Toronto have struggled to make sure people in encampments have the basic supplies the city has refused to supply—water and tents, ice, sleeping bags, fire safety equipment and food. The closure of businesses and drop-in centres means more social isolation and an increase in risk as sex workers barred from buildings lose their incomes or are forced into riskier ways of working, and the spread of coronavirus in these dense, impoverished neighborhoods—where many people already struggle with staying healthy—would be catastrophic. The tent community at the DTES's Oppenheimer Park is mostly urban Indigenous people, and of course struggle with the social distancing and hand-washing measures suggested to flatten the curve.

Mainstream Canadian news has barely touched on the conditions and experiences of Indigenous peoples in Africa and South America, except to present the tired racist dichotomy of "remain on your lands and die or move to the city and die," as if those are the only two possible outcomes for Indigenous peoples there. All peoples on the continent of Africa are particularly vulnerable to the virus because, in the afterlives of colonialism, there are only two thousand ventilators on a continent where 1.2 billion people live, with some countries having none at all. Indigenous peoples and their communities in African countries also face the conditions of the ongoing legacy of colonialism and theft: a "fragile" health care system and lack of infrastructure and resources to contain the virus through sanitation. Hindou

Oumarou Ibrahim, coordinator of the Association of Peul Women and Autochthonous Peoples of Chad, also reminds us that physical distancing is tantamount to starvation in communities where people need to go to the market to buy and sell their products. "If they don't, they basically don't have any food for the day," Ibrahim says. "Our agriculture is already vulnerable due to climate change impacts and now this crisis is adding poverty to poverty." Organizations in Angola, Botswana, Namibia and South Africa have reported similar problems with regard to Indigenous peoples—inadequate health services and COVID-19 information, the devastating impact of stay-at-home orders on livelihoods and food insecurity, a lack of government response measures, and lack of inclusion of Indigenous voices in the development of measures to address COVID-19. All of these issues disproportionally impact the continent's Indigenous women in Angola, Botswana, Namibia, and South Africa for example, because, like Indigenous women across the globe, they are facing discrimination on the basis of race, ethnicity, gender and economic status, an increase in gender-based violence during the pandemic, and are often the main providers of food and nutrition for their families.

The situation is similar in Latin America and South America. Indigenous peoples in the Amazon are already coping with the brink of environmental collapse because of illegal mining and deforestation on their territories, with the invading miners and loggers carrying the virus into their communities—communities that are often days away from an increasingly overwhelmed Western medical system. In Brazil, faced with gross inaction from the right-wing

Bolsonaro government, some Indigenous nations, such as the Paiter Suruí and Parque Indigena do Xingu peoples, have placed themselves in voluntary isolation since March of this year, 2020. The situation is similar everywhere because four centuries of colonialism creates similar conditions for Indigenous peoples, whether you live in Africa, Europe, the Americas, Asia, or Australia. Our land bases have been ecologically destroyed. We have been removed and dispossessed of our homelands. We live in a planned and enforced situation of poverty with less access to the necessities of life than our colonizers have. Our bodies carry the consequences of the physical and emotional violence of colonialism, making us more vulnerable to new viruses. We are made vulnerable and fragile by the ravages of capitalism and colonialism.

Still, we persist. Organize. Endure. Resist.

In Canada, the experiences of Indigenous peoples with COVID-19 are different from, yet interlocked with, the experiences of Black peoples. Writer, activist, and academic El Jones took on the state's anti-Black response to COVID-19 in the *Halifax Examiner*:

> Black women are concentrated in frontline health care work. The agricultural industry employs large numbers of Black migrant workers who are affected by border closures. New State of Emergency declarations raise concerns about the intensification of racial profiling directed at Black communities. Black people make up a disproportionate amount of precarious workers, people in the gig economy, and home businesses such as hairdressing. Prisons, known as an epicentre of infections, disproportionately incarcerate

Black people. The socio-economic impact of health means that COVID-19 will have a serious impact on Black communities and seniors.

Jones, quoting Beverly Bain, a professor in Women and Gender Studies at the University of Toronto, also highlights a fact that rings true across Canada—Black people have been absent from reporting on COVID-19. Not only have Black people been absent from the public health-care messaging; their work on the front lines as health care providers, cashiers, and cleaners has been all but erased, as have their experiences of the pandemic under Canadian anti-Blackness—including increased police surveillance targeting Black people, evictions, and lack of income support. "We are invisibilized in the discourses of protection and safety but hyper-visibilized in punitive discourses and practices invested in Black death," says Bain.

Both of our communities face overcrowded living conditions on reserves or in urban centres, housing and food insecurity, and increased exposure to the virus in prisons and detention centres and lack of access to quality health care. We have witnessed increased police targeting and surveillance of Black people; increased exposure from frontline work with a lack of personal protective equipment; and deplorable living and working conditions on farms, and in prisons, and in detention centres. For both our communities, the structural and systemic nature of anti-Blackness and colonialism and their deliberately planned and enforced poverty position our relations as the most vulnerable to COVID-19, all the while obfuscating this fact. We know the inequalities and injustices of pre-COVID-19 life in Canada will only become more intensified and entrenched during the crisis. Our past lived experiences tell us that it will be the most vulnerable segments of our communities who bear the brunt of this pandemic. No matter how many times the state says, "We are in this together," we know we most certainly are not.

Imperialism and ongoing colonialism have been ending worlds for as long as they have been in existence, and Indigenous and Black peoples have been building worlds and then rebuilding worlds for as long as we have been in existence. Relentlessly building worlds through unspeakable violence and loss. Building worlds and living in them *anyway*.

I've been thinking about the affirmations in your letter: Our histories, presences and futures are different and intertwined with one another. Our world-making projects of abolition and decolonization are enmeshed. We are globally positioned as the first to die and when crises hit, and their solutions always preserve the systems that produce these conditions. Our communities are already post-apocalyptic experts and can best imagine worlds beyond our current realities, but in order to imagine, some of us have to first survive.

Wabakinine

Prior to the pandemic, I imagined actually taking our kids and physically walking along the route from your home to places on Bay Street where our collective genocides are always being mapped out. I thought it would be interesting to walk the land, and walk the city together, with our

Indigenous and Black loves from different generations. I was interested to see how our kids would find joy *anyway*, because that is the gift of young people. I was interested to see how we would find joy anyway. I was interested in how we would each uncover signals from and of our communities and separate these signals from the noise of the city. I was interested to see the Black and Indigenous worlds we would together create along the route. I was interested in developing this as a practice over time. Perhaps taking different groups of people with us, collectively coding and decoding the city. What would happen if we took the land-based practice of walking the land, walking a part of our intertwined worlds together? What would be our experience and what would we learn? How would we deepen our relationship to each other and to this place?

Now, given the pandemic, we are at least a year away from being able to walk anywhere together. Underneath the visible Toronto, or maybe not underneath, maybe beside, is an Indigenous Toronto. A Michi Saagiig Nishnaabeg Chi'engikiiwang. A Haudenosaunee Tkaranto. A Wendat Ouentaronk. One that exists today, and one that used to exist in relation to the buried and forgotten creeks, the island that didn't used to be an island and the rivers Chi'Ziibi (Rouge River), Cobechenonk Ziibi (Humber River), Waasayishkodenayosh (Don River), and Mazinige Ziibi (Credit River).

When the kids weren't paying attention because we'd have loaded them up with ice cream, and we were standing where the St. Lawrence Market is today, I'd ask first, because there is sexual violence in this story, and then I'd whisper:

On August 20, 1796, a small group of Michi Saagiig Nishnaabeg came to York (now Toronto) from the Credit River to sell salmon in the area around what is now known as the St. Lawrence Market. Wabakinine, together with his partner and his sister (women whose names the colonial historical record did not record), camped for the night on the waterfront, across from Berry's Tavern, just east of the market block. The remainder of their group camped on the peninsula which eventually evolved into the Toronto Islands.

Just before midnight a Queen's Ranger, Charles McEwan, approached Wabakinine's family. At some point that evening, McEwan had given Wabakinine's sister a dollar and some rum to "induce her to grant him certain favours." McEwan arrived with two compatriots to rape Odawemaan (Wabakinine's sister). Wiijiiwaagan (Wabakinine's partner) awoke to see McEwan dragging Odawemaan from the canoe she had been sleeping under. Of course, she woke Wabakinine for help.

Wabakinine confronted the three white men, and McEwan murdered him and then physically assaulted Wiijiiwaagan.

Their relations on the peninsula heard the terror and rushed to Wabakinine, Odawemaan and Wiijiiwaagan.

The white men who had viciously attacked the Michi Saagiig Nishnaabeg had left. The Nishnaabeg collected their loved ones and carried them to the peninsula. The next day, they took them home to the Credit River. Wabakinine died of his injuries on the way. Wiijiiwaagan died of her injuries shortly after. They were buried soon after.

When this story spread across Kina Gchi Nishnaabe-ogaming, Michi Saagiig Nishnaabeg were outraged and demanded accountability and justice and they mobilized. McEwan faced a grand jury in mid-December for the murder of Wabakinine but was promptly discharged as a result of "it not having been proven that the Chief with whose murder he was charged is dead."

No white authorities had seen Wabakinine's body, which the Mississaugas had buried soon after his death.

The Michi Saagiig Nishnaabeg refused to appear in court to give evidence, I assume because they had zero faith in colonial judicial processes to bring about justice, accountability or a rebalancing of relations. I assume because a conviction in the face of violent systemic dispossession would do nothing to destroy the systems that were destroying them.

Despite having conversations with their allies, including Six Nations, the Michi Saagiig Nishnaabeg were unable to launch a military attack on Fort York; they were ultimately too overwhelmed with death from infectious diseases, dispossession, and the colonial-induced collapse of their economic, social, and political systems.

My re-telling of this story, based on both historical accounts and Nishnaabeg ethics, reveals several differences between the two. I have chosen not to erase or minimize the sexual violence that initiated the confrontation between Wabakinine and the three white men, nor the death of Wiijiiwaagan. I have chosen not to highlight that alcohol was consumed by some of the people involved in the violence because that is not an excuse or a mitigating factor in sexualized or physical violence. I have chosen to name both Wabakinine's wife and sister even though their names are not recorded in history. I have chosen to tell this story differently, because we do not have any accounts written by Michi Saagiig Nishnaabeg.

This story is eerie. The methodic, deliberate—almost rhythmic—repetition of violence from Fort York in 1796 to Toronto in 2021 is infuriating. As you know, a different but related set of events took place sixty-two years before these murders: the horrific torture and murder of an enslaved Black woman in 1734, Marie-Joseph Angélique in Tio'tia:ke (Montreal), as told to us by Afua Cooper in her meticulous work *The Hanging of Angélique: The Untold Story of Canadian Slavery and the Burning of Old Montreal*. Angélique was arrested, tortured, and publicly hanged for attempting to flee from her white mistress, and she was accused of burning down Old Montreal. Both you in *Policing Black Lives* and Cooper compel us to remember or learn that this story is one of resistance and revolt. You go on to remind me, quoting the work of Peggy Bristow, that in the nineteenth century there were "hundreds of free Black people in Southwest Ontario that risked state and populist repression by forming vigilance committees that resisted white American slave catchers' attempts to re-enslave Blacks who had escaped their bondage and fled to Canada."

We have been together in this place for a long, long time.

As I write this, I'm thinking of the murders and the resistance of Marie-Joseph Angélique and Wiijiiwaagan, and their families and communities, in Toronto and Montreal. These stories are not the same or equivalent. What is overwhelming to me in bringing these two stories into conversation, is that these same narratives have been repeated over and over and over in the years since 1734 and

1796, and there are now thousands upon thousands of Black people and Indigenous people who have experienced eliminatory sexualized and gendered violence, particularly trans and queer people.

This is Canada.

There were three fatal police shootings of Indigenous people in Winnipeg in ten days at the beginning of 2020, including Eishia Hudson, Jason Collins and Stewart Kevin Andrews. Between March and June 2020, the height of the first wave of COVID-19 in Canada, we have witnessed the deaths of Maurice Cardinal, Jacob Sansom, Rodney Levi, Jimmy Cloutier, Chantel Moore, Regis Korchinski-Paquet and D'Andre Campbell at the hands of police or white people. While British Columbia is touted as a COVID-19 response success story, there has also been a 93 percent spike in overdose deaths amongst First Nations people, meaning eighty-nine First Nations people have died from overdoses in the province between January and May of 2020, with a fraction of the societal and state care or response mechanisms deployed to manage COVID-19. The colonial world we are forced to live in, at least part-time, is built upon sexual and gendered violence and the death of Indigenous and Black peoples, and this death is carried in our bodies and recorded on the land, if you know where to look.

After our walk, I wanted to invite you and your child to Nogojiwanong (Peterborough) which is more of my home than Toronto. I would have told you the story that made me. Instead, I'll write you a version of this story, a version that speaks to epidemics and loss, hope and resistance, family and land, and the love that binds us together.

Civil Twilight

In the 1930s my grandmother Audrey was a ten-year-old Nishnaabekwe living on Wolfe Street in Peterborough, Ontario, having recently moved into town from the reserve, but still spending glorious summers on the lake in her home community of Alderville First Nation. Her father, and my great-grandfather, Hartley Franklin, most often a fishing guide on Rice Lake, had found more stable employment building canoes for the Peterborough Canoe Company, necessary in part because of lost hunting and fishing rights in the wake of the fraudulent Williams Treaties of 1923. The life he created was itself a feat—an intact Michi Saagiig Nishnaabeg family with children in the home, living in our homeland with food and shelter—but the calm would not last.

A decade before the discovery of antibiotics, Hartley contracted tuberculosis and was quarantined in a sanatorium more than two hundred kilometres away in Kitchener. Audrey, her mother and little brother moved to Galt to be closer to him. When Audrey's mama Agnes also got TB, my grandmother and her brother were apprehended into foster care with white families. Hartley eventually died in the sanatorium when my grandmother was fourteen. She remembers standing by his casket in Grandma Ida Smoke's living room on the reserve in Alderville while her mom was fighting for her life in the sanatorium. Two years later, Agnes recovered, but my grandma was forced to quit school when their living allowance was cut off. She got a job at Galt Wood Heel, gluing heels onto shoes for ten hours a day.

In the span of a decade, my family went from living on the reserve immersed in Nishnaabeg life and community to being alone with grief in a city several hundred kilometres away. Tuberculosis succeeded in removing my family from our territory, away from our land, family, culture and language, and pushed us further into the wage economy, meeting Canada's political goals of eliminating Indigenous peoples through either death or assimilation.

I live a few blocks away from the house my grandma lived in as a child in Peterborough. Every night at eight o'clock, my daughter Minowe and I run through our neighborhood. The streets are quiet. Min likes the colour of the sky at civil twilight. She practises her vertical leap by attempting to high-five a giant white pine. I think about how each week she gets faster and faster while I stay the same. By the time we're back at our house, away from the motion-detecting lights of our neighbours, we can see the first stars. She points them out and names them, while I just listen, which I now realize is always the most important job.

A strong part of me wants to use these half-hour runs to lecture my captive audience of one. I want Min to carry within her body a sharp knife. I want to assign her Robyn Maynard, Andrea Ritchie and El Jones's recent writings on COVID-19 in the dominating structure of anti-Blackness, and then discuss them on the nightly run. I want to talk about Eabametoong First Nation, a remote, Nishnaabeg fly-in community 362 air kilometres north of Thunder Bay, and how, ever since they confirmed their first case of COVID-19 on April 5, they have been fighting through the bureaucracy of government for testing kits, a field hospital, doctors and nurses, PPE and emergency support. I want to talk at her about communities like Grassy Narrows and how they will face COVID-19 with all of the same challenges as other remote First Nations will: food insecurity, lack of adequate housing and health care, and the endless fumbling bureaucracy of Indigenous services agencies, in places where community members already have compromised health from mercury poisoning in the 1970s, TB exposure in residential schools, and a host of other chronic colonial-induced diseases.

I want her to know the situation for urban Indigenous peoples is challenging in a different way under COVID-19. Our families, too, experience high rates of housing and food insecurity, but also police surveillance and violence, incarceration, intimate violence, substance use and street-affected realities, and, for our gender non-conforming, non-binary and trans relations, navigating a mostly hostile medical system committed to the gender binary and transphobia.

I want her to know that the oil and gas industry has continued to endanger Indigenous peoples in Wet'suwet'en homelands, by continuing work along the pipeline route and housing hundreds of workers in work camps.

I want her to know that we and everyone we love are more vulnerable because of colonialism, and that in crises, vulnerabilities are amplified.

I want her to know "we" are not "in this together."

The empty streets of our neighborhood under social distancing and stay-at-home orders remind me of the loneliness Hartley Franklin must have felt, quarantined in an institution for years far from everything Nishnaabeg and all of his loves. I wonder if he would feel the same relief I do watching Min harvesting wild rice or splitting spruce roots for a canoe or standing in traffic in solidarity with the Wet'suwet'en or running with the stars through the neighborhood where he brought his family in the precious moments before Nishnaabeg life was stolen.

I wonder if he could still find meaning in twilight or stars or in the frozen lake of grief that inevitably blanketed him.

Minowe is living through a pandemic at the same age my grandma was when she lost her dad to epidemic TB.

She is teaching me not to crush her joy.

On our nightly runs she demands I stay in the moment, breathe in sharp air and listen for the drumming of our shoes on the cement against the rhythm of our breathing. She reminds me to look forward to the crew at the end of the street that meticulously chalks Scooby-Doo characters onto their sidewalk each day, to not aimlessly veer into traffic when I see another human on the sidewalk, and to maybe even practise my vertical jump, too.

Each night Minowewebeneshiinh pulls me out of myself and insists I remember that running through inky bruises seeking light from the moon and beside someone you love is one of the best parts of this life. She reminds me that maybe if you are a fourteen-year-old Nishnaabekwe and you can find the will to reach up to our tree of peace, you don't always need the lecture and the sharp knife, maybe you've already beaten COVID-19, and are in the midst of dreaming beyond colonialism.

PART TWO

Making Freedom in Forgotten Places

Hi Leanne,

I've been wearing the yellow-and-black checkered Dechinta flannel that you gave me in January like a hug. When I first wrote to you, I could not possibly have foreseen this moment: the stay-at-home orders, the closures of schools, daycares, workplaces, the empty streets, and the packed emergency rooms. Though we had already committed to be in relation and communion, to engage with how to build life amidst the already-underway crises of our times, I'd not imagined we would be contending with such an immediate and dramatic up-ending of the lives we'd grown accustomed to.

A few weeks back I was folding my son's clothes and texting with you, feeling overwhelmed by the demands of parenting, rapid-response organizing, chronic pain, yet glued to the CBC News App and its minute-by-minute tracking of rising hospitalization rates. We were mostly just checking in. I was pretending to be a tough guy, as I do. You wrote back something vulnerable, though, that reminded me it was okay for us to feel momentarily shattered at a time when the world we have come to know is shattering.

I've been worried about you, too. I know you've lost Elders and likely fear losing more. I feared this for you as soon as the age vulnerabilities of the virus were announced. I know, from a deep understanding of this country's history, that those you have valued and learned from most may fall subject to the tyrannical abandonment that comes from being evacuated, continuously, from the conception of the "public" whose health is being prioritized and protected during this pandemic.

We have just lived through—are still living through—a moment in which one catastrophe enfolded into another. Because, of course, the crisis that is this pandemic is by no means separate from the ecological crisis. It's not that we weren't warned: as so many scientists have noted, a shifting climate made another pandemic nearly inevitable. A 2010 study in *Global Warming* described how climate change facilitates the conditions for a new and possibly deadly pandemic: how the thawing ice, changing bird and animal migration patterns, and a travel-based world of constant human migration create ideal conditions for the spreading of viruses new to humans. The study's authors posited that "climate change and globalization" could create the next pandemic, adding that "[a]s the climate becomes more unstable, its role increases," leading to multiple ways to increase risks of pandemic illnesses. This is not to say that pandemics are new to this time, or that they are *solely* created by a heating planet and capitalism. But these factors make pandemics far more possible and likely.

So here we are, as scientists predicted and as #Octavia ToldUs. I'm re-reading all of Butler's works to salvage my imagination through this bleakness. Published in 1994 and 1998, Octavia Butler's two-part *Parable* series focuses on an emergent community, led by a young Black woman named Lauren Olamina, working to build lives anew in the wake of total social collapse. The years preceding the collapse are described as "the Pox"—a period of widespread contagious illness, mass death, and scarcity. The society's reliance on unceasing corporate greed, unrelenting ecological destruction, racism, and ongoing warfare led to "accidentally coinciding climatic, economic, and sociological crises." In *Parable of the Talents*, the coinciding crises are described as stemming from North Americans' "own refusal to deal with obvious problems in those areas," stating that "we caused the problems: then we sat and watched as they grew into crises." This sounds familiar, of course.

Describing the series, Butler told an interviewer twenty years ago that "there isn't anything in [these books] that can't happen if we keep going on as we have been." In other words, the books were a warning. A warning that went unheeded. In a moment when a world that was already plagued by preventable droughts, famines, and food shortages is now in the midst of a global pandemic that has devastated global south economies, where residents of North American cities face mass evictions as billionaires become trillionaires, the *Parable* series can only just barely be categorized as science fiction. Butler had an ability to project, with eerie accuracy, the possible futures born of the present. It's hard not to feel that the text was used as a playbook by the ruling elite: I cannot imagine her reaction had she lived to see the scenes of her novel play out so literally. Because twenty years ago, her narrative described the rise of a demagogic right-wing US president who came to power—in the 2000s—with the slogan "Make America Great Again." This—while the story's characters navigate a California landscape ravaged by wildfires, caused by global warming. Because of this, Butler is often described as a prophet, in a semi-mystical fashion. I think it's more helpful to understand her as highly well-read, and as an uncannily astute political theorist who understood where the logics of racialism and unrelenting extraction of all living things could take us, if they continued uninterrupted. Her texts were based on, in her own words, "the sociological aspects of our future lives." And *Parable* was an "If this goes on . . ." series, bringing to life the long-term consequences of the status quo: increasing corporate control over all aspects of animal and human life; uninterrupted ecological destruction, racism, and labour exploitation rendering so many lives disposable. And it did go on, of course.

So as #OctaviaToldUs, we are facing, today, a climate crisis that is a health crisis that is a crisis of racial capitalism. Living through a pandemic that did not create but *reveals* the violent hierarchies that define our world's asymmetrical determinations of access to life—and vulnerability to death.

For what is COVID-19—and the massively uneven exposures to death that have proliferated since it emerged—but a conglomerate of the "coinciding climatic, economic, and sociological crises" described in Butler's text?

And here we are.

As you've outlined so lucidly, few—if any—crises exist that are untainted by racism, colonialism, Indigenous genocide, and anti-Blackness. Which of course structurally positions our communities on the razor-sharp edges of vulnerability and disposability in the COVID-19 response. And as you've also shown, for our communities, this is "[a]nother crisis amongst a multitude of crises, from police and carceral violence to pipelines and global warming to the missing and murdered to opioids." Exactly!

I'm honoured to have received what you have shared with me. That you have entrusted me with the story of Wabakinine, of your own family's dispossession from the land—itself mediated by yet another racially stratified "public" health crisis. Reading these words awakened in me the dull throb of anger that lives, most days, in my lower chest cavity—the place where I hold my rage—which at times pulses through my arteries and competes for space with the oxygen and threatens to overtake me if I don't purposefully direct it outside of myself. This is a throb that is activated each time I turn on the radio and, after fiddling with the dial, learn of another young Black person robbed of their best years, meeting too-soon with a death that was preventable but for this country's structural and societal abandonment. It is in the family of anger, spanning from dull to acute, that comes from the knowledge that all of this loss is not a bug, or a failure, but part of the design of this place called Canada. Together, the stories you've re-told for me so keenly illuminate the sexual, racial, and gendered violence upon which this nation was and is built. The biological and ecological warfare against your peoples serving, in your words, to "eliminat[e] Indigenous peoples through either death or assimilation." Your grandfather Hartley's illness and death, the fallout that ensued for the rest of your family, bring to light and to life the direct line that tethers the state brutalities of the past to those of the present.

It's so essential that we collectively refuse the purposeful absenting of these enduring histories from the public memory, that we refuse to forget the ways in which illness— smallpox, TB, syphilis, now COVID-19, has been allowed— and encouraged, in some cases—to proliferate in those racialized outside of the "public" of public health.

The pandemic is unfolding along the racially delineated lines of the crisis of the past five hundred years. Could we have expected anything less?

Ruth Wilson Gilmore has highlighted the ways in which vulnerabilities of all kinds—to illness, environmental harms, to state captivity—come together in sites that she describes as "forgotten places": places where peoples who have been abandoned by the state are vulnerable to state captivity and poor health. Places whose demographics are delineated along racial and economic logics established long ago.

And I have been thinking, as I wrestle with your letter, about the forgotten places of the COVID-19 crisis. The high rates of infection in places like homeless and refugee shelters, of Black neighborhoods in the west end of Toronto, of Montréal Nord, home to a large and economically disenfranchised Haitian population (though it stands to note they are not, not ever, forgotten by the police). You've highlighted others: Oppenheimer Park, the Downtown Eastside, northern Indigenous communities.

"Forgotten places," as a descriptor, makes sense of how and why, despite Canadian public-relations clichés that "we are all in this together," some peoples—our peoples—have been abandoned altogether.

A friend of mine, Zoë Dodd, a long-time outreach worker and advocate for street-involved and drug-using communities, texted me recently. She was asking if I could, if need be, help raise support for the largely Black residents of Moss Park in the likely event that they were to face eviction by the city of Toronto. Black people—who are 30 percent of the homeless population in Toronto—have been, as she describes, the last to be re-housed by the city, and thus represent the majority of the encampment residents at this time. This community of largely poor Black men have been living in tents, or more accurately, in tent-based encampments, a result of the confluence of the housing crisis and the pandemic. Of course, the housing crisis is not new, and dozens of people die preventable deaths here every year; I live in a city where high-rises lie empty, but housing is unaffordable—capital chosen over people time and time again. Yet the contours of the city's priorities of wealth over human beings have become more sharply visible, an already-deadly calculus that is now all the more acute.

Because as Black residents are facing possible evictions from these makeshift but vibrant homes, the COVID-19 risks in congregate settings, and in the shelter system in Toronto, are well-known. After multiple and constant outbreaks it's clear to many of the homeless residents of this city that tents are safer; they allow for social distance. Encampment residents have been discerning, have made choices about their own lives and safety, and have selected the best of the limited available options. And they are laying claim to a public space (so-called) in a city that is hostile to Black life, staking out survival in a context where even the very basics of virus prevention have been denied to them. Still, in the face of this industriousness, of this lived and wide-spanning knowledge of how to survive in a context of urban warfare and multiple epidemics, of the sheer force required to maintain community safety despite endemic state neglect, city officials have denied them some of the basics of health protections. The city has not, and apparently will not, turn back on the public water fountains— shut off during the COVID-19 closures—denying both clean drinking water and any possibility for handwashing.

I have just watched a video that Zoë sent me over text, recorded moments before. In this clip, a city official tells the Black men on camera that they will need to leave the premises, letting them know that he will call the police if they don't leave. The city employee's voice is tense, high-pitched. He is seemingly exasperated, perhaps simply unable to fathom people's refusal to leave the community and comparative safety they have fashioned from the wreckage of a failed housing and health response. He nervously cites trespassing and municipal bylaws, the now-routinized avenues of criminalizing poverty, Blackness, Indigeneity.

And yet, the resident in the centre of the frame holds tight. He is not intimidated, he holds his shoulders squared, with pride, he is a pillar of strength and vitality as he responds to the city worker's outright bureaucratic cruelty, asking: "Am I not a human being or something? Am I not a human being?"

Exactly.

He moves not. One. Inch. He is not leaving. His question, his refusal, exposes the violent racial exclusions of the municipal COVID-19 response, just as his insistence on his own humanity reveals a dignity that cannot be stolen, even when pressed up and against the cruelty of a city policy that negates it.

This video too clearly illuminates that Black people are left out of the city's nominal commitment to *leave no one behind in the COVID-19 response*. Or to put it differently, it reveals just who has been decreed "no one." Reveals who makes up the multitude of *no ones* who will be and are being left behind every day.

And this is only one of many forgotten places. There are a multitude of Moss Parks, of Oppenheimer Parks, that are less well known, where Black, Indigenous, and other dispossessed peoples are abandoned, yet claiming public spaces, living anyways, insisting on their own health anyways.

This same weary drama is being played out, too, in jails and prisons, which feature centrally among the forgotten places of the COVID-19 response. To date, 600 prisoners and 229 staff have tested positive across forty prisons, at infection rates vastly disproportionate to non-incarcerated peoples (five times greater in provincial jails, and nine times greater in federal facilities). In some institutions, one-third of the prisoner population has tested positive for COVID-19. And perhaps unsurprisingly, this end of the health crisis has been altogether muted within dominant society. Canadian media has hardly reported on the conditions in prisons since COVID-19 began, as compared to long-term care and other congregate settings. We have of course some understanding as to why: the health and well-being of Black and Indigenous communities had *already* been, for all intents and purposes, abandoned by the state into carceral institutions during pre-pandemic times. For the state's captives, illness was already prevalent. And little was said, less was done, by the state or the broader public, where prisoners' lives register hardly at all.

A while back, in the first few weeks of the pandemic, I was in touch with another young Black man incarcerated in a provincial institution. I spoke with him and his family, all of whom were deeply concerned: he and another Black prisoner—very young, an adolescent, just over eighteen and hardly a man—had been transferred, despite the temporary stay on transfers between prisons. In their new location, they had been in lockdown for three days, for twenty-three hours per day.

It's since been revealed that the lockdowns like these two young people faced are a normal feature of the COVID-19 response, part of the routinized violence that is "health prevention" for those held captive by the state. Even the prison guards have described this—solitary confinement, that is—as torture. The continual use of this practice stands in stark opposition to the other clear possibility. That is: it was always possible to say "Listen, it's a pandemic—it's a fucking global pandemic and we never thought we would see something like this, and we are not sure how, as a society, we will be able to survive this. So the time has arrived to empty jails and prisons and let our community members come home, shelter in place, and stay alive, and wait this out with their loved ones."

It's still possible now.

But instead, COVID-19 has made it all the more clear that, to paraphrase Angela Y. Davis, prisons exist to disappear from social and political life the people whose very presence otherwise asks us to account for the social, racial, and economic inequities of our societies.

The treatment, under the pandemic, of Black people, Indigenous people, homeless and trans and drug-using and sex-working and poor and migrant people, shows what it means to be rendered expendable. And it exposes quite clearly that we live in a society that is structured around mass expendability.

And amidst all of this, even as cities and nations are nominally "closed down" to flatten the curve, the police still find time to kill us—Chantel Moore and Eishia Hudson and D'Andre Campbell. They are, it appears, not satisfied with letting us die first and fastest, but are committed to accelerating the process.

There is an apparent contradiction when it comes to Black people's roles in these times. We are not only making up the forgotten places of the response, but are also deemed, somewhat incongruously, "essential." Without any sense of irony, undocumented Black women are being called the "guardian angels"—in the term of Quebec's premier, François Legault—of the pandemic. You are correct, Leanne, if you remember that Legault won his election partly due to a campaign that represented the (largely) Black families who had crossed the border in 2016 onward as a threat to the province, the nation, to society as a whole, sparking a man-ufactured and racist "crisis" over immigration. And you are correct too that now, these same women are working to care for ailing Québécois families in long-term care homes, and the same men are cleaning the medical clinics and taking out the trash. The *anges gardiens* are falling ill, and dying too, while struggling for the right to stay in the coun-try, because they do not have the right to health care, to sick days. Because they are deemed "illegal" by those whom they are structurally forced to serve. There is an entire book to be written about the re-branding of this subjection and coerced sacrifice as "angelic." But anyways.

I'll move forward instead to note that the apparent con-tradiction in how this nation positions Black peoples is no such thing. Because for Black peoples, expendability does not and has never ruled out our usefulness in a white supremacist society. Anti-Black logics are not challenged by the presumed usefulness of Black people's *labour*: our use-fulness does not contradict our disposability. This is what it means to exist in the afterlife of the commodity.

M. NourbeSe Philip, in a vigil organized by BLM-TO about Black grief in a time of COVID-19, spoke to the conditions governing Black life in these times. She spoke these words:

Our lives have always *mattered* for white supremacy, but they have mattered for the wrong reason—for use value, expendable and disposed of once no longer needed.

Exactly.

It is this flexibility, the ease, the interchangeability by which we are positioned and re-positioned, purposed and repurposed for the needs of Canadian society, that actually lays bare the specific logics governing our lives as Black peoples in this nation. Because all at once, we are surplus peoples, abandoned and forgotten in prisons and encampments; we are dangers to society whose calls for support in crises are met with (always legally justified) murder by police. We are the "essential" and disposable workers, we are the "guardian angels" whose deaths from COVID exposure are a tragedy with no author, we are thanked for our structurally mandated "sacrifice." And all the while, we remain detainable, deportable, killable. Endlessly useful, endlessly unnecessary: *this* is what it means to be fungible.

I am thinking of you and your loved ones so much right now, as discussions are turning toward "re-opening" the economy. I'm thinking about what this re-opening means for our communities, for our survival. As we speak, the economic impacts of the pandemic are being deemed unacceptable. As a result of this calculation, a certain amount of human loss appears to be requisite to this re-opening. This has been deemed acceptable, though this half never makes the headlines. The re-opening of economies, of course, only exacerbates what is already underway. Because our peoples' collective exposure to the virus was already present during the period described as lockdown—including the Indigenous communities living near resource extraction camps, pipelines, and other supposed economic essentials. Even before this pandemic, our health, our living spaces, our labours, our bodies, our communities, have continually—as a matter of practice—been sacrificed for the economy. Our ritualized sacrifice has been the engine of economic growth, and its precondition. So it is hard not to fear what, in the hell, "re-opening" will bring us.

Perhaps what is more novel is the expansive reach and scope of the sacrifice that is demanded by re-opening economies and going back to work during a pandemic: we may be *first* to die, but no one is invulnerable to a highly infectious and deadly virus. The level of human sacrifice that our communities have endured for centuries has now been extended, more broadly than ever before, into white working-class and white middle-class families, all of whom, of course, stand to experience the deadly impacts of the virus as *all* children are slated to be sent back to school and daycare, as restaurants and gyms are slated to re-open.

It's hard, and by that, I mean it is a labour, not to allow myself to turn to cynicism, as we witness the horror of some white liberals who wonder *how the government could do this to them (!!!!)*, the shock—real, genuine shock—that *their* lives and *their* families could be put at risk, as health ministers freely admit that re-opening is occurring not because it is safe to do so, but for economic reasons. Their shock shows an unfamiliarity with history, of the reality that the policies originally crafted to sacrifice *our* (Black, Indigenous, racialized) respective peoples inevitably boomerang back onto the broader (white) public. (Structural Adjustment, anyone?) I'm dismayed, angry, horrified, at times. But to be surprised requires a level of naïveté, of feigned innocence, that is not possible if one has attended, even briefly, to the lived realities of Black peoples and Indigenous peoples globally.

And yet.

You might think I'm being overly optimistic—I have been accused of this before. But I don't want to capitulate to cynicism here. Even though I will dip my toes into cynicism now and again, I won't let myself reside there. Because of course (!) it is difficult not to feel, rightfully, skepticism, irritation, anger with the surprise of the general (i.e. white, middle-class) public, when they realize that the government, like the corporations it works in the service of, *does not give a shit about (most of) them, either.* Du Bois warned, after all, in 1935—nearly a century ago now—that the privileges of whiteness (the "wages of whiteness") are most importantly psychological privileges, even as they are undoubtedly lived in a material sense as well. He warned that only precious few, even white, would escape the ravages and violence of an economic system predicated on the exploitation of nearly all of us, if unevenly distributed across racial lines. It is absurd, monstrous, that it has taken a global pandemic of all things to bring this reality to light, and even then, only partially. But still: I am less invested in a critique of the long-standing refusal to see, refusal to know, than I am with what to do with the new possibilities that emerge from this new, illuminated understanding of the true nature of this economy, of this society. Regardless of what it took to get us here. Because I feel, or perhaps I hope, that this is the beginning of a broader reckoning. That perhaps something profound is occurring, being revealed, that despite the efforts of the political ruling classes, few will be able to unsee with any ease. And crucially, I am invested in what it means to turn this surprise, this anger, into protracted and organized struggle toward a different, more livable future that includes all of our survival.

This society is being forced to see, in no uncertain terms, the violently exclusionary ways in which it has constituted the social—the "public"—within public health. These dominant ways of thinking are being undermined, though, and pathways being re-written from the very grounds of the forgotten places. As true as it is that I've never witnessed such a cruel mathematic of life and death as the tragedy of Black and Indigenous vulnerability to death under COVID-19, it's accurate, too, to say that I've never seen, in my own lifetime, such strong attunement, across different publics, many for the first time, to the need to collectively craft responses to support and protect one another, and those long abandoned by the state. A society that turns towards, rather than away from its forgotten places stands to produce new ways, too, of understanding "public" and "health."

In this moment, communities are creating, building from, and experimenting wildly with forms of collective care at an entirely new scale and scope. Forgotten places are not, after all, forgotten by all. And in those places forgotten—abandoned—by the state, people have their own visions for freedom, for their own multiple struggles to make life livable, to strive for a different and more collective way of organizing human life, and of distributing care.

Of course, while there is a newness to the scale and scope of this crisis, the world-making practices we are seeing now are far from novel. In sharing the re-telling of Wabakinine, you have shared, too, how the death-making logics and practices of the settler state were refused, fought, even amidst unbearable loss. The story of Wabakinine, Odawemaan, and the Michi Saagiig Nishnaabeg who tried to avenge their deaths serves as a reminder both that this society's logics are murderous, and that we make our own logics all the time. Freedom is continually being forged in and across forgotten places.

I am being transformed by witnessing, in these times, the multiple and often decentralized forms of community and collective care that stand to interrupt age-old patterns determining who is able to live and who is left to die.

I have witnessed and contributed modestly to a network of abolitionists across the country—former prisoners, families with loved ones behind bars—supporting prisoners who are working, with the support of peoples outside, toward their own release in the context of COVID-19. From here we can see, in the demand that we #FreeThemAllForPublicHealth, a call to release prisoners from jails and federal institutions. This is necessarily linked to an insistence that prisons and jails were always-already a public health crisis. And that they need to be abolished. I've been moved and inspired by the labour of Free Lands Free Peoples, Indigenous prairie community members coming together to build abolitionist futures, end incarceration, and fight for the return of Indigenous lands. People have been showing up in previously unimaginable ways, in times of enormous difficulty and loss, to bring our people home from sites of captivity. Some of this effort has borne fruit: thousands of those held in provincial jails were released in March, a major, if still woefully incomplete, victory.

Major because the release of thousands of prisoners meant tens of thousands of community members got their loved ones back: no one is an island of one. Family members of incarcerated peoples and their supporters learned together that we can bring people back home into our communities. And that, if this was not already crystal-clear, if people in jail could be released over the span of a few weeks due to health reasons, no one should have been in cages in the first place. The state was warned, too, that we will fight like hell to see that our people are never, ever, taken from us again.

Of course, people pressed to the edges of state and public abandonment consistently show the most courage and take the largest personal risks. It is those who are forging liberation from sites of captivity who model what it is to make liberation a fleshy, lived, concept. I was on a Zoom a few weeks ago with some of the formerly detained Black migrants who had led #HungerStrikeLaval, and feel I there bore witness, truly, to the full social livingness of the Black radical tradition: mutual aid and self-sacrifice for the well-being of the collective. History, here, being made and written from inside of one of Canada's most infamous migrant prisons.

Immigration detention has always been a scene of anti-Black captivity in North America. Migrant detention centres, like jails and prisons, have proliferated from and with the logics and practices of anti-Blackness. This spans from the hold of the ship to the detention of Black radicals like Claudia Jones at a reformatory in Alderson, West Virginia and C. L. R. James on Ellis Island; the use of Guantanamo Bay to house Haitian asylum seekers in the 1980s; and the long-standing detention of largely Black migrants in Canada. It is one of the disinheritances of North America. And so from their captivity in migrant detention, Black peoples have continually forwarded expansive visions of freedom.

On March 24 of 2020, one week after delivering a handwritten petition signed by dozens of detainees, migrants in the Laval Immigration Holding Centre, largely Black, undertook a six-day hunger strike. (The Canada Border Services Agency callously described this as a "food action.") With support from those on the outside organized by Montreal's Solidarity Across Borders, significant pressure was levelled by public health and civil society organizations and medical doctors like Nanky Rai, and detainees began to be slowly released. And by early April, all the hunger strikers, and many, many more state captives had been temporarily freed. They had, by this time, received messages of support from across Canada, including from the Black prisoners who had been part of the Black August prison strike of the year before, who wrote: "Like the hunger strikers, we know the unclean conditions, the impossibility of social distancing, the lack of access to health care, and the health problems already caused by incarceration. These things make prisons dangerous at all times, but especially during a pandemic." Solidarity across forgotten places.

Over the Zoom, their easy smiles and laughter were incongruent with the hell they had just endured. And the risks. *The Lancet* has described the possible impacts of hunger strike on the human body as "starvation-induced effects of electrolyte imbalance, vitamin and mineral depletion, infection, hypothermia, and renal failure." Abdul, Mr. S (these are chosen pseudonyms to protect their identities), and others risked their lives—quite literally—to protest the cruel conditions of holding people captive in close quarters with no ability to social distance in a global pandemic. On strike for their own release, and for the release of *all* migrant detainees.

By way of contrast, I am hearing reports of white Canadians who are refusing to wear masks, who are vehemently opposed to abiding by the public health measures that would help protect vulnerable peoples from contacting this virus. Refusing a sacrifice so small, a slight physical discomfort, to protect this society's elders—*their* elders, too!—its health care workers and its immunocompromised. Simply because they are drunk on this society's individualism, and do not wish, I suppose, to be inconvenienced for the sake of another, not if it means being "told what to do."

There are two different visions of freedom at play here. One is the freedom to evade, to deny one's responsibility to a collective social body; the other forwards a freedom that is relational, holds up freedom as collective safety. As some uphold the "right" to refuse to inconvenience themselves, the hunger strikers have risked their legal status in this country, and their own health, and in doing so have demonstrated for all of us what it means to sacrifice oneself to keep one another safe. I would like to hope, yet of course cannot know, having not been tested, if I would have the strength to show one fraction of this level of courage, should it be asked of me. I do know that this is what grass-roots heroism looks like.

I have been trying to talk to my son L. about what I do when I'm busy during parts of the day, now that we are home together. I want him to know me, and I want him to absorb some of the beauty and the loss of this moment we are living through. I tell him that our family, along with families all around the city, the country, and the world, are working to get people out of detention, out of jail and prison, working to make sure people get out of cages and get to be home safe with their families. I'm teaching him that we're fighting the bad guys, that it is kind of like being a superhero in the shows he watches, except in real life there are hundreds of thousands of us—millions of us, maybe— and that we are ordinary.

L., too, loves to run. He and Minowe would get along, I think, at least on this front, despite the age difference. He has loved to run since he was able to walk—insisting on it well before he was physically capable. He was floppy, clumsy, constantly falling, covered in bruises, but he insisted, he could not be stopped (this remains a facet of his personality that I deeply admire even as it makes parenting a challenge). He now says he loves running so much because it makes him feel *free*. Because of that I—I who had always hated—*hated*—running, do it too. I join him and we run together, every day, as our allotted exercise break from the stay-at-home orders. I know we, Black mom and kid, are not living in a world in which Black freedom can be easily actualized. Because of this he needs to feel something that resonates with him as a space of freedom inside himself. He needs to smell and taste what liberation could be like: I want him to know it, to feel it in his body, to revel in it, so that one day when we truly experience it, he will recognize it and know he has come home.

Robyn,

It's already July and I'm writing to you today on the thirtieth anniversary of uprising and resistance at Kanehsatà:ke,
commonly known as the "Oka Crisis." This of course was
a resistance mobilized by the Kanien'kehá:ka people to protect their land and community, which consisted of sacred
pines and burial grounds, from the expansion of a nine-
hole golf course and the construction of condominiums.
Canada's response was a violent show of force—first by the
Sûreté du Québec (SQ), Quebec's provincial police force,
then by the RCMP, who were replaced a week later by the
Canadian army.

Ten years ago, my family and I were invited by Ellen
Gabriel to attend the twenty-year commemoration of the
"Oka Crisis" in Kanehsatà:ke. I was there in part to launch
This Is an Honour Song: Twenty Years Since the Blockade—
a collection of narratives, poetry, and analysis I co-edited,

from writers outside of the Kanien'kehá:ka communities involved, in celebration of the positive impacts the resistance had on us as individuals and as communities. My family and I walked up the famous hill, past the golf course, to the Pines. It was hot and humid, and not everyone on the route through the white town of Oka was happy to see the procession. I worried for my kids' safety, as I always do, but I wanted them to be present as part of the legacy of resistance that all Indigenous children are born into. The day before, I had sat in the gymnasium of the École Rotiwennákéhte to witness and hold the words of warriors of every kind as they spoke about the seventy-eight days in the summer of 1990. I learned about pain, sacrifice, persistence, and the trauma those individuals took on and have been forced to carry with them. I learned about unspeakable targeted police violence, never reported in the media.

I also learned that very little has changed. No Kanien'kehá:ka community has control or influence over their territories in the face of ongoing encroachment, environmental degradation, and development of all kinds. I learned that all of the root causes that led to the "Oka Crisis" still exist, and that there is no political will on the part of Canada to talk about our land—apart from terminating our Treaty—or our Aboriginal rights, for these Kanien'kehàka communities or for anyone else. In ten more years, very little has changed.

Standing up, speaking out, and protecting Indigenous lands and bodies is one of the reasons Indigenous peoples exist today. At every point in Canadian history, Indigenous peoples have been articulating this importance with diplomacy. We have been willing to take on personal and collective sacrifice to protect what is important to us, and throughout our colonial relationship with Canada, we have been pushed to put our bodies on the land. And even though we know that our bodies on our land between the white colonizer and his resources will end in police and military violence sanctioned by Canadian law, we do it anyway. This comes from a tremendous, unconditional love of our people and our families, our culture and languages, and the land that sustains us. Yes, it comes from love. We have learned to use our righteous anger and resentment to protect and create Indigenous spaces where our kids can grow up to be the very best kind of people. This makes me proud. Without this kind of deliberate resistance shown by the ones that have come before me, I wouldn't be here today as a Michi Saagiig Nishnaabekwe. I wouldn't exist.

Indigenous struggle rarely makes it into the minds of the Canadian mainstream, and when it does surface, it is often without proper historical context. In the recent past, Canadians caught glimpses of this during the 1969 mobilization against Trudeau's White Paper, and again in the mid-1970s when the Dene successfully voiced their critique of capitalism and industrialization in opposition to the Mackenzie Valley pipeline development, both through the Berger Inquiry and in their brilliant articulation of the Dene Declaration. We saw it at several points in the 1980s, whether it was the Haida-led blockade of Lyell Island, which led to the creation of Gwaii Haanas National Park; the ongoing struggle of the Algonquins of Barriere Lake; or the resistance and subsequent raid at Listuguj over salmon fishing rights preceding the "Oka Crisis."

But our resistance goes deeper than this. It's present when we teach our children our languages. When Two-Spirit and queer youth organizers discuss harm reduction with their peers; when the women of the Downtown Eastside of Vancouver organize tirelessly through the decades against the gender violence in their lives. It is present when we shatter the stereotypes Canadians have been taught; it's present when we speak back to racist comments in coffee shops and racist sports logos.

When I think of the "Oka Crisis" I think of the hundreds of Kanien'kehá:ka women from Kanehsatà:ke, Kahnawà:ke, and Akwesasne and across the country who organized the logistics to support the blockades. I think of the food, the medical supplies, the childcare and the worry. I think of their tremendous spiritual and political influence. I think of the principled leadership Kanien'kehá:ka women showed us from behind the barricades. I think of Ellen Gabriel, and how during the summer of 1990 she taught me about righteous anger, love, and to come at injustice from a place of unapologetic strength.

The summer of 1990, for me and many other people of my age, was the most profound political education of my life. It has influenced my professional, artistic, and activist life in a way I couldn't have predicted. I learned the value of direct action. I learned the value of articulating our histories, perspectives, and realities in a clear way. I learned what it looks like when Indigenous peoples live and act by using our own political traditions, systems of governance, and values. I learned what principled action looks like. This was never a crisis; it was a radical transformation—and to realize the full potential of that transformation, when Indigenous peoples act with such conviction, we should all listen and ask, What can I give up to promote peace?

Andrea J. Ritchie, in *Invisible No More: Police Violence Against Black Women and Women of Color*, also writes that the Kanien'kehá:ka resistance was her "initial awareness of police violence against women of color on Turtle Island." Having grown up across the river from Kanehsatà:ke, Ritchie was one of the women who organized to support the blockade by helping to get food and supplies behind army lines, and by joining the camp and acting as a human shield outside of the community. Ritchie writes that these events laid bare for her the continuing violence of colonialism and the role of police and military violence in the maintenance of the settler state, violence that she saw repeated in the recent uprising at Standing Rock.

I know, Robyn, that you are likely too young to remember these events—you will have different actions that you witnessed during your coming of age that changed you. The "Oka Crisis" is transfixed in my mind because this was the first time that events like these were televised over and over again. This was the summer of 1990—before the internet and the nine-hundred-channel universe. It was before cell phones and social media and before everyone had a video camera in their pockets. I knew that this kind of violence existed in the world—it existed in the intimacies of my world—but I had never seen it enacted on Indigenous people five hours down the highway from me, repeatedly on the news. This seems so innocent and naïve in the media-saturated world where we now live.

Two years after the "Oka Crisis," I witnessed from afar another act of horrific violence and another community uprising against that racialized violence—this was the Los Angeles Police Department's brutal beating of Rodney King. Ritchie also writes about witnessing this. I remember seeing the righteous anger in mobilizations in the streets when those same police officers, whose trial had been moved to a white suburb known as a popular place of residence for LAPD members, were acquitted. I remember the 1992 protests in Toronto in response to the acquittal of those officers and in response to local police violence in the city—just two days earlier, Raymond Lawrence had been shot and killed by a plainclothes white police officer. All of the events and circumstances that created these two uprisings have been repeated over and over again over the past thirty years. There is a responsibility that comes with witnessing and with truth.

Very little has changed since 1990 and 1991. Very little, except that on the thirtieth anniversary of the Kanehsatà:ke resistance, we are in the midst of a global uprising for Black life, the latest in five hundred years of Black resistance. An uprising and a movement grown from a tremendous, unconditional love of peoples, families, cultures, and places and lands that sustain Black life. Zoé Samudzi and William C. Anderson foreground Indigeneity on the African continent in *As Black as Resistance: Finding the Conditions for Liberation* in their discussion of Black identity and the many ways it is inextricably linked to land. The Twa people around the Great Lakes, Zambia, and western Uganda; the Maasai and Samburu peoples of Kenya and Tanzania; the

Nuba people of Sudan; the Khoikhoi (or Khoi) and the San of southern and southeastern Africa; and the Dogon of Mali and Burkina Faso—these are all peoples whose homelands do not conform to the enclosures of nation-states. And, like Indigenous peoples in the Americas, Indigenous peoples in Africa organize and fight the nation-state for their lands, cultures, bodies and minds (their "rights") through state-sanctioned mechanisms, transnational bodies and international means.

To fully understand the post-Columbus world, I believe one must think through Indigenous genocide in the Americas and in African contexts alongside the commencement of the African transatlantic slave trade. We must also consider the vast bodies of brilliant resistance Black and Indigenous peoples have generated through engaging in centuries of resistance.

I've spent nearly all of my adult life articulating in one medium or another the importance of land to the Nishnaabeg. Although three generations of my family were removed from our reserve community, and much of our culture and our language, I have been able to spend the past twenty years living in our fractured and injured homeland, and struggling to learn language, culture, ceremony, and knowledge. There are many, many Nishnaabeg who know more than I do, whose land is more intact than mine, who can think inside our language with ease. There are also many Nishnaabeg who have not had the same opportunities.

Land is so important to me, and to Indigenous peoples, that all of our uprisings and resistances hold land at the centre.

Land is of unquestionable importance to Indigenous peoples and land is of unquestionable importance to Black peoples.

These are different sorts of diaspora. A rootlessness based on common and divergent experiences. In common, our ancestors having lived in and built healthy and sustainable Indigenous societies; diverging, a distinctiveness in history and experience perpetuated by the mass kidnapping and genocidal trafficking of Indigenous peoples from the African continent and the genocide and near-genocide of Indigenous peoples in North America. It echoes the crucial corrective of Robin D. G. Kelley, using Cedric J. Robinson's work to critique Patrick Wolfe's *Traces of History*, in which Wolfe argues that settler colonialism operates through the logics of elimination. This corrective has been useful in my own thinking in understanding the colonizer's desire to desecrate everything sacred and meaningful to my people— our lands, bodies, families, ethics, governance, and intelligence—primarily because they want land, and Indigenous attachment to land is an impediment. And, as Kelley points out, Wolfe's assertion that Indigenous peoples were colonized for land, and Black Americans for their labour, is problematic, and has caused harm in our relationships inside and outside of academic thinking. Wolfe erased African Indigeneity through the logics of elimination in the transatlantic slave trade, and did not address settler colonialism as a structure and a process on the African continent. I now think of this every time I see or type "settler colonialism."

Samudzi and Anderson continue, "Much of the identity production of Black people in the US [and Canada] both from descendants of enslaved Africans (African Americans) and otherwise has stemmed from a yearning: an attempt to reconcile a diasporic self with roots and a sense of African groundedness, a sense of homespace." Here again, there is both a congruency in yearning, of piecing back together, and also a distinctiveness. My Indigenous ancestors were not part of the transatlantic slave trade and the mass kidnapping and genocidal trafficking that violently severed Black peoples from their homespace. My Indigenous ancestors are part of a different genocide, a severing of self from land, body, mind, spirit, culture, and language that took place and continues to take place *in* our homespace. Still, I am writing this from my homespace, the homespace of my ancestors. I'm not sure my ancestors would recognize it as home because of the successive world-endings that have taken place over the last four centuries; but, nonetheless, there are fragments. There are glimpses.

I feel homespace most completely in the bush, in a sweat or fasting lodge, surrounded by my closest Nishnaabeg relations. A feeling of homespace is nearly non-existent when I am confronted as an "Indian" on a white, manicured cottage lawn while trying to launch my canoe and harvest wild rice, or when I am arguing with sales clerks in a downtown Toronto shopping mall about status cards and sales tax, or when I am the target of sexualized or physical violence. And there is a grounding from the former experiences of home and place. An ephemeral belonging that inoculates me in some ways from the struggle of later experiences. Sometimes I think that it is those more beautiful Nishnaabeg experiences that have kept me alive.

NourbeSe Philip recently reminded me of this. We had been invited by the brilliant artist scholars Andrea Fatoma and Tania Willard to be in dialogue with each other as part of a Contingencies of Care virtual residency hosted by Graduate Studies at OCAD University, the Toronto Biennial of Art, and BUSH Gallery. At the suggestion of Andrea, we began the dialogue by reading each other's work; I read an excerpt from the beginning of NourbeSe's essay entitled "The Ga(s)p."

> We all begin life in water
> We all begin life because someone once breathed for us
> Until we breathe for ourselves
> Someone breathes for us
> Everyone has had someone—a woman—breathe for them
> Until that first ga(s)p
> For air

She ends the essay by quoting, and then responding to, the final words of Eric Garner:

> I can't breathe;
>
> I will breathe for you.

NourbeSe read the beginning section, "Solidification," from my book *Noopiming: The Cure for White Ladies*. We talked about breath, what it is to breathe for someone else, ideas of care and reaching out to each other; but it was NourbeSe's first observation that I want to repeat today. NourbeSe had asked me how to pronounce the names of the seven main characters, several of which are in Nishnaabemowin:

I want to speak about my experience with this poem, and I hope I can without crying because so much of it, even though it comes from another reality, another experience, speaks to my own experience. So, if I go to what you just identified when I read "I believe everything these seven say because ice distorts perception, and trust replaces critique, examination and interrogation"—and, even before that, the seven—those seven words. For me when I was repeating the words this morning earlier and then saying them, what it did for me was take me to this place of grief, of not having any other language but English. And while I understand in this corporate, capitalized world, having English is useful—"*Akiwenzii is my will . . .*"—and I would think, What word would it be in another, African tongue for me? What is *Sabe* in my own language?

NourbeSe went on to describe a panel discussion some years ago where one of the participants broke down a non-English word to reveal its deeper meaning. She said she is "at times a little envious that Indigenous peoples can re-learn" our languages very easily.

That stayed with me, because so often I've been discouraged and frustrated at how difficult it has been for me to re-learn a tiny bit of my own language and how unfair it is that French is taught in schools, while Indigenous languages are left to die. I have felt ashamed and angry with the violence that all but eliminated Nishnaabemowin in Michi Saagiig Nishnaabeg spaces. Still, in spite of the history of linguicide, I still have access to fluent speakers, online dictionaries, and language classes. Those sounds, however rare, still exist in my homespace. And as NourbeSe said in that same exchange, language is "breath linked to sound linked to meaning."

Language = breath linked to sound linked to meaning.

After the Zoom event ended, and as soon as it was posted on YouTube, I went back to this moment and watched the video over and over. I wanted to spend more time with this moment, and with this equation and with this group of thinkers. I wanted to watch NourbeSe and Andrea's meticulous and generous engagement with my work, and I wanted to watch their brilliance generate new meaning for me, meaning that extends and travels far beyond my work and my offerings in the panel.

Of course, this is the brilliance of Philip's book *Zong!* For those unfamiliar with it, on November 29, 1781, the captain of the Dutch ship *Zong* ordered the murders of 150 enslaved African people, a massacre by drowning that took place over the next ten days so the ship's white businessmen could collect insurance money. The legal decision *Gregson v. Gilbert* documented the colonial discourse that ensued, and provided the text for NourbeSe to build a world in which the urge to make sense of the senseless is refused in favour of "telling a story that must be told by not telling." This requires the writer and the reader to be "implicated and contaminated by the untelling." NourbeSe locks herself in the legal text, mirroring in method the way Black people were locked in the holds of the ship. She uses silence and space to draw the reader's eye into a circus of typography, forcing us to try to order and make sense of something that cannot be made sense of—mimicking what it was like to be an African person aboard that ship. She "whites out, black outs, mutilates and murders the text," randomly picking them, grammatically forcing them to work together, doing to language what was done to bodies, minds and souls aboard that ship. The result is a book that refuses to be confined by the page. When I stopped reading and listened, I heard a ceremony, "chant, moan, shout, oath, ululation, curse, sound, mourning."

On November 30, 2020, Philip presented her annual durational reading of the book, and because of the pandemic, this iteration was both global and virtual. This year's reading, held over ten days, echoed through the space created by the global uprising of movements for Black life, through a global pandemic disproportionately impacting Black and Indigenous communities, and at a time where many of us are reconsidering the work our writing does in a world preoccupied with Black and Indigenous death. *Zong!* teaches us to write differently, to think differently, to read differently, and in NourbeSe's refusal to conform to the foundations of telling, the world of *Zong!* could not be more relevant.

NourbeSe created a new language out of sound and breath and meaninglessness. She created a new language, new sounds and new meanings out of a legal discourse in English, out of nothing.

Language = breath linked to sound linked to meaning.

After the section of the durational performance of *Zong!* I attended, I listened to the recordings of Inuksuk Mackay and Tiffany Ayalik's collaboration, PIQSIQ, and then to Tanya Tagaq's album *Retribution*—to hear the language of Inuit women linking breath to sound to land to meaning and creating new frequencies that disintegrate the noise of colonialism. These sound immersions reminded me of this section of poet Natalie Diaz's "The First Water Is the Body":

> I carry a river. It is who I am: 'Aha Makav. This is not metaphor.
>
> When A Mojave says, *Inyech 'Aha Makavch ithuum,* we are saying our name.
>
> We are telling a story of our existence. *The river runs through the middle of my body.*

Diaz is 'Aha Makav and an enrolled member of the Gila River Indian Tribe. The Colorado River runs through the middle of her body. The Great Lakes are my internal organs. = Our existence, our bodies, minds and spirits are of the land, part of the land, from the land, inseparable from the relationships we have to air, water, soil, fire, plants, animals, and spirits. I am umbilically attached to this place. I carry an ethical imperative to live and build in a way that promotes more life—all life.

These listenings lead me to a re-reading of Tiffany King's work in *The Black Shoals: Offshore Formations of Black and Native Studies* on Black fungibility, and then of course to the bodies of work by Saidiya Hartman, Hortense Spillers, and Sylvia Wynter. These three brilliant theorists made me sink into myself and think more deeply about the ethical imperatives Nishnaabeg Elders have taught me with regards to homelands, space, and the deep sharing that comes with being a part of the land. Ethical imperatives and responsibilities to protect both land and life from exploitation, and to share that same land and life across complexities, violence, and oppressions. The afterlives of transatlantic slavery, current manifestations of anti-Blackness, fungibility and colonialism might complicate these ethics and responsibilities, but it doesn't mean we abandon them or ignore them. It means they require more presence, more work, more intention, more consideration, and the vision and wisdom of our respective ancestors to move through with grace, and in ways that support a continuous rebirth of Black and Indigenous life and freedom and shared politics and ethical practices responsive to the needs of living beings. Land will always be an important analytic for me and Nishnaabeg thought, although I don't think of land as enclosed patches of dirt with armed borders around it and I do think my love of my land is compatible with Black liberation. If we engage deeply with these complexities perhaps we can find more than what has been relegated to us by four centuries of white violence.

What if Black and Indigenous relationality refuses settler logics and centres the dismantling in a grounding of the very best practice of Indigenous and Black radical politics? What does it look like if we are all engaged in generating theory, organizing to the specificities of our lived experiences, but we are deeply linked in our distinctive world-building relationalities to ensure the worlds we build do not restrict, enclose or eliminate Black and Indigenous life? What worlds do Indigenous and Black land-based politics give breath to, and how do we connect these to anti-colonial movements outside of North America and beyond? What does it mean to equitably share land, time, space, and the gifts of creation? What does this look like? What does it feel like? Can we make Indigenous and Black futurities against occupation and social death relationally responsive to each other? There is no justice in Land Back if it is not in concert with the destruction of racial capitalism, and if Black people remain landless. There is no justice in Land Back if we are silent with regard to the radical imaginings of Black futures and Black struggles for freedom, just as there is no justice if Black liberation is framed through the ongoing dispossession of Indigenous peoples.

We know that in our respective communities, notions of land and nationhood (outside of the nation-state) can cause tension, and these tensions can and have led to incommensurability. I wonder if thinking through these tensions, of holding these tensions, can also be generative and closen us in terms of our unique and interlocking projects of justice. Similarly, Samudzi and Anderson use both abolition and settler colonialism as lenses through which to think about political affinities between our communities.

Following their example and moving outside of settler logics and dispossession, what could relationally responsive projects of Black and Indigenous liberation look like?

I've often used the Dish with One Spoon treaty relationship with the Kanien'kehá:ka on the east side of Lake

Ontario and our relationship with the Wendat as examples of political relationships that draw on wisdom of distinctive peoples to create ways of living together that respect separate jurisdictions, sovereignties, and self-determination over a shared territory. I've also used examples of Nishnaabeg treaties with the deer and beaver nations as examples. Nishnaabeg nationhood and territoriality, within our political practices, was *never* exclusive and was never about enclosures. Our homespace was and is shared with a multitude of self-determining plant and animal nations and peoples. Our homespace was always shared, particularly around overlapping places of presence, with other self-determined nations. Our homespace was and is always shared with our ancestors, our children yet to be born, and spiritual beings. A deep and complex relational sharing has always been our foundation of existence, and the way we are able to organize ourselves to live in a way that brings forth more life, more breath. Yet, this seemingly open and endless sharing isn't naïve or utopian. There isn't a place in my homespace for capitalism and its evil siblings because of their continual ending of worlds, their continual death march where self-determining beings become resources, property, or are eliminated altogether. It is under these circumstances that the ethical imperative to protect life-generating processes becomes greater than the imperative to share.

There is urgency in this work. The global climate emergency, what Françoise Vergès calls the "Racial Capitalocene," is the backdrop for all of the other world-ending consequences of conquest. Our relationships to land and place are as always of paramount importance to our collective freedoms and continuity as peoples. Both of our communities live with the consequences of uneven resource distribution, food insecurity leading to chronic colonial-induced health conditions, lack of drinking water, house insecurity, environmental racism with regard to contamination, and the surveillance and removal of black and red bodies from the land when they are a threat to capital.

In many ways, our practices of resistance are already doing this work—when the Freedom School visits Six Nations on a field trip, or in #BLMTOTentCity, or when we come together in the territory of the Yellowknives Dene to share fish and dream of trips to Barbados and the sugar bush. In many ways, there are people in our movements who have always been doing this work—when organizations like the Native Alliance for Red Power (NARP) visited with the Black Panthers Seattle chapter in 1968 to discuss solidarity, for example, or when Black feminists continue to write the Indigenous present into their work and organizing. There are many more contemporary and historic examples of productive relationships of insurgence and co-resistance and there are lots of shortcomings and failings as well. My point here is that this work is not without historical and contemporary precedent, and it is work being done by an assemblage of organizers, intellectuals, activists, artists, cultural workers and people using practice to generate theory from the ground up. My point is that, as Cedric Robinson points out in *Black Marxism*, the fact that Black people exist today is not a miracle but rather a product of the collective intelligence developed over five centuries of struggle. The same could be said of Indigenous resistance. Perhaps, Robyn, you and I are able to have the particular conversations in this book because so many Black and Indigenous thinkers and doers have already had these conversations or are building practices and thinking together as we are writing this. It strikes me that this collective insurgent intelligentsia and practice of resistance that Indigenous and Black peoples hold, then, is immense and unprecedented.

On Sunday, October 2, 2016, I was invited by a former student of mine to take part in the evening program of the Justice for Abdirahman Community Conference in Ottawa, alongside Yusra Khogali, Hawa Y. Mire and Kim Katrin Milan. The event was a response to the tragic killing of Abdirahman Abdi by Ottawa police on July 24 of the same year, and was an intentional space designed for his family and community to discuss and share knowledge around anti-Blackness, state-sanctioned violence, mental health and xenophobia. This was a diverse Black Muslim–majority space of mourning, prayer, peace, anger and right relations in Algonquin Anishinaabeg territory. It was a glimpse of the potential of Black and Indigenous world-making, even though it may have only lasted a few hours. It felt different. I felt Nishnaabeg and it felt like my homeland, but it also felt like I was an invited visitor and guest in someone else's homespace, a community that was not mine, but to which I was profoundly linked.

I am reminded of this practice when I think about the #BLMTOTentCity created by queer/trans Black activists in front of Toronto Police Service Headquarters for two weeks in the spring of 2016, in response to the announcement that no charges would be laid against the Toronto police officers involved in the homicide of Andrew Loku.

I remember photos of the encampment community in the media, and I remember seeing a Mohawk Warrior flag and a Haudenosaunee Confederacy flag. This caught my attention. As I learned more about the Tent City, I learned that there was space within the community for Indigenous peoples. I learned that Indigenous activists took on a care-taking role, sharing medicines and smudging practices. I learned that Indigenous activists respected the goals, decision-making and plans for the community.

This community reminded me that when we are intentional and attentive to the settler colonial and white supremacist logics, encampments and other forms of occupation can become rich sites of theory generated through shared practice, reminded us of our potentiality together. Our truths, layered, nuanced and rooted in different historic and contemporary realities, can be an asset when our relationship building, movement building and community building is intentional, attentive and committed to not replicating the logics of capitalism, colonialism and slavery.

Theory generated from land, from practice, from experience, from collective minds and bodies coming together in formation and achieving something synergistic that, as individuals, we couldn't have achieved otherwise. Theory generated from action propelled by the social conditions and material needs of our peoples. Tent cities and encampment communities as shared homeplaces are microcosms of mutual and treaty relations between Black and Indigenous peoples. Tent cities and encampments build a practical alternative to live in while generating shared Black and Indigenous meaning and theory that could not have been generated otherwise.

White supremacy has a vested interest in keeping Black and Indigenous movements apart and competing. Colonialism benefits from these two genocides. Capitalism benefits. Deepening our relationships with each other in tents, in the bush or on the street, behind barricades and while dismantling barricades, and even through letter writing, opens up endless possibilities for dismantling the white supremacist, colonial and capitalist present in synergy with each other.

What do liberated lands look like?

PART THREE

A Summer of Revolt

Hi Leanne,

It's 4:30 a.m. right now. I can never sleep anymore. I'm beginning this letter to you as I'm scrambling, doing some of that behind-the-scenes movement work, love work, that keeps things flowing smoothly. Due to being part of a very high-risk pod, I am not out in front of Station 22, but I'm helping out as a movement auntie, with the logistics of legal and media support, from home. You're probably aware that in Toronto we are in the midst of a battle on many fronts to defund/dismantle/abolish the police, along with other monuments to racist violence. What this looks like in this exact moment, though, is that many of us are collectively fighting in defence of arrested comrades: numbering Black, queer, and/or disabled folks who've been taken into the station for booking, held for what has felt like an eternity. This is, of course, the latest saga in the grossly disproportionate state response to BLM-TO's artistic disruption of the Ryerson statue, among a few others. The arrests were and are polit-ical: the alleged offence involves some pink paint (he hon-estly looks better than ever), and a sign that reads "Tear down monuments that represent slavery, colonialism and violence." Yet here we are with what seems likely to be crim-inal mischief charges. Propelled to action by the ridiculous-ness of these arrests, railing against the criminalization of dissent in a moment of historic mass Black-led uprisings, hundreds of people have been out on the streets all day and most of the night outside of the cop shop, demanding that the arrestees be let go. And we know how to turn up, of course, Black folks in these times. DJs, speakers, poetry all being a part of the occupation of the public space outside the police station. As it turned out, the arrestees were not all at this station, but had been spread across all corners of the city. For hours we could not find our people, the police were not answering the phones, let alone telling us where they were being held. I have made dozens of calls, so far, to Mike Leitold, a lawyer with the Movement Defence Committee who has been supporting the day's action. I have dubbed him my New Best Friend, given how much we've spoken in the last twelve hours. He has been patient with me as I have continued to call and text him through to 4 a.m. until we've known that our arrested comrades are safe, out, freed (albeit constricted by the conditions attached to their crimi-nal charges). As I'm settling down now into writing to you, the last arrestee has just been *found*, released, safely brought home, and the crowds have dispersed. I've been scribbling notes to send your way between calls, between updates, etc. It's been all too fitting to be sitting, tonight, with your letter printed out on my kitchen table. Thirty years since Oka. Because here we are in the midst of yet another period fraught with militarized police response to dissent, the criminalization of liberation-oriented organizing across North America. On the front lines of a general strike against carceral racial capitalism.

When we were hit with the pandemic and the corresponding shuttering of the day-to-day, I was awestruck by the courage and principled struggle emerging at encampments, behind bars. But I was also mourning, and scared, to be honest, for how this period of quarantine and social and physical distance would impact the foreseeable future of resistance struggle. The possibilities for the public arm of organizing had suddenly been vastly, dramatically constricted, and I worried that we'd reached an indefinite end of the vibrant street culture of resistance that had propelled so many of the recent years of struggle. There were discussions, across many organizing communities that I am part of, about how we could do "public" actions, now that all sense of public had disappeared. Car demonstrations outside of prisons and detention centres, for example, took on a new life, yet I worried at their limited effectiveness. I was happy to contribute to strategy, mobilizing, where and what I could, as this is what the times demanded. But looking back, I realize now how much I was doing so out of habit, and urgency, but lacking the general sense of guarded optimism that usually sits with me. I held on to hope as a discipline, a practice that I've learned, along with countless others, from Mariame Kaba, and moved forward out of a sense of principled commitment, rather than giving in to despair. But I see now that I was doing so without my usual underlying belief that somehow we will get to where we need to be; that I was lacking the cautious optimism that normally lives below my sternum. I feared that the months ahead would be nothing but slow announcements of the deaths of our people. I was worried that even though we'd fight—we always do—the fights would be siloed from one another, silenced by dominant society. I worried that all of the emergent struggles to keep one another alive, to keep each other safe, would simply not be enough. And I was afraid that we were losing, losing harder and faster and altogether *more* than we could bear to lose. It seemed to me that I was a closeted heretic, within movement spaces. Said no—I had to, I felt—to most public speaking invitations, because I knew I could not be what people seemed to want or need me to be, because optimism had gone beyond my purview. I felt sure that my doubts would show through despite the confidence implied by the red lipstick, eyeliner and the "work sweater" that serves as my professional drag.

What I had not anticipated, of course, was the wave of revolt, the massive surge of street-based uprisings, that was to come, that is now upon us. While history had trained me to be aware of the ongoing possibility of public executions such as that of George Floyd, what I could not have foreseen was how this event would spark off these revolutionary Black-led but multiracial uprisings that would launch an attack on the dominant episteme, on the very symbols of racial domination and violence of our society: police stations, prisons, statues, and all other monuments to racial violence and brutality. I had not anticipated hundreds of thousands in the streets every day for months. The moment we are in right now was unthinkable, unimaginable. It's believable only because it's still happening, and I still wake up worrying sometimes that I only dreamed up this part.

But you're correct, Leanne, that each wave of struggle builds on the last. Resistance to the settler, police, and military brutality at Oka inspired three decades of struggle in its wake. Idle No More did not end but planted seeds. And, as this moment is making clear, the Black Lives Matter movement born in Ferguson in 2014—BLM 1.0—did not end, either, but saw the creation and expansion of root systems that would be ready for the next act. That would prepare us for the fire this time. Preceding moments of struggle that led us into this moment did what so many of us could only hope they could: they have turned into a movement. Including but extending well beyond the formal organizations in the Movement for Black Lives, new formations of struggle in defence of Black life seem to be emerging daily, organized and informal, across cities and towns, together forming a life-affirming crescendo impossible to ignore.

As I'm sure you're aware, in the US, people have been in the streets, in cities like New York, Portland, and Minneapolis, defying state-imposed curfews and massive levels of police violence for over thirty days, demanding not only an end to violent policing but an end to a society governed by racism, governed by violence. Demanding a society based, instead, in care. At my most recent count there were, over a period of three or so weeks, seventy protests across Canada related in some way to calls to defund/disarm/dismantle/abolish police. For over two weeks, a new collective called Afro-Indigenous Rising has held down an encampment, with tents labelled "abolition camp," hosting teach-ins on police abolition. The new queer Black formation Not Another Black Life, born in the wake of the death of Regis Korchinski-Paquet in a police interaction, led a march of ten thousand through the streets of Toronto. Halifax saw its largest street protests ever, and Winnipeg held a week (!) of actions in support of police defunding and against anti-Black and anti-Indigenous racism, one in which mostly young, mostly Black people took over the Convention Centre, riding up the escalators chanting "No justice no peace! Black Lives matter!" Intergenerational gatherings of people—Black-led, broadly, but with mass multi-racial support—are taking to the streets risking their health, in a time of a global pandemic, to demand a new world.

As is usual for me, I'm writing you, but I'm also distracted. And so in another window of my computer screen, I'm re-watching the footage from the protests earlier tonight. Rajean Hoilett, a member of Toronto Prisoners' Rights Project, takes the mic at the street occupation: he's just stated that so far this summer, there have already been five hunger strikes in Ontario's jails. Five!

This is a summer of revolt.

This is the summer that we collectively breathe light into a new world. Or at least, the possibility of one.

I've hosted a few community Zooms, trainings on police abolition work, and in doing so I've met incredible, brilliant, cross-generational but broadly young, new, and extremely committed Black peoples working to overturn the violence of policing in all its forms. Over Zoom and the thousands of new WhatsApp and Signal threads that have started since this all began, I've learned enormously, have heard from Black and Indigenous peoples in the Yukon who are working to defund the RCMP, and from young Black activists in Kitchener-Waterloo, Edmonton, Hamilton, and Vancouver who are working to get police out of schools. Many have been successful, and many more likely will be.

I have never seen a more exciting time.

It's more than the numbers, mind you. The very grounds from which we stand and from which we wage our struggle have been altered. Cedric J. Robinson wrote, in 1975, that in periods of mass unrest, we bear witness to a "revolutionary attack on the culture." In order for movements to be successful, in his analysis, a mass collective of people needs to be able to reverse the language, the symbols to which they are opposed, and to instill them with new meanings. Put differently, a sign of success within movements is when we are able to intervene in the dominant logics of the times and to collectively produce new meanings. And I believe strongly that this is what we are experiencing in this moment: a revolutionary attack on the culture, led by everyday people, self-organized communities, by the formal organs of social movements, working together in long-term or short-term, and even in momentary capacities.

So many taken-for-granteds of the institutional violence woven into daily life are not only being exposed, but overturned, including the state-sanctioned terrorizing of Black children in public schools across North America. School boards in Minneapolis have severed their contracts with the Minneapolis Police Department, Oakland passed the

"George Floyd Resolution to Eliminate the Oakland Schools Police Department," the Denver School Board voted this June to phase police out of its schools, San Francisco and San Jose voted to suspend or disband school police contracts. And all of this is possible because there is an ever-expanding understanding in our streets and communities at this time that it is not only police violence, but policing itself, that is a source of harm in our society. Large swaths of the population are mapping out the meaning of *safety* beyond/without the police, prisons, and all forms of surveillance and captivity, and demanding nothing less than liberation.

This has occurred because of a revolutionary shift in the very meaning of safety. And in this instant, policing has been de-linked from its association with public safety, from being upheld as the site of public safety, has been exposed as its anathema. Consequently, it is no longer taken for granted that policing is a natural, necessary, and permanent feature of society. That has been ruptured, perhaps inalterably.

This is a wildly generative breach. Because as it has been increasingly understood, across North America, that policing is itself the *opposite of safety*—safety's negation— much else has been made possible. It is hardly radical to desire safety, to believe that we deserve safety. And once we understand that safety does not come from the police, especially not if you are Black or Indigenous, it becomes possible for large numbers of people to ask, *If not this, then what?* And in this very questioning, to begin to generate expansive alternatives, to undertake a meaningful study of, and experimentation with, what safety could look like, otherwise. Because of course, if safety does not come from the police, then it is only reasonable that we must support the creation of real safety, of felt, embodied, and lived forms of security, with all that we have. That safety could be reconstituted as care is indeed a revolutionary proposition.

People are revolting for wildly imaginative things: for worlds radically transformed, for the end of policing, the end of prisons, the end of ICE and the CBSA, of militarism and colonialism. At the same time, people are revolting for what are considered—or what should always have been considered—the most basic of things. The hunger strikers in the Ottawa-Carleton Detention Centre, for example, are asking for decent food, clean water, phone calls to their loved ones. This highlights yet again that basics, "givens," are not given but purposefully withheld. Of course, it is *because* this systematized neglect is so endemic that we are faced with the demand for something new. It's the consistent and structural refusal to meet people's basic needs that *is* the status quo; the ongoing and structural denial of meeting basic needs is in fact the reality which underlines the necessity of a broader transformation. Mass uprisings like these are truly simple, in this sense: a demand for the necessities of life exposes how purposefully these are denied.

And if you've been reading, as I have, the demands being forwarded on these streets, the demands that have proliferated across North America, it is clear that not only are police budgets under attack, but there is a massive groundswell geared towards funding community supports that are not rooted in the surveillance and punishment of our communities, but in truly allowing our communities to flourish. Because "the opposite of a carceral society is a care-based society."

And yet so crucially: while there is a *newness* to this world, this life, this summer—it's built from generations of intellectual and political labour.

This revolutionary summer with its even more revolutionary demands felt like it came out of nowhere. Yet in many cities across North America, work to divest from police, abolish police, had been part of a daily grind of struggle outside of the public eye for years, even decades. Outside of public moments of attention, of course, organizing does not sleep. Before this summer of revolt, work had already been underway in Minneapolis, Chicago, LA, Toronto, to decouple police from schools, to remove police from Pride parades. In Toronto's case, in fact, this work was highly successful: efforts by LeRoi Newbold of Freedom School Toronto, LAEN, Education Not Incarceration, and BLM-TO had already achieved the end of School Resource Officers (SROs) in the Toronto District School Board, Canada's largest. BLM-TO had already *won* the struggle to remove police from Pride. Working with Randy Riley and other Black prisoners, El Jones, Black liberation visionary and long-time prison abolitionist, was nourishing abolitionist freedom dreams for years before the public would listen. This movement, though, had been seeded, nourished, too, from longer traditions of Black radicalism: from abolitionist organizing in North America against the prison-industrial complex; by the women of colour–led projects of INCITE!; by Critical Resistance, founded by Beth Richie, Angela Y. Davis, and many others in 1997; by the intellectual and political labours of incarcerated Black political prisoners; by the Quakers; by survivors of sexual and gendered violence;

by my formerly enslaved ancestors. Generations of political and intellectual labours have informed and are informing the visions and worlds that are being fashioned in our present moment. I say this to highlight the sometimes unseen and uncredited *work* that made possible the emergent logics of these times: the public education and organizing that was required to get us, as a society, into a position from which a movement to defund/abolish police could emerge.

And it feels unbelievable that we are where we are. I remember, at a police abolition conference earlier this year, facilitated by long-time Black feminist activist-scholar Rachel Herzig,[*] a few of us joking about how we hoped, but did not expect by any means, that we would live to see a time where our people would be penning op-eds about police abolition, talking about it on the news, bringing it into mainstream conversations. I don't think any of us imagined or even dared to fantasize that we would be reading, and sharing, only a few months later, Mariame Kaba's "Yes, We Literally Mean Abolish the Police," published in the *New York Times*, of all places.

And listen, when it comes to reform, we have tried, and we have been tried. The first crescendo of Black Lives Matter resulted in a series of public statements and piecemeal changes by lawmakers and some politicians. More diversity of officers, "implicit bias training," all of this meant to sell us on the idea that tinkering with the system of policing would

---

[*] This conference was hosted by a number of organizations, including Interrupting Criminalization and Criminal Resistance, both founded and led by Black feminists.

be enough to foster change. When the police in Minneapolis murdered George Floyd, the city had already had an Indigenous woman as its chief of police. George Floyd was killed under the leadership of a Black chief of police, was killed by police who were wearing bodycams, by a police force who had gone through trainings that explicitly taught them not to hold people detained in prone positions such as that experienced by Floyd. We have lived and died for generations now within the limited and limiting promises of reform.

I was educated by my elders about the energies extracted from past generations of Black radicals into police reforms. Movement elder Brenda Paris, a Montreal-based Black feminist now in her late sixties—who fought the arrests and deportations of Black students under the 1969 Concordia computer riots—schooled me on this. She helped me see just how long they have been dodging us, avoiding meaningful change by means of tiny "reforms" explicitly designed to waste our energies, to wait out the moment of public scrutiny while maintaining the status quo. She taught me about how after police killed a Black teenager, Anthony Griffin, in 1987, and the city was aflame in protest for days, Black folks—Black women especially—who had protested, like herself, had been pulled in by the city to train the police on racial bias. They entered into this work begrudgingly, of course, yet wishing to do anything that could put an end to the unrelenting violence of the policing of Black Montreal. She described to me, with a weariness in her voice, the bone-deep disappointment when the early 1990s brought us more of the same: the deaths of Leslie Presley, Marcellus Francois, Fritzgerald Forbes, Trevor Kelly.

I would learn, later on, about the Black Action Defence Committee (BADC)'s push for the creation of the independent oversight of police. This activism emerged in response to the 1970s police murders of Buddy Evans and Albert Johnson in Toronto, and the epidemic of police killings of Black folks that went on to shake the community in the 1980s. While BADC surely dreamed of far more than the creation of a *new* racist institution, that is what they got. Ontario's Special Investigations Unit (SIU), ostensibly a "police oversight unit," would be staffed by ex-police who would exonerate 99 percent of the police who killed. Kikélola Roach, daughter of BADC co-founder Charles Roach, spoke of her father's rebuke of the so-called oversight body, stating on Twitter that "[BADC's] activism is credited for creating the SIU. But he always used to say the SIU was like getting a car but with no steering wheel and no gas. It never took us where we needed to go."

In my own time, working in a group called Justice for Victims of Police Killings with Bridget Tolley, an Indigenous woman from Maniwaki whose mother was killed by the Sûreté du Québec, alongside many other family members who'd lost loved ones to police, we tried. And tried. When Gladys Tolley—Bridget's mother—was struck and killed by a Sûreté du Québec patrol car in 2001, the brother of the man who'd struck Gladys presided over the investigation. Marches, vigils, public education; more family members of loved ones killed joined us, and we worked, from 2010 onward, to end the practice of police investigating police, to get a *non-police-based* investigation body set up, only to see, in 2016, the establishment of a so-called independent police investigation body, staffed largely by former police officers, à la SIU.

Throughout my twenties, I, like so many others who work in community and harm reduction, have had to eat shit, time and time again, as tinkering with the system, senseless by design, stood in for transformative change. Have sat on countless neighborhood meetings where we decried ongoing police abuse of Black and Indigenous women, while the community police officers—who were inexplicably invited to all municipal neighborhood meetings—promised they would "look into it." Have, again like countless others, even skeptically and begrudgingly run educational workshops for police officers-in-training about racism and sexism to try to convince them in advance not to beat and rape our people. Have helped collect data for study after study. Black women have been doing this since before I was born. As I said: on reform, we have tried, and we have been tried.

What is being demanded on the streets in this moment is not police "reform." It is not another study, more diversity training. It is not body cams. It is not more police oversight, it is not putting the police who kill behind bars, even. It is not more Black cops/Black prosecutors/Black heads of state. It's the end of police, and of policing. And the creation of a society that would not need police and policing.

In this moment, I feel a sense of vindication for my ancestors, and for my comrades and elders and aunties in the movement for Black Lives, as many of their visions are pulled front and centre, scaffolding the freedom-oriented demands in a moment of historic revolt.

Yet Indigenous radicalism, in its multiplicity of traditions, has, too, been foundational in the development of my own belief in what is possible, and has helped many of us see the kind of intellectual and political work that is possible, necessary, to make this world livable.

You're right, Leanne, that I was too young to have any lived memory of the Oka crisis—or, to use Ellen Gabriel's term, the 1991 Siege of Kanehsatà:ke. Still, its legacy had a long-standing ripple effect on my life; it diffused into all movements that would come afterward. The Mohawk response to the siege was a substantial part of my own political education, and everyone's around me. The entirety of my early adult life was spent in Montreal, just under an hour from Oka, so my involvement with organizing at that time meant, fortunately for me, that I was able to absorb, if vicariously at times, many of the lessons of Mohawk struggle. Ellen Gabriel made frequent appearances on a no-borders community radio show that I used to co-host. I learned from her and many others about the collective organizing, tactical strategy, sacrifice, and enormous courage demanded of those who struggled for over two months in the face of vast, militarized state repression.

One of my most formative early political experiences was, in fact, witnessing Mohawk resistance, though it took place nearly twenty years after Oka. This time around, though, the resistance to the state was taking place in the community of Akwesasne. There I saw first-hand the power of mass collective resistance against the violence of the settler state that I reside in.

In 2009, the Canadian government announced that the US–Canada border would now be armed: that Canadian border agents would now have guns with live ammunition, after generations of one of the longest non-militarized land borders in the world. The Mohawk community living in Akwesasne—a territory cut in half by the US border— refused, quite simply refused, to allow the border that cuts through their territory to be militarized.

The border, and the Canadian state's ability to control movement across it, has been a site of struggle for over a century. As Audra Simpson has detailed carefully, the Indian Defense League of America had been organizing against— and indeed rejecting—the border's imposition, and fighting for Indigenous freedom of passage since at least the 1920s. Community members rightly opposed the militarization of a border that had, already, been viewed as an illegitimate imposition on their territory, making it difficult—illegal!— for family members to visit one another without the formal permission to cross that is the prerogative of Canadian border agents. The border's militarization, though, was the last straw. I was invited to join a delegation in support of hundreds of community members gathered at the border to oppose its militarization. To my surprise, by the time our delegation had arrived, the Canadian Border Services Agency had abandoned the border station entirely.

I don't know that I can describe for you the feeling of awe that worked its way through my body when our car pulled up, when I looked at the border station and realized it was un-manned, and when I looked up and saw the vibrant purple and white of the Mohawk flag soaring in the air against the skyline, having been raised on the pole in front of the CBSA station where the Canadian flag had been. A celebration, now, of nation, not nation-state. The border guards, who I can only assume were told to depart by higher-ups wishing to avoid another shameful international incident, had simply up and left. Instead, a large community gathering was taking place: speeches, fires, song. This was a celebration, a militant affirmation of life: we were hosted, fed, and educated. It was more than the negation of a carceral and militarized zone, more than a border closure: it was the creation of communities, otherwise. (And as I think through this, Ruth Wilson Gilmore's voice whispers in my mind once again: "Abolition is about presence, not absence.")

This was not a full victory, of course, given that the border itself remains. Given, too, that the border guards are, in the end, armed, albeit in a new station that is a few miles away from the old one. And of course, we are writing to one another in territories that are still occupied by the Canadian nation-state. But nonetheless, here I had witnessed a *demand*—not a request—made upon the Canadian state. And one that was met with a level of state surrender that my twenty-two-year-old self, a baby Black radical, in but not of the Canadian state, could not have foreseen or envisioned. It briefly made visible, too, that there are other ways to organize human life, that we can hold space alongside one another, in the absence of harmful institutions. This was a pivotal period of development, when I had bestowed on me lessons which would take years to truly sink in and are certainly sinking in still.

Even as Black radicalism has for me always been the centre from which other forms of learning were supplemented, Indigenous resistance struggle has been foundational to my political development, being, as you've termed it elsewhere, "the longest running resistance movement in Canadian history." Indeed!

And about solidarity across communities, despite zones of political or strategic difference, I learned this from a 2009 phone call with Ashanti Alston, former Black Panther, a movement elder and a survivor of the war that came before: "If people in Puerto Rico are fighting for independence, you don't necessarily have to agree with all the ways that they envision that, and the way that they fight, but you know that they have the right to conduct their struggle in the best way—that they need to do it to get the boot of imperialism . . . off their neck. You support that."

He went on to say that in the US, "our Black liberation struggle is still in so many ways an anti-colonial struggle, a five-hundred-year-old struggle." Solidarity across anti-colonial struggles, within and across communities working to get the boot off of our collective necks—I feel fortunate to have learned about this at a young age. There remains much to learn about solidarity from people who came up against the boot of the empire and survived.

In what now feels like lifetimes ago, the last trip that I've taken out of Toronto was about one week before the stay-at-home orders hit. Along with a few other Freedom School parents, I went up with a carful of kids to the blockades at Six Nations in support of the Wet'suwet'en land defence. That moment had become, as Katherine McKittrick described on Twitter, "a network of anticolonial struggles" traversing wide-spanning geographies. Because 2020 was ushered in with solidarity blockades that spanned the whole of Turtle Island, across so-called Canada and up to Standing Rock. It felt like the beginning of something massive. It was *already* something massive, transformative, historic, radical anti-capitalist Indigenous resistance to extraction. Standing up against the sheer weight of colonial violence and extraction, staring down the settler police force, defending traditional lands and inspiring a generation of young people.

And when the many solidarity blockades ended, seemingly overnight, with the announcement of the global pandemic in mid-March, I feared for what this would mean for the possibility of land defence going forward. I feared that we were entering an era where not only would all forms of protest, rebellion, and emancipation be aborted, but that pipelines, fracking, and other forms of racial ecocide would continue unabated (and of course, that part turned out to be true).

But today, we find ourselves in a moment where police stations have been burned to the ground, where city governments are talking about dismantling entire arms of the state (though we'll see). And while I have no unfettered optimism that the state, out of benevolence, will redefine its own structure and functions, I am no longer pessimistic about the future of protest, in this time. How could I be? I feel, too, that the Wet'suwet'en solidarity blockades midwifed our world—or at least those of us in North America—into the next phase of struggle, from one transnational anti-colonial nexus to another: a historic year of protest for Indigenous land, for Black life, and for a new world.

Importantly, in this moment, I'm seeing our communities fighting together. This struggle touches close to home, of course, for our people. Indigenous feminists like Pamela

Palmater and Emily Riddle have been supporting the #DefundThePolice movement and expanding its scope, forwarding a call to #DefundTheRCMP—an institution born to clear Indigenous peoples from their lands in the West. They have been foregrounding, too, how policing connects to the violent theft of Indigenous territories that continues to this day. This chorus of voices, spanning both our communities, is reflected, too, in emergent struggles on the ground. Black and Indigenous communities are, in this moment, coming together to challenge the very institution that has relegated so many of our peoples to early death.

Defunding is not just slashing the funds allotted to policing, it is creation: it is Mad co-led mental health response, a safe drug supply and housing for all, and free public transportation and status for all, and education and childcare and the conditions for vitality and life and life and life and life and life.

I believe it was at David Chariandy's book launch a few years ago that I was speaking to Dionne Brand. Probably blabbing on nervously, I was enthusiastic, describing how, surely, something was in the air—Black radicalism, Black thought, Black writing, was having a renaissance like I had never before witnessed. Because that was a year: we were anticipating the release of her *Theory* and *The Blue Clerk*; David's *Brother* had just come out and *I've Been Meaning to Tell You* was on its way; Desmond Cole was well into *The Skin We're In*, then still in process—all of this nourished by and nourishing Black struggle on the streets, in our schools, across our communities. She responded, and I'm paraphrasing her slightly here, "Sure. But what we need to do, what we really need to do next, *is to change the air*." That correction, the crucial distinction that she had forwarded, continued to sit with me for a long time.

And it is this change in the air that is upon us right now.

In real time, our communities are rescuing the term "safety" from where it had been languishing within the carceral regime and bringing it into as expansive a realm as possible. Insisting that if we want safety, *really*, we can, and will, attempt to resolve social, racial, gendered, and economic inequalities that are the root cause of harm; that we can and will choose to resolve the issues rather than police the people most harmed by them.

And we're closer to winning than I have seen us! On the cultural level: What other word but "winning" describes the fact that 50 percent of Canadians support defunding the police—nearly three-quarters of my generation? This is substantial: by way of comparison, in 1964, a majority of white New Yorkers surveyed by the *New York Times* said they believed that the civil rights movement had gone too far.

I'm not one to declare victory prematurely, though. While we've changed the air, collectively, it's of course too soon—far too soon and far from accurate—to declare that we're winning on the political front, on the institutional front. Because while the public's thoughts are changing, those in power are not changing alongside them. Amidst widespread calls to slash the police budget, Toronto has upheld a motion to *increase* police funding by investing in body cams, a move echoed by Montreal mayor Valérie Plante, and Prime Minister Justin Trudeau on a national level. Culture is only one front of the struggle: if we are changing the air, we have not yet radically transformed and rebuilt institutions that harm and maim into conditions that heal and sustain. But this does not and should not diminish the importance, the historic nature of this moment.

Changing the air is vital. It is a precondition to the possibility of systemic transformation; it's integral to struggle; it helps us, as Toni Cade Bambara describes it, to "make revolution irresistible."

Audre Lorde says, "social protest is to say that we do not have to live this way." It is a rejection of "the inconsistencies, the horror, of the lives we are living." And this generative rejection, this demand for another way of living, is louder and more vibrant and more wide-spanning than I thought I would live to see, especially in these times.

Abolition is world-building. It is building the worlds we want and need. I know that we are not yet there, and that so much can still happen to undo this moment of possibility. But I am savouring it, still. Because I don't know what lies ahead, I want to commit to memory what it feels like to be sitting so close to the possibility, at least, of such large-scale transformation.

We haven't had a chance to speak in person since all of this has unfolded. And every day is a fucking month, right now, so it feels like it's been years since I've heard your voice, seen your face. I miss you, Leanne. Right now, Mark Saunders and Justin Trudeau are kneeling on my neck but I love writing you, and won't let those clowns impede this communion. As I look back through my phone, almost all of our photos sent over text messages in the last few months are pictures of our kids at protests. I sent you pictures of L. and a dozen or so other Black children in Freedom School, holding up a banner we'd made that says: "Black kids in solidarity with Wet'suwet'en." A bit later on, you sent me one of your two young ones holding up signs that say "Nishnaabe Solidarity with Black Lives." I think, or rather I know, that this is because we are mutually committed to one another's lives and one another's living, working to build a society in which that living, period, is not so continually threatened.

But of course you and I are talking about world-making all the time, have been since we first met a few years back. At the time you invited me to Dechinta, I was in one of the many burnout phases that plague me even though I am technically old/wise enough to know better. I was looking forward to the visit but felt a bit apprehensive: of having to pretend not to be a wuss about the cold, of my own shyness and extreme awkwardness in group settings. That nervousness quickly fell into the background, though. As I remember it, there was not so much an itinerary as a plan, as Glen said, to "let the land do the work for us." And that is exactly what we did. What it did.

I remember sitting, with an early-morning coffee you'd brought me, in an old fur-lined canoe attached to a snowmobile, legs covered in a blanket and looking into the blue sky. It wasn't as cold as I had feared. I will not forget soon, maybe ever, the feeling of holding on tight as we took off from Yellowknife and sped over the (mostly) iced-over river towards Denendeh, me always slightly worried that Glen would accidentally drown us all, but mostly trusting the process. I remember us discussing our communities' respective histories of radicalism, of struggle. And I remember my usual social anxieties dissolving as we discussed our own understanding of ethical relations, commitment to political struggle, and world-building.

By the end of the two days on the land with you and yours, and me and mine, I was giddy, if ill: in my enthusiasm, I had chain-smoked continuously and my body hates when I do this. I had eaten muskox, kept good company, spent time on the land. I had witnessed, by watching and by speaking with the program's Elders, a tiny fraction of the immense wisdom that they hold; the complex knowledge required to live and make life in this territory, built over centuries; the nuanced perceptions required to understand the positions of fish, the use of animals to nourish and of plants for medicine; the knowledge required to subvert the constant threat of terror from violent white settlers. Witnessing and experiencing all of this alongside you and our other comrades, I felt, for a rare moment, invincible.

I'm bleary-eyed, truly; it's not even nighttime anymore but morning. But I feel committed to this moment. I want to do what I can to struggle through this time, alongside you. To experiment, try, fail if we must, learn, regroup, try again. I want to contribute, to the best of my abilities, to all of this ambient frenetic energy that surrounds us right now. I want to do my part to help "shape change," to think with Octavia Butler again, to help in any way I can to guide this moment toward the most liberatory possible ends, while this energy is still here, still with us.

In this time that our communities, collectively, are changing the air, have changed the air, I want us to win as much as is possible, to use this window as well and as wisely as we can. It's in protracted struggle alongside one another that we get to the heart of what it means to get free. It's you and I eating muskox in Dene territory, it's watching these second-gen Bahamian kids screaming—in equal parts joy and terror—as they see a net filled with dozens of fish emerge from under the ice, carefully pulled up by Denendeh's Elders. It's me bumming all of Glen's cigarettes as I learn about Dene anti-capitalist struggle, and it's T.'s Indigenous Freedom School and L. and N.'s Black Freedom School exchanging tips on pedagogy, planning exchanges, and mapping out the terrain of future liberation, abolitionist futures for the young ones. It's Black folks supporting Wet'suwet'en and vice versa, it's Black and Indigenous abolition camps in Toronto parks, it's tent cities, police stations aflame, and statues of slavers thrown in the sea and it's our communities, in a chorus, forwarding a collective call to defund/disarm/dismantle/demilitarize/abolish police. It's #*reconciliationisdead* spray-painted overtop of every billboard, it's letters, and hushed conversations at dinner, it's *this*, all of it, and so much more.

As I said, I can never sleep anymore, but I don't think that matters right now. No Black woman I know is sleeping, not well. I think we are awake, collectively, because the energy of this moment of revolt is residing in our bodies, because our ancestors are keeping us awake, using any energy stores that we have available to transfer this energy to our comrades waging struggles in Minneapolis and Wet'suwet'en and London and Cape Town. I think we are awake because none of us wants to sleep through the closest many of us have ever come to feeling like maybe we could truly *win* this thing called liberation.

Robyn,

Yesterday, I was in a Zoom webinar discussing the idea of queering in general, and queering land-based education in particular, on a platform that could not be farther away from the one in the bush on the island in Denendeh I described in my previous letter. One of the participants was the very brilliant Kanaka Maoli (Hawaiian) scholar, Manulani Aluli Meyer. We were talking about the pandemic and how, as Indigenous peoples, this crisis and this pandemic are not unprecedented. We have been "here" many times before. She talked about the pandemic in terms of her own Hawaiian cosmology, moving effortlessly between her language and English, explaining that right now, in this time of pandemic, we are also in a tremendous time of upheaval, amplification, intensification and conflict. She spoke of the pandemic as an opportunity for unfolding coherence or awareness, as a stimulation for the concept of aloha, and reminded us

"Ulu a'e ke welina a ke aloha. Loving is the practice of an awake mind." Her people were organizing, reattaching themselves to Kanaka Maoli practices. Noelani Goodyear-Ka'ōpua, a Kanaka Maoli political scientist, describes *huli-hia*—an "over-turning, [a] massive upheaval, so great that when the churning eventually slows, our lives will be permanently altered." These Kanaka Maoli thinkers are moving through the pandemic as an opportunity to strengthen their communities. I imagine there is something similar in Nishnaabeg thought, because "massive upheaval" is part of the natural and ecological cycling of the earth. Both Noelani and Manulani remind me that our peoples and our living relations have experienced over-turnings before, several times actually, on both micro and macro scales. It reminds me there are ancient bodies of knowledge that can provide comfort, meaning and guidance through this turbulence. It reminds me of the generative and degenerative energies working in reciprocity with the forces of upheaval. The practice of an awakened mind. Witnessing with clarity. Using sadness, anger and conflict to awaken, amplify, intensify, or what Cree scholar Alex Wilson calls queering—and quoting Kalaniopua Young—the practice of making medicine out of trauma.

There are moments.

This morning I'm listening to part two of a podcast called 'Give Your House Away, Constantly': Fred Moten and Stefano Harney Revisit *The Undercommons* in a Time of Pandemic and Rebellion." *The Undercommons* is a book that has always spoken to me, as someone who works primarily outside of institutions, because of Moten and Harney's insistence on centring Black intellectual pursuit outside of the academy and inside a plethora of modalities—from listening to music, to watching sports together, to kitchen-table discussion. As I've witnessed universities move to further entrench Indigenous Studies in the academy, I've witnessed similar tensions and losses as our Elders and their knowledge, land pedagogies, and languages are absent and as the majority of our communities and more radical politics are largely missing from these institutions. As Moten points out, Black Study is trying to generate knowledge through an endless process of asking, What are we going to do and how are we going to live? This cannot be reducible to reading and writing and talking about books.

Robyn, how are we going to live and how are we going to live together?

Today Moten begins the conversation talking about the idea of home and homelessness. He talks about how for white Americans (and Canadians), home is thought of as a sovereign place, "home is your castle," an enclosed space that you own and put a fence around, surveil and guard. He contrasts this with his own experience of home as a Black child with a mother who was a schoolteacher who continually brought students home with her, and how his feelings of missing home are missing the "constant violations of the boundaries of so-called home" as his relations came through the door without knocking. He goes on to explain homelessness as "not a condition of where you have no place to stay. Homelessness is not a condition where you don't have a house. Homelessness is the condition in which you share your house, you give your house away constantly as a practice of hospitality. Home is where you give home away."

This resonates strongly with my own Nishnaabeg feelings of home, nationhood and territory. This continual practice of hospitality is spoken about in my culture, and other Indigenous cultures, as an ethic of sharing. Share everything you have. It is repeated over and over in story after story. It is demonstrated and embodied by fluent speakers, Elders, and Knowledge Holders. It is practised by harvesters whether they are hunting animals, fishing, or picking medicines and berries. It is practised in the face of extreme poverty, on reserves and in the streets of inner cities. It extends past material possessions to include time, space, emotions, and labour. It is ritualized in ceremony, where food and material items are literally given away. It remains strong and steadfast in our communities today, whether those communities are reserves, in the city or everywhere in between.

Last March, I was hoping to share the experience of making maple syrup with you and your relations as a continuation of the work we did together in Denendeh, but this time in my territory. So much of the politics of sap and sugar are about sharing. In the origin story of how maple sugar came to the Nishnaabeg, a squirrel, whose nation, homespace, sovereignty co-exists with mine, shows a child how to chew on a maple twig in spring and find sap. This in turn leads the young Nishnaabeg to enter the homespace, the nation, the sovereignty of the maple, to ask for the consent of the maple through an offering, and the maple agreeing to share their sweet sap with the child. The child then shares their new knowledge with their parents and family. The family then prepares an evening meal, which again is based on the sharing of another nation, the deer clan, this time the body of a deer which is cooked in the sap. The sap boils down to sugar and again, this new knowledge is shared with the larger community, as the child relays the origin story.

If you had been able to come to the sugar bush, land would have figured prominently in our experience, as would have water, which, like us, is part of land. March in Michi Saagiig Nishnaabeg territory is wet. The snow is melting, it is sometimes snowing and sometimes raining, the rivers and lake are full of meltwater, the air is humid in contrast to the dryness of winter. We'd begin by collecting the tree water from the trees in the bush. We'd spend hours boiling sap, immersed in steam, taking maybe ninety litres of sap and reducing it to three litres of syrup. There would be a bit of mild struggle over keeping the heat from the fire at the right intensity to keep the sap boiling but not overflowing, another sharing that is a constant negotiation. Another metaphor that emerges from experience. We would insist you take the syrup home to share with your community. We likely would not have talked directly about sharing, but all of our interactions would have been enmeshed with the practice of sharing—you sharing your time, labour, emotional space and intimacy with me. The trees sharing sap with us. The fire sharing heat with sap. Me sharing this intimate practice and my time, labour and emotional space with you. There would be so much sharing braided with care and kindness that we can't really do what I'm doing here—predict how our relationship might have deepened or the kinds of things we would have talked through during the process. We haven't yet been able to share in this experience in

Nishnaabeg territory because we were all under stay-at-home orders this year during the pandemic, but I know we will.

This politic of sharing is a continual divestment of individuality and a perpetual deepening of the communal or the wider network of life. It is anti-accumulation. The politic of sharing is intertwined with a practice of caring—caring for oneself and for all of the other relationships that form the community, the nation, and the worlds that are overlapping and being continually generated in time and space. Greed is simply unacceptable because of the damage and harm it causes our relations. Withholding one's time or labour to someone in need is simply unacceptable because it damages our relations and therefore our home.

Sharing is also a foundational practice of the Dene, and one of the reasons we are writing together today. Our solidarity gathering was forged on the practice of sharing— land, water, knowledge, food, labour and a tremendous skill set and collective wisdom that spanned from hunting and fishing to navigating ice conditions to a retelling of Dene history and presence to an embodied practice of Dene law. We were welcomed into Dene homespace with generosity, kindness and care and, in turn, were able to give it to each other. The plants and animals had shared their bodies with our Dene hosts, and they in turn shared everything they had with us. The land and waters are constantly sharing with us, and in that sharing, more life is generated. Visiting is paramount in the politic of sharing as a mechanism to nourish and strengthen relationships, as a medium to exchange knowledge, as a structure that builds and maintains homespace. I've seen and felt variations of these practices in

Indigenous lands all over the world: the Inuit, Kanaka Maoli, Maori, Kanien'kehá:ka, Mi'kmaq and the Haida. I've felt the safest and most cared-for outside of Nishnaabeg lands as a visitor in a Native home.

I've recently read the graphic novel *Paying the Land* by Joe Sacco, a Maltese American journalist who is maybe most well known for his work about resistance in Palestine. Sacco's new work is about Dene resistance, and so I was reviewing the book to see if it would be useful for my students in Denendeh. I knew the students would be eager to discuss the positionality of Sacco and the ethics of a non-Dene writing about Dene culture and history, and I thought both the students and our Dene staff would find joy in seeing familiar faces and stories in the images in the book. What is clear to me in spending time with this book is that Sacco has forged relationships with Dene Knowledge Holders, and that he spent time in their communities and learning from them on the land. Land-based politics, led by the Dene, are prominent in the stories Sacco re-tells. The acknowledgements section in the book demonstrates a back-and-forth consent process with particular Dene experts. The book for me also is a demonstration of the generosity of the Dene. I can see the Dene ethic and law of "share everything you have" over and over again in the book, from the sharing of food, equipment, and time to the deep and careful sharing of knowledge and the most intimate of stories.

The book is also a sharp reminder that the exploitation of this ethic has been a cornerstone of colonialism. We shared our homes, medicines, food, technology and knowledge with the first colonial invaders so they didn't die.

Sometimes, in the face of five centuries of viciousness and violence in return, I feel ashamed of sharing, as if not sharing and not caring for, as if eliminating the first invaders and colonizers would have stopped colonialism. It would be easy, particularly in the logic of colonialism, to frame sharing as naïveté and a not-knowing—as is often done with regard to the Native, even sometimes in the more radical Indigenous circles that travel within my mind and in my work.

Returning to Moten, I am hearing him say, home is never just your home. It is not an enclosure. It is not *property* with a picket fence and a guard dog. It is a space created by relationality, constantly visited by insects, mice, squirrels, bears, spirits, winds and rain, plants and medicines, and this visiting forms the network that is the container of home. So yes, we are homeless, not in the sense that we don't have a house, but in the sense that homelessness is, in Moten's words, "a condition in which you share your house . . . in which you give your house away, constantly, as a practice of hospitality." When practised collectively, this builds the most beautiful responsive formation, continually being remade and morphing to meet the needs of individual beings.

There are requirements, however, for this to work. Requirements that the viciousness (Moten uses this word, and it resonates with me) of white supremacy and the practice of colonialism refuse to fulfill and so, as the old metaphor goes, the settler moves into the Indigenous home, confines us to a closet, and proceeds to take ownership over the house, building a picket fence, acquiring a guard dog and security system. Ah! So in our practice of kindness and sharing and deep care, we will clearly outline our expectations and we will agree to share the space, take care of the space, and respect each other's decision-making processes, working diplomatically to negotiate solutions to conflict. We will enter a treatied relationship, to be clear.

I'm drawn to the way Moten uses the term "homelessness" as a refusal of homelessness in one sense, as an assertion of homelessness in another sense, and then, finally, as a remaking of what homelessness or homespace means as conceptualized by Black people. I use terms like "self-determination" and "nation" as a way of pushing back against the state and the forces of dispossession—as a refusal of state definitions and Western political definitions and an assertion and remaking of those terms based in Indigenous thought. Similarly, I use the word "nation" both as a push back against colonial understandings of the word and as a way of affirming Indigenous collective and relational formations as legitimate—more legitimate, I'd argue, than settler nation-state formations. It is possible in Nishnaabeg understandings to hold "sovereignty" and "jurisdiction" over land while also affirming the "sovereignty" and "jurisdiction" and "self-determination" of others on the same space, and this requires an intense, intimate and ongoing relationality and shared political understanding. In my mind, this idea of homelessness, to come back to Moten's term, also extends to territory and nation. Nishnaabeg think of our nation as a home or homespace.

I understand Nishnaabeg nationhood to be a formation of deep relationality, with all of the communities of living beings sharing a particular time and space for their place-making. It is a network, cycling through time. A web of intimate connections where bodies are hubs forming vital pathways and links between plants, animals, rivers, lakes, the cosmos and humans, blurring the boundaries between body and individual in favour of interdependent communal systems—indeed, the spirits of living things are believed to transcend the enclosures of bodies and commingle in realms other than the physicality of the earth. Our homespace is an ecology of relationships in the absence of coercion, hierarchy or authoritarian power.

Kina Gchi Nishnaabeg-ogamig, the place where we all live and work together, the "we" meaning living things, not just humans, is connectivity based on the sanctity of the land, the love we have for our families, our language, our way of life. It is relationships based on deep reciprocity, respect, non-interference, and freedom. It is relationships based on bodily sovereignty and communal sovereignty, so groups of living things can make decisions to best support the overall system in bringing forth mino-bimaadiziwin, in bringing forth a continuous rebirth, in bringing forth more life in all of its different forms. This formation not only makes possible, but actively nurtures and supports the conditions that make possible a diversity of life—the incredible awe-inspiring ways life finds to be in this world. Collectivity is continually generated from individual self-determination and self-actualization, based on political processes that allow divergent and minority voices not only to be heard but, when it is beneficial to the communal, to have profound influence.

Human is not centred. In fact, I'm not even sure I understand the enclosure of "human" within Nishnaabeg thought, other than as a different formation of life and living that isn't more important or integral than a mouse or strawberries or a lake or a butterfly. And that formation makes capitalism unthinkable—we are taught to give up what we can to support the integrity of our homespace for others with whom we are sharing and for the coming generations of life. We must give more than we take.

This is what I understand our diplomats were negotiating when settlers first arrived in our territory. This was the impetus for those very first treaties: freedom, protection for the land and the environment, a space—an intellectual, political, spiritual, artistic, creative and physical space where we could live as Nishnaabeg and *where all living things could do the same.*

In radical Indigenous circles, "nation" has come to be a push back against the racist characterization of our communities as being without complex political and governing structures and practices. My use of this term is in line with that tradition. It is a refusal of nation as a Westphalian nation-state and a remaking of the term that is conceptually more similar to larger political formations within Indigenous thought. It is *one* articulation of an Nishnaabeg homespace. I am also reminded here of Dionne Brand's comments in her 1996 NFB documentary film of herself in conversation with poet Adrienne Rich: the word "nation," she says, may just be too contaminated and corrupted by states to be of use, or for us to use the word to mean anything more than nation-state.

In my mind, Indigenous nations, Indigenous homespaces, Indigenous homelessness must be engaged in a radical and complete overturning of the nation-state's political formations and a refusal of racial capitalism. My vision to create Nishnaabeg futures and presences must structurally refuse and reject the structures, processes and practices that end Indigenous life, Black life and result in environmental desecration. This requires societies that function without policing, prisons, and property. This is a Nishnaabeg formation that must align with radical Black freedom struggles. My world-building must support the world-building of Black freedom struggles. This requires me, like Black feminists and organizers before and alongside me such as Tiffany Lethabo King and Sefanit Habtom, and Moten and Harney in this work, to refuse the opposition of Blackness and Indigeneity. Nishnaabeg formations of nationhood mean a radical over-turning of the current conditions and configurations within which we live—an absolute refusal of capitalism.

Going back to Meyer's insistence that this pandemic is a time of clarity, intensification and thinking, I wonder about how we are creating homespaces. On July 4, 2020, Dionne Brand wrote an article in the *Toronto Star* entitled "On Narrative, Reckoning and the Calculus of Living and Dying." Like Meyer, Brand diagnoses our present:

> I know, as many do, that I've been living a pandemic all my life; it is structural rather than viral; it is the global state of emergency of anti-Blackness. What the COVID-19 pandemic has done is expose even further the endoskeleton of the world. . . . The x-ray that is the novel coronavirus exposes once again the bare bones of the social structure in which for Black and Indigenous people governance equals policing.

For Indigenous peoples colonialism is dispossession, a usurpation of political power and the mechanism that attacked our bush economies and replaced them with capitalism. I've been thinking about those words of Brand's, "governance equals policing," and how this relates to Indigenous experiences with land and homespace. State governance requires policing in all its forms to maintain expansive Indigenous dispossession. Dispossession that is not only expansive, but also recursive.

"Recursive dispossession" is a term Robert Nichols uses in *Theft is Property!: Dispossession and Critical Theory* to describe the conversion of Indigenous belongings to land into property as a precursor to colonial theft. Using the thinking of Black feminists, Indigenous scholars and the Black Radical Tradition, Nichols makes several interventions regarding dispossession. He uses the idea of recursive dispossession as a theoretical and practical way to move through the dilemma of "If you don't own land, how can it be stolen?" He argues that "in the specific context with which we are concerned [Anglophone settler colonialism and Indigenous resistance], 'dispossession' may be coherently reconstructed to refer to a process in which new proprietary relations are generated but under structural conditions that demand their simultaneous negation. In effect, the dispossessed come to 'have' something they cannot use, except by alienating it to another." In other words, colonialism converts Indigenous attachment to land into property as it dispossesses us of it and steals the property. A particularly Indigenous experience of property as theft, as Nichols says.

Reading Nichols' book got me thinking about how these ideas play out not only in the realm of the academy, but in my own life and in Indigenous life in the present. It got me thinking about ways to push back against expansive and recursive dispossession from within Nishnaabeg thought. It got me thinking about how much I've learned about my body and its experience of dispossession from Black feminists—thinkers like Hortense Spillers, Katherine McKittrick, and El Jones, and all of the organizing from the most recent summer of revolt.

Following Moten's refusal and remaking of the idea of homelessness, I resist the logics of property, meaning I'm not interested in *taking* property back, but *pushing* property back. I'm not interested in thinking about getting land as property back, but rather about rejecting the kind of desecration or defilement of the broader life systems that generate Nishnaabewin. I'm interested in refusing the logics of property. Let me explain.

I have a canoe made of Kevlar and carbon, made by "Canada's Oldest Canoe Company," in my backyard. It is red. I bought it with my first paycheque from Trent University, twenty years ago. It took all of the paycheque. I most definitely should have paid off student debt or bought professional-looking clothes, but I bought a canoe. Now in my language, this canoe would be considered an inanimate object. Because it is made out of Kevlar, because I bought it, paid for it with money I had earned by engaging in wage labour, I own it. It is my possession.

Let's imagine, for the sake of argument, I have another canoe in my backyard. This one, I made out of four trees:

birch, spruce, cedar, and ironwood, with an Nishnaabeg Elder and canoe builder. In my homespace, I share both time and space with these four trees and many others, as living sovereign beings. I am ethically required to seek out their consent and engage in reciprocity with these trees as a way of living in this world. I am required to nurture and maintain a meaningful relationship with them—from harvesting and using their medicine, to protecting their access to the things they need to live, to defending their habitat from life-ending forces, to engaging in conversation or prayer with their spirits. I take on the responsibility to learn what time of year is best to engage in harvesting practices, and which methods of harvest cause the least harm to the wider community. I'm required to use everything I take, to share everything I've gained from these trees, and to take only what I need. I am required to braid these four trees together into a canoe the best way I can, putting good emotion and positive thought into the making process. In short, in order to harvest these trees, I am required to engage in an ongoing intimate relationship with each of these living beings. Put another way, I am required to carry the responsibilities for these relationships throughout the entire time I'm in relation to the canoe. When the canoe can no longer fulfill its purpose, I'm also required to return it to the earth, so that life can break it down into its constituents and make more life anew. If I can no longer fulfill my responsibilities to the canoe, I must find someone else who can.

This canoe, this jimaan, is very much alive. It is not a possession. It is not my property. I do not own it. I am attached to it. I am related to it. We come from the same place, breathe the same air, and drink the same water. I have responsibilities to the life it is made out of. I have responsibilities to use it in a way that provides for me, my family and my community. I have a responsibility to share it with those that may also need it. I have a responsibility to care for it, to repair it and to maintain it. I have a responsibility to protect it from those who might misuse or harm it or commodify it outside of those original agreements between myself and those four trees, those Elders that shared their making knowledge with me, and the water and heat that allowed us all to combine this life into a new life. Just as those trees have the responsibility to protect the original agreements with air, soil, light, water and the ecology of the forest that gave them life. The same could be said for the tools that I would have fashioned in order to make the canoe and to move the canoe. The same could be said for the water, indeed the aquatic ecosystem that would hold me up when the canoe and I pushed off from the shoreline. Perhaps we would set nets and fish, thus engaging in another set of ethical and consensual relationships. This is a cascading, ever-expanding series of relationships, of attachments, of belongings, that generate meaning from connectivity.

This canoe is not my possession. It is not my property. I do not own it.

It is my relative. I am attached to it. We belong to each other and a network of other relations. I am responsible for caring for it and it is responsible for caring for me—providing me with safe passage on rivers and lakes.

Can you steal something that is not property?

Of course. It seems obvious. If you take something or do something without consent, it is a violation, a theft.

If both of my canoes were stolen from my backyard I would experience the first canoe, the red Kevlar one, as theft, because I relate to it as property.

The circumstances or the context of the taking of the birchbark one from my backyard would matter. If, for instance, the canoe was taken by an Nishnaabeg friend or acquaintance who upheld the original responsibilities, the event might not even register in my consciousness as an event, but rather a normal part of living life in community. If that same person had taken the canoe, and then was unable to care for it because of sickness or theft or some other sort of complication, I might be able to approach the situation with empathy and compassion and work to regenerate the relationships that had been harmed. Indeed, this practice is the basis of Nishnaabeg restorative justice.

On the other hand, if a white person had taken the canoe and cut it up with an axe and lit it on fire because of their intense hatred of Indigenous peoples, as so often still happens, the impact on me would be much greater. In fact, the stealing of the birchbark canoe would feel like a tremendous violation in comparison to the loss of the Kevlar one because it would violate more than just me—it would violate the cascading, expanding series of relationships and responsibilities that allowed the canoe to come into life. The harm of that theft is intimate, and of a different order of magnitude than a loss of a possession.

Consent in this context is about whether you trust someone to uphold the responsibilities to the reciprocal relationships within which life is enmeshed. I consent to share land
with the Haudenosaunee or Wendat because I know they will
ethically engage in the relationships that make up my land. I
will not consent to share land with the French and English
and Canadians because over and over again, they have demonstrated they will agree to these responsibilities on the surface, and then set up a series of life-ending systems designed
to accumulate wealth for the very few.

This point of conversion of land into property, one that
took place historically and takes place continually, requires
reinforcement in Euro-Canadian law, policy. When Indigenous peoples push back against recursive dispossession,
placing our bodies on the land between the colonizer and
the resources they are about to exploit, we are met with
state violence in the form of policing, like the Haudenosaunee
land defenders faced at 1492 Land Back Lane in Ontario, or
the army, in cases like the 1990 resistance at Kanehsatà:ke.
More recently, lobster fishers from Sipekne'katik First Nation
were met with white violence from white vigilantes.

We know this already. We know the structure of colonialism was maintained and is maintained by policing and
authoritarian power over us, and Indigenous thinkers like
Sarah Hunt have pointed out that this violence is asymmet-
ric, landing on the bodies of Indigenous women and Two-
Spirit/queer people and trans people more intensely and
more often than others. Indigenous feminists know that
we have been dispossessed of not just our land, but also

our bodies and intimacies, our languages, our thought, our spirituality, our creativity and all of our meaning-making practices as a targeted and strategic way of breaking our attachment to land and to each other—as an attack on belonging, as an attack on meaning, as the complete annihilation of homespace. Dispossession for Indigenous peoples, then, is both expansive and recursive; it has attempted to turn our relationality into property and commodity and then taken our minds, bodies, spirits and homespaces away from us. It sells ourselves back to us in various forms of recognition and rights.

Black feminists have taught me a great deal about bodily forms of dispossession. Of course, slavery and anti-Blackness have a different history and set of experiences with dispossession than I have as an Nishnaabekwe because under slavery, Black (and sometimes Indigenous) people themselves, and their kinship, were owned by white people. Black feminist writing has helped me more fully understand my body and how I live in it (or don't). Hortense Spillers writes:

> [T]he socio-political order of the New World . . . with its human sequence written in blood, *represents* for its African and indigenous peoples a scene of *actual* mutilation, dismemberment, and exile. First of all, their New-World, diasporic plight marked a *theft of the body*—a willful and violent (and unimaginable from this distance) severing of the captive body from its motive will, its active desire.

Anti-Blackness and colonialism are different and multiple modes of violent severing—bodies from land and bodies from will, desire, self; bodies from each other. A severing of ourselves from, as NourbeSe Philip might say, breath. The making and remaking of ourselves, our homespaces and our worlds in exile, amongst the severing, is our normal. Indigenous and Black life is a persistent process of taking back our bodies, our minds, our spirits, our relationality to land and a reclaiming and remaking of our homespaces in spite of constant erasure and elimination.

Black and Indigenous peoples have different and linked experiences with expansive and recursive dispossession of land and bodies. Our different and linked struggles for freedom as a place, as Gilmore reminds us, involve land and bodies. We have been living in successive waves of the pandemics of anti-Blackness and colonialism, in the ever-intensifying crisis of global warming, and, as Ruth Wilson Gilmore says in speaking about abolition, we must change everything—"Abolition is deliberately everything-ist; it's about the entirety of human-environmental relations. Where life is precious, life is precious. It's a theory of change."

Where all life, not just human life, but *all* life is precious.

I wonder, then, if it would be helpful to foster a different practice to talk about land, territory, nationhood and home-space. Maybe land and our relationships to it can become a listening, a thinking, a speaking in a different register, a different starting point for Black and Indigenous relationality, just as land has become such an important way for me to relate to you, Robyn. Maybe Black and Indigenous land-based politics holds potential for our world-building and freedom struggles; or, as Samudzi and Anderson write, "the actualization of truly liberated land can only come about through dialogue and co-conspiratorial work with Native communities and a shared understanding of land use outside of capitalistic models of ownership."

Maybe in our practice of liberating lands and peoples, we can be homeless, but together.

PART FOUR

One Hundred Forms of Homespace

Dear Leanne,

I've always been a nerd. Specifically, a sci-fi nerd. And more specifically still, the kind of sci-fi nerd who, as a child, tried to learn to speak Klingon from her father's *Klingon Dictionary*. And so as you can imagine, *Star Trek TNG* has been a balm to my pandemic insomnia. I was likely influenced by episode 63—the one where the *Starship Enterprise* passes through a temporal rift and inadvertently creates two timelines, two ships, two futures—when I would find myself, during my walks down a largely empty Bloor Street in late March, musing that perhaps somewhere out there, too, was a timeline in which you and I were making syrup on your land. Where we hadn't even continued to write one another letters, in the end, because we were too busy speaking in person, riffing ideas, discussing movements and thinkers that were moving us, inspiring us. Where we had maybe taken our kids together on the walk we'd discussed, and otherwise taken a bit of joy and comfort in one another's presence, small transitory moments amidst otherwise very separate and hectic lives. And as you can imagine, this sort of speculative exercise naturally leads to a contemplation of other timelines, which are never far from my mind, anyways.

For instance, what and who would be here instead of my landlord's house, the paved streets named after bandits and burglars, here on the lands of Haudenosaunee, the Anishinaabeg, and the Wendat? And what else might the human and ecological landscape beneath my feet have become, if not for the long-standing and ongoing occupation and administrative control of the British and French empires, the settler state? Not to mention, of course, where would I be had my ancestors not been kidnapped *en masse* and used as fuel for the unsettling of this side of the Atlantic world? It's hard not to focus on the sheer weight of the timelines aborted, globally, by slavery and colonialism, and their afterlives. These timelines seem to bulge inadvertently into this plane, the alternative homespaces and modes of organizing life, the multitudinous other ways that this world and its inhabitants could have been structured. I like to think that they accompany us, glimmering planes of reality alongside our own.

To pick up here where you left off—your words running through my mind and coursing through my veins as always: *an awakened mind*. An awakened mind, too, is to know that there is nothing natural or inevitable about any part of contemporary governance, about "policing as governance," per Brand. It is a spiritual and bodily rejection of the egregious violence of the quotidian. It is a refusal of the everyday humiliations of anti-Black surveillance, of the unceasing representations of Black peoples as pathological, of the (attempted) negation of all the richness, beauty, and fullness that is Black life. And it is a felt refusal of the racial and gendered violence that is constitutive of the settler state. And it is an awareness of other possible timelines, alternate futurities, of a liberation not yet arrived.

But in this timeline, I'm sitting in my kitchen, as usual, trying to use this communion to write my way out of a mood, one caused all too predictably by reading the news. You will not normally find me using my energy to point out how this or that piece of writing has failed to meaningfully address racism. Not because it's not true, but because it's true so often that it rarely gets a rise out of me anymore. This is how the media operates, with a few rare exceptions. And yet somehow, I've been arguing in my mind with a *Toronto Star* article ever since I first read it over my morning coffee on June 13, when their editorial board published a piece called "Let's save some outrage for treatment of Indigenous people."

I'm certain it was intended to be well-meaning, the ostensible goal being to highlight a politic that you and I are both clearly invested in: ending anti-Black racism matters, and so does ending racism against Indigenous peoples. It seems clear that neither of our respective communities is the target audience of the piece (more on that in a moment). However, Black people are being, here, not-so-subtly scolded for an apparent singularity of vision. This is part of a broader disciplining of the Black liberation struggle that Canadian media cannot do without, and one that is rarely levelled at other communities struggling to liberate themselves. The words "Black lives matter" are taken to mean that we wish only for Black lives to matter, and that others do not, or should not. Which disappears both historic and current forms of co-resistance with Indigenous and other communities, as well as the way that Black people's freedom struggles, even when standing on their own, have historically liberated broad swaths of people. But this kind of misunderstanding, by which I mean misrepresentation of the movement, its maxim, is so classic so as hardly to be notable. And so this is not the place I am focusing my attention—my own outrage, so to speak. Because another subtext that is somewhat more novel in this piece is its deliberate obfuscation of other facts of the matter: that Black and Indigenous struggles are interlocking and interconnected. That all of us stand to gain from the growing movement to defund and abolish policing. That in many instances, our communities have been, in these times, working together to dismantle organized violence and rebuild the world anew. Instead, this analysis, which is by and for white Canadians, pits Black and Indigenous communities against one another as we organize—often collectively—for abolition, decolonization, and a police- and prison-free world. It obfuscates, and thus licenses continued negation of the overarching reality that our unfreedom is wrapped in one another's, and further, that it is these interlocking unfreedoms that are in fact constitutive of the Canadian state—and capitalist states everywhere.

Perhaps what keeps drawing my attention back even more, though, is that phrase in the title: "let's save some outrage." Because this forwards the notion that white Canadians' outrage needs to be saved, neatly portioned out, and carefully preserved, lest it be wasted all in one go (*and on the Blacks!*). And it is this aspect of the editorial that I cannot shake. It reveals something about the structure of Canadian society and its affective capacities; and, perhaps more importantly, about its structurally limited capacity for in-depth solidarity. Because for your average Canadian there *is* a limited amount of outrage that can be distributed across the vast injustices of our time. We live in a society that requires that we tolerate a certain—significant—level of violence and death. People dying of overdoses, of exposure, at the hands of police: this is the collateral damage of the mode of governance that we live under. Outrage, then, is finite. It necessarily has an end point, lest the discomfort lead to a broader demand for the always-possible, continually deferred transformations that would be required to shift the tyrannical racial logics of our time. And so outrage needs to be carefully portioned out, in moderated doses, in order to preserve the status quo. The media functions, and the public along with it, such that Indigenous genocide and anti-Black violence erupt into the national discourse only in moments of brief national attention, allowing them to appear to be episodic. Rather than endemic, enduring. And mutually constituting. Outrage needs to be rationed precisely because only a limited amount of "justice" is, in fact, possible, or achievable, for this country to go on as it has. Which is of course the unstated goal of liberal outrage, trimming here and there at the worst and most visible excesses of harm, while leaving a violent system intact. *Too much justice*—the liberation of Black and Indigenous peoples—would make Canada, as it stands today, impossible.

You would not know from reading this op-ed of the turbulent insurgencies of this time, of two mutually unfolding and as-of-yet unfinished liberation projects that stand to shake the very foundations of this society. But, of course, it is the obfuscation, the misdirection, that is the point. Regardless of intent, the purpose and the function of such an intervention is to cast our struggles in competition, in moments of mass unrest, using colonial fictions to uphold, rather than undo, white supremacy.

And clearly this editorial was not written with us in mind: each of our communities holds enough rage (not outrage) to power the next five generations of freedom struggles.

I have enough rage for Ahmaud Arbery and Colten Boushie and Eishia Hudson and Wabakinine and Wiijiiwaagan and Regis Korchinski-Paquet.

You and I live in a country that is reliant on either our violent exclusion from, or genocidal inclusion into, the nation-state. In cities and in a country where governance as violence and abandonment is the defining feature of daily life. The sheer weight of our respective communities' presence across the state zones of capture and abandonment make all too clear that we are living and dying in a formation that was not designed for us, but built top of us, to facilitate the exploitation of lands, labour, but not to facilitate life. And most certainly not Black and Indigenous life. The nation-state requires the dispossession of Indigenous peoples' lands and lives; it requires the destruction of Black peoples' lives, our flesh, our personhood, our timelines of otherwise. And most of all, the Canadian state requires the destruction of Black and Indigenous freedom struggles, seeking at each instance to undermine and reroute liberatory social transformation by means of criminalization, co-optation or, most often, an admixture of the two. Canada, as it exists today, cannot be recuperated.

The refusal to take things as they are as inevitable or a given: this *itself* an act of radical imagination, of conjure work. It is its own form of warfare, and of life-making, as well. Because to be attuned to the wrongness, too, is to hold within ourselves the multiplicity of different possible futures, of worlds that are not yet born, of forms of governance based not in violence, but abundance. It is insisting on the possibility of a new timeline, and suggests, too, that they may already be on the horizon. If we care to look.

Last year, I came across Dionne's short story "100 musicians at Jane and Finch?," originally published in 2007 in the *Globe and Mail*. The story revolves, at first glance, around an argument between lovers. The protagonist, June, wakes up with a start, joyously. She has heard, as she exclaims loudly to her lover, the CBC radio host announcing that the mayor would be sending one hundred musicians to Jane and Finch. She is elated: it is brilliant, she says. Her lover, at first amused and then increasingly irritated, insists otherwise, insists she has misheard, that she is mistaken. They have announced, he says, that they've found funding to send one hundred *policemen* to Jane and Finch. June refuses to capitulate. The unnamed lover becomes increasingly frustrated, he can see no sense in what she has heard, what she is celebrating. He tells her "Don't be naive. They're gunmen. They're sending police for the gunmen." To this, June replies, "The gunmen are children. They need music. They could use some bicycles, some painters, some soccer balls, some trees. The place is pure post-industrial dreck. Who wouldn't want to murder somebody? A hundred trees, a hundred teachers, a hundred trips out of there, a hundred anything, not a hundred policemen. Why are you so fucking pessimistic?"

At the story's end, June and the lover have not bridged the chasm. Both have concluded that the other will only hear what they choose, and the lover's final, chastising inner monologue sums up June as follows: "Like she's not living in the same time as the rest of us." The closing of the story leaves us with two timelines, one which moves toward an end to want, and another where we are left with the same old, same old.

Yet an awakened mind, June's, in this case, rejects that things must go on as they have. June will not concede anything inevitable about the murderous status quo of this city, this country. She will not concede to governance as violence.

This, the discordant visions between June and her lover, is a drama that replays with astonishing regularity in this city and in this country. The competing visions occur between communities and those who hold the power to govern Canada's Jane and Finches, Montréal Nords, and North Prestons. Each day, modes of living otherwise are violently rejected in the service of more of the same. It is a political choice that is made daily by elected officials whose political imaginations have been so stunted by generations of reliance on "law and order" that they cannot conceive of choosing differently, literally cannot fathom a homespace, a form of governance that would affirm Black life.

June's lover cannot perceive what Tory and Ford and their supporters refuse to see, which is that their imaginations are impoverished, undernourished, dead or dying. And as a result, the solution to rampant racial and economic inequality is, and can only be, more armed men with guns and cages. More private property and more hired agents to protect it. That this barren vision seems practical to so many, that anything beyond this seems preposterous and naïve, speaks to the banal monstrosity of our times. They simply cannot imagine, as June can and does, that there can be—and must be—more for us.

We, too, must hold tightly to our insistence that there are, always, one hundred otherwises to the violence of contemporary governance.

I'm with you, Leanne: How are we going to live together? And in this place? Those that run this society have tried to lay that out for us. But Black queer folks, radicals, feminists, and other outlaws, I think, have long known that the nation-state form was an insufficient container to hold our most expansive dreams for freedom. And accordingly, that our appeals to the state—for belonging, for the protections of citizenship—would be met with silence, and worse.

This is captured in a discussion between James Baldwin and Audre Lorde at Hampshire College in Amherst, Massachusetts, in 1984. They discussed the possibilities—and the limitations—of Black people's freedom within the United States.

Baldwin says this to Lorde:

Du Bois believed in the American dream. So did Martin. So did Malcolm. So do I. So do you. That's why we're sitting here.

To which Audre Lorde replies:

I don't, honey. I'm sorry, I just can't let that go past. *Deep, deep, deep down I know that dream was never mine.* And I wept and I cried and I fought and I stormed, but I just knew it. *I was Black. I was female. And I was out—out— by any construct wherever the power lay.* So if I had to claw myself insane, if I lived I was going to have to do it alone. Nobody was dreaming about me. Nobody was even studying me except as something to wipe out.

Their disagreement is instructive. While Baldwin still held out for the possibility of Black freedom, held that perhaps the American dream could, if cajoled strongly enough, be made to stretch itself out to enfold him, Lorde understood the limitations of the nation-state. She knew that its promises were not meant to be extended to all of us, and could not be made to do so. I don't mean to be ungenerous, here: James Baldwin was no dupe and he was nobody's fool. He knew of the unrelenting and merciless brutality of US capitalism, racism, and militarism, knew that "the system is doomed because the world can no longer afford it." Yet we bear witness, in his discussion with Lorde, to Baldwin's faith that there remains something, somewhere, somehow recuperable about the United States: if not in its past or present, in its future. And it is this possible recuperation that Lorde altogether refused. As a Black lesbian, a social-ist, a descendent of Caribbean migrants, she resided, in more ways than one, on the constitutive *outside* of the American nation-state. On the outside of belonging, and of protec-tion. Outside by design. Outside of the patriarchy, the racial logics of the citizen, she knew there was no iteration of the USA in which she could belong. And thus for her the American dream was unsalvageable.

I have come back to this discussion quite often. For Black women like Lorde, and for so many others made outlaws of North American society, the home, the nation which is its metonym, emerged historically as a space to actualize the freedom of white, propertied men. And if this promise would later be extended, partially, to white women and prom-ised, if never delivered, to Black men, it would not reach all the way to us. Because "home" has not been safe, after all, for most Black women—neither from the state surveillance and harm, nor from male violence. It is especially not safe for Black queer, trans, gender non-conforming young people for whom ejection from the family home is a fact of life. And it is criminalized, quite literally, for those involved in sex work or drug economies, and others who make ends meet, who forge other kinds of intimacy and family in the grey economies of our cities. And so these formations, home, nation-state, are not elastic enough to enfold those deemed radicals, outlaws, defectors, and deviants. Our dreams have lain elsewhere by necessity.

It's not only the white-supremacist settler state that poses the problem: the nation-state, as a form of governance, itself needs to be rethought. It *requires* the production of the outlaw. And it is this outlaw—the migrant, the radical, the queer, the artist, the sex worker—who is criminalized, incarcerated, deported, forcibly "rehabilitated," set to work in exploitative conditions. And so surely, we can imagine other ways to live together. *Other than this.*

Dominant Western historiography is replete with fictions that are meant to numb our ability to dream up alternatives, to keep us from breaking up with the timeline we've been conscripted into. It crafts narratives of European, North American benevolence, where there has been none, tells a teleology of a steady march toward progress where there has been, instead, unchecked brutality. Accompanying this, we are educated to believe that today's dominant forms of governance—the nation-state, capitalism, hierarchy and inequality—were and are natural, were and are part of the evolution of humankind, exemplifying the forward march of the universal human spirit.

While these are fictions, without a doubt, I would argue that they are fictions that derived not from the imagination, but from its absence.

I won't deny that it is highly ambitious to dream of conquering the globe, enslaving entire peoples, wiping out others and indenturing the rest. It is even more ambitious to have fastidiously worked to make this dream a reality. In extending the arms of colonial administration ever outward, the European ruling classes did nothing short of undertaking a project to remake the world—our worlds!— in their image, and to suit their own desires. But ambition toward domination, deliberate obfuscation, these are not the same as imagination.

A lack of curiosity: this is what differentiates the violently speculative project of Western civilization's last five hundred years from what I would call imagination. We're speaking, after all, of a worldview so insecure, so based in ambition and domination that it was unable to imagine even the existence of our lifeworlds—except as suffused with pathology, degradation, and lack. This worldview saw our ways of organizing life, our forms of kinship and knowledge of the natural world and wondered at nothing! Saw nothing but empty space, "savages," resources to be stolen and hoarded.

And worse still, when they encountered the complexities and richness of earthly life, they chose to impose their worldview upon it, with all alternatives dismissed, persecuted, and driven underground. As they steadfastly remade the world— our worlds—they extinguished or nearly extinguished thousands—more!—of other modes of life, of governance, and all their inherent possibilities. Broke up our societies, nearly *all* non-European societies, at random, slaughtered some, displaced others, re-organized long-standing forms of social and political organization into imperial outposts that served, broadly, as resource colonies, upheld and supported by colonial police and prisons, stamping out other possibilities each time they emerged. Worked to build not just their own homeplaces on top of ours but a world based on civilization as enclosure, freedom as property, and happiness as the amassing of violently extracted wealth. This drive toward sameness and violent hierarchical inclusion would have required a paucity of imagination matched only by an arrogance that is difficult to comprehend.

And it's from this vacuum of imagination that we were left with the nation-state: the geopolitical administrative units under which our lives are now governed, regardless of our consent.

Black revolutionaries have consistently struggled with the tensions between nation—as a largely de-territorialized way of conceiving the relationships between Africans and the world's Black diaspora—and the nation-state, in the project of Black liberation, particularly at the height of anti-colonial struggle. After being expelled from Algeria due to his role in the anti-colonial uprisings with the Algerian National Liberation Front, Frantz Fanon dictated *The Wretched of the Earth*. In this work, it is clear that he saw national liberation struggles in Africa as a step toward a broader African unity, and yet the African nation-state was not the endpoint of anti-colonial struggle. Writing in Tunis while he was in remission from leukemia, he warned that if we constricted our dreams of liberation into the limiting confines of the nation-state, Black people's freedom, too, would remain bound "within certain territorial limits." He thus lamented the expulsion of Africans between one nation and another. And this warning served to be true, both on the continent and well beyond, in multiple registers. Thirty years later, Ogoniland defender Ken Saro-Wiwa, who was part of the Movement for the Survival of the Ogoni People (MOSOP), one of the many Indigenous groups facing land expropriation by the Nigerian government and multinational companies, wrote a scathing critique. He wrote that the nation-state, on the continent and elsewhere, was born of "European will, European desires," and continued to serve only the needs of national elite, multi-nationals, and Western nations. He reminded us that "in virtually every nation-state there are several 'Ogonis' being subject to environmental and cultural destruction, and mass poverty."

I would never deign to collapse the distinctions between the nation-states in Europe and North America—imperial states and their settler colonial outposts—to the post-colonial states that emerged in the wake of anti-colonial nationalist struggles. Because for the non-European-world, the colonial state was literally built on top of us: and national sovereignty—home rule over the territory represented the only possible mode of governance available to those of us who would free ourselves. Black-run nation-states—the only grounds upon which freedom struggles were recognized as legitimate—entered a global economy that was rigged from the start. Parity with Europe and North America was a farce. A new version of dependence awaited Black peoples' entrance into a global governance structure that was unequal by design.

The nation-state, wherever we find it, is a problem: Black people are still living and dying from the vestiges of colonially-imposed states and the carceral mechanisms installed to support them.

The fact is that Black peoples, formal citizens or no, experience few of the protections of citizenship wherever we live. Gunned down in North American streets by police, mass deported from the USA, Canada, and the continent of Europe. Despite the best intentions of young Kwame Nkrumah, Pauline Opango, Claudia Jones, and countless others who envisioned a freedom of movement across the African continent and the Caribbean region, the logics and technologies of nation-state have prevailed. As M. Jacqui Alexander so aptly described, "not just any (body) can be a citizen" in a nominally decolonized Caribbean. Lesbians, sex workers, and others deemed deviant for non-heterosexual sex were cast outside of the nominal promises of citizenship in post-colonial Trinidad and Tobago. Undocumented Africans from Mozambique, Chad, and Zimbabwe face rampant labour exploitation, populist violence, detention, deportation, and police violence in South Africa, while non-status Haitians in Bahamas were told to leave the country or be "forced to leave" by Bahamian prime minister Hubert Minnis after Hurricane Dorian. It's not my intention to collapse under broad strokes the demonstrably unique historical and geopolitical contexts of these places. But these occurrences represent a broader pattern: organizing Black life—and human life—into nation-states forecloses the actualization of freedom for Black peoples. Globally, the colonial nation-state, and the logics and carceral practices that it relies upon to function, have not served as an adequate container for Black liberation. Our citizenship is everywhere precarious and contingent, when it exists at all.

Of course, against this barren structure, clumsily but violently implemented across the world, much survived. And our most imaginative thinkers have consistently worked to organize life, to envision emancipation well beyond the terms of governance-as-violence imposed upon us by Europeans. Reading your work has consistently reminded me that while unidentical, our respective communities' multiple traditions of radicalism have consistently worked to usher in more collective ways of organizing and governing life.

Métis activist and academic Howard Adams, in his 1975 book *Prison of Grass,* makes it clear that for Métis and broader Indigenous communities in Canada, it is not only colonialism that is the enemy, but the "forms and institutions of colonialism." The very best of our respective traditions of radicalism have always, anyways, insisted on seeing the *wrongness* of the world that Europe built on top of us, and dreamed of building old/new forms of home, of governance, new terms under which we could live and work, new ways of advancing and defining our relationships to the land and its human and non-human inhabitants.

Gifts and offerings in your work, my dear. Sovereignty not as ownership and property, but sharing; nationhood as a "series of radiating responsibilities," over and against the logics and institutions of the nation-state. *Outside* of the normative definitions of European epistemologies. These formations, and the politics that underlie them, derive from political formations based in non-domination that preceded, have endured, and work to undermine the colonial nation-state. It demonstrates another way for us to live, together.

To recognize that something was built on top of us is generative because it serves to remind, too, that there is no inevitability to the current formations that we reside in. Helps us to hold on to the knowledge that the nation-state, a colonial inheritance, often prevailed *despite* Black peoples' labours to build forms of homespace and governance along different lines. Black radicalism is replete with communities working to create forms of organizing life outside the shackles of capital, and outside the limited and limiting structures imposed by European formations. Panther visionary Kwame Ture, for example, clearly identified the United States as a settler colony, as occupied Indigenous lands. He forwarded a vision for a Black nation that transcended geography entirely, from landless Africans in the domestic colony inside the US to the Caribbean and the continent. Black freedom extended necessarily beyond national borders, encompassing a global Black life to be freed from the tethers of police, capital, empire.

Even during the era of mass national liberation struggles, the freedom dreams proffered through Black anti-colonial struggles held a kaleidoscopic array of possibilities for alternative formations of organizing human life, and had not yet calcified inside the nation-state formation. Offered us something else. In this period of radical experimentation with liberated territories, beginning in the twentieth century, decolonization, as Adom Getachew describes it, was more than nation-building, but a project of *worldmaking*, intended as a radical rupture. Anti-colonial struggle, as she traces it, was not meant to find its culmination as Black leadership over a Westphalian state system in a world still characterized by massively uneven wealth distribution. She details the experiments in re-ordering the world toward the liberation of the *global Black world:* the Caribbean's West Indian Federation, Africa's New International Economic Order. An attempted timeline ushering in Black homespaces the world over, grounded in communalism, socialism, a world free from hardened and impermeable national borders, and untethered by the global racial hierarchies of previous centuries. Which is to say that Black people the world over worked to build a global society that you and I have been raised to believe could only exist in *Star Trek* and other utopian science fictions.

And yet I do not wish to romanticize away the fact that many conceptualizations of Black nationalism re-affirmed, or at last failed to challenge, patriarchy, and other forms of domination and hierarchy. Cast Black women as the mothers and caretakers of the race. Tried to reify gendered subordination into Black freedom by acting as if it emerged from our very bodies, tethered it to semi-fabricated, mythologized patriarchal "traditions." Perhaps it's for this reason, then, that it is from the feminists—the outlaws of the outlaws— that we have continually witnessed some of the most expansive ways to map the world anew. Looking to Claudia Jones (1915–1964), we find an outlaw on multiple fronts, as well as a visionary: a Trinidadian-born Black communist feminist, journalist, and organizer, committed to organizing human life on different terms. She held a wide-spanning vision for Black, liberated territories that extended beyond the yoke of the nation-state. This politic was likely influenced by her experience of being incarcerated, deported from the US, barred from re-entering Trinidad, and finally exiled to the United Kingdom, for her radical politics as a Black woman and openly identified communist. Jones believed that being split into small nation-states would render Caribbean peoples unable to stand up against the colonial forces of British and American imperialism, and instead had an expansive vision for Black and multiracial homespace. She fiercely advocated, in the newspaper that she edited, the *West Indian Gazette,* for "an end to all restrictive practices towards minorities, an extension of civil and cultural rights and freedom of movement" for people across the Caribbean. Up to the last years of her life, she saw a united, socialist Caribbean as a necessary move into the future, toward a world that could be free of its vast geopolitical racial inequities, free from American and European imperialism. Her vision for liberated Black territories stemmed from the outside in: Black women, mothers, workers *in the colonies* being the centre from which a global economic and racial justice could be re-organized. In her words and in her vision for the West Indian Federation, we find a liberatory timeline mapped out, if never born, of Black life beyond the narrow confines of nation, beyond the ongoing violence of capitalism and empire. Beyond the limiting structures of patriarchy. Arising from the needs of those rarely considered within Black liberation projects of the era—the lives of Black women, mothers, and workers in the colonies—were timelines toward new terms of belonging, of mobility, of liberated territories for Black peoples. I like to hold on to the timeline in which Jones grew old in the liberated Caribbean she worked so steadfastly to manifest in her writing and organizing.

These dreams, however, were not realized. The Federation collapsed; Jones died a few years later. Yet many more had come to see how the nation-state formation was limited, despite formal decolonization and work to escape the limitations it imposed on Black struggle. Trinidadian by birth, C. L. R. James, too, was made an outlaw by multiple nation-states: detained and expelled from the US and held under house arrest in post-colonial Trinidad, experiencing the blunt arm of the state on multiple occasions, he was a Black radical exiled, broadly, from any particular vision of home. The first edition of James's *A History of Pan-African Revolt*—published in 1938, in the early years of Black anti-colonial struggle—is wildly optimistic, tracing the legacies of Black struggle and filled with liberatory visions for a Black world which had freed itself from (formal) slavery, and would now free itself from the yoke of colonization. Reading the later edition of the same text, published 1969, I imagine the new lines along his eyes as he penned a new epilogue to the book, writing that "the newly independent state was little more than the old imperialist state, only now administered and controlled by the black nationalist." By this time many anti-colonial struggles were beginning to sag under the weight of bureaucracy, of obsolete European imported institutions, of "flag independence" and neo-colonial subjugation under Black faces. James—and multitudinous others—held firm, imagined more for *all* unfree Black peoples, believed in the new formations to come.

The artists, radicals, the revolutionaries, activists, and visionaries presented alternative ways to orient life and alternative forms of governance that did not come to be, at least not in this timeline. Every attempt to build something else, fashion new forms of global belonging outside of the terrors of capital and empire, was assassinated by Western imperialism, and in many instances, with the support of the national bourgeoisie. Nation collapsed into nation-state. And from Ghana to the Congo to Grenada to Haiti, from

Philadelphia to Montreal, each new possibility has been extinguished before our eyes. In the words of Alexis Pauline Gumbs, "a home controlled by black people who refuse capitalism is a dream that is too dangerous for reality."

How could decolonization have wrought freedom while largely leaving intact the colonial state, and all of the violent, carceral institutions that colonialism put in place: the police force, the prison, and the border guard? Black liberation was never and could never have been fully achieved within these confines, which are so hostile to collectivity, so reliant on hierarchical forms of sovereign power, so antithetical to human life. Especially not for those who are "out"—to think with Lorde—*by any construct, wherever the power lay.*

Black queer, trans and gender non-conforming folks' very lives—the preservation and the protection and the proliferation of our bodies and our imaginations and our ontologies: these are not possible on the terms set out by the nation-state.

We are left instead with the husk of freedom struggles past: the colonial and carceral nation-state endured. And so, nation-state thinking threatens, always, to stunt our imaginative and speculative capacities.

Our freedom will not take place as a triumphant entrance into the nation-state, and there is nothing to be celebrated when we join the ranks of its murderous institutions. This rejection is generative and propels us into new forms of living.

To riff on Derek Walcott, *My only nation is the imagination.* And yet I have a responsibility, too, to the place where I live. To you, and the nations, not nation-states, within which I reside. Here on stolen land, creating places for belonging, insisting that Black peoples belong here as much as we do anywhere, this is not the same as asking to belong to the nation-state. It is not the same, or rather it does not need to be, and ought not be the same, as vying for equality, inclusion, "settler adjacency," to think with Zoé Samudzi and William C. Anderson, in a nation-state that is hostile to Black and Indigenous life. Because as much as this place accords no value to my own life, the Canadian state, as you and Audra Simpson have both illustrated so clearly, *requires* violence against Indigenous women, as part of the dispossession of the land. This is what she means when she writes that "*the state is a man.*" Her work, and yours, illuminated for me that dispossession relies on an asymmetrically gendered violence: of lands, peoples, and the attempted eradications of knowledge systems. I want to belong *otherwise,* on altogether different terms.

Leanne, *how are we going to live?* There's no going back. But because we continue the work of our ancestors to work for new timelines, new kinds of homespace outside of capital; we take up the visionary love work of worldmaking that we've inherited from our predecessors, even as we imbue their freedom dreams with new meanings.

For now-departed Lorde, for you and I, for so many other queer, radical, Black, Indigenous peoples, the knowledge that we are "out—by any construct" of state power is a valuable site of knowledge, from which to develop a shared politics.

Of course, this is a kind of conjure-work: to refuse the state that refuses you. Because it is not only a rejection, but an act that is geared toward liberated presents and futures.

As outlaws of this nation-state, Black and Indigenous communities, especially those on the far reaches of the power structures inside our communities, are uniquely poised to develop a shared politic based on an expansive protection of life, an expansive protection of the outlaw, to make emancipatory claims that go well beyond the formal equalities that we are continually proffered and just as continually denied.

And this is, of course, what is happening right now. The turbulent urgencies of this time are making clear that new kinds of governance are on the horizon, new futures being mapped in the present.

Cree-Métis-Saulteaux author and art curator Jas Morgan describes in *Canadian Art* how the arrest of Anne Spice, an Indigenous queer writer, at the Unist'ot'en camp sparked a new orientation of Indigenous radicalism, led by queer Indigenous young people, leading to the phrase that has defined the next phase of this movement: #ReconciliationIsDead.

By which Morgan meant that the "reconciliation" extended three years after the emergence of Idle No More, with the publication of the Truth and Reconciliation Commission's report in 2015—and intended to be promise of a "new relationship" between Canada and Indigenous peoples—was a lie, and would now be treated as such.

Spice, as told to Jas Morgan, says this:

> We're in this highly destructive system, and it's built on heteropatriarchy. It's built on colonialism. And breaking out of that means having the imagination to think through other alternatives. For queer people and for Indigenous

people alike, we're already living those alternatives. And so the constructive project of building a different world is something that we're already practicing. It's not just saying "no" to the pipelines. We're engaged in that world-building project already. And I think that's what draws us to land defence. We know we need to protect the territory, but we also need to build something else that's going to continue to feed our relations into the future.

To build something else.

#ReconciliationIsDead holds lessons for us all, in which queer, young Indigenous peoples' demand for the return of land and an end to violent extraction, their seeking of not new or better relationships with the state, but to build something else, extends a promise for a future on different terms.

I learned from Ojore Lutalo, who spent twenty-eight years in a New Jersey state prison, that "we are our own liberators. We have to define our own reality." Leanne, I'm with you here: we deserve forms of homespace that allow life, in all of its forms, to proliferate. This belief—a shared *politic*—is what grounds my solidarity with you and yours. It is not contingent on reciprocity. I will forever choose to align, politically, with those who would continue to work toward liberated territories, bodies, lives, and homespaces, in whatever form that takes. Against any form of governance that relies on land dispossession, that renders some of us criminal, alien, or forced to the constitutive outside of belonging.

I believe in forging a shared *politic*. Undergirded by the knowledge, and belief, that "where life is precious, life is precious," and forging political solidarities to value *life*. I believe in forging a politic that is centred, too, on the multivalent needs of those who least have access to a livable life. We start from here and move outward.

I believe that I am able, that we are able, to commit together to demanding the impossible because we are steeped in old-new, future-oriented political traditions that show us that there is nothing inevitable about the present, that it need not be permanent. We are able to demand alternative timelines because consciousness is born of generations of struggle, because we are so very fortunate to come from political traditions of radicalism that are collective, and communal, that are against accumulation and individualism. These not only expose the lie of Western historiography but offer a vastly expansive vision that is so much richer than the death cult that is proffered by a white supremacist society.

Abolition is imagination work, anti-colonial struggle is imagination work, conjure work, science fiction in real time. It is daring to see that the world now did not need to be as it was, does not need to be as it is, and certainly, most importantly, need not—will not—remain this way. It is *too much justice*, re-imagining and refashioning governance as abundance rather than enclosure. The timelines being forwarded by the land return projects of the hosts of the *Métis in Space* podcast, the Métis futurisms sketched out by Chelsea Vowel's writing, Camille Turner's Afronautic Research Lab, and the reparations struggle of Lynn Jones and other Black elders in Nova Scotia: all of these sketch out alternative futures right here in the present.

As described in Sun Ra's *Space is the Place:* "We live on the other side of time."

Toward the end of "100 musicians at Jane and Finch?," despite the insistence of her lover, June hears—she is certain!—the radio announcer saying these words: "The mayor has decided to send one hundred musicians including flautists, guitarists, bassists, saxophonists, drummers and pianists to the Jane-Finch corridor to help curb the violence in the neighborhood. The plan was approved by City Council . . ." June's timeline is well underway; her city, her home and world are exponentially expanding outward with possibility.

It's late summer now, so the stores are open again. Bloor Street West is no longer nearly empty. I prefer, going forward, to linger my thoughts not on the spring/summer as I had planned/hoped it to be, but to choose differently. I hope I can continue to maintain the courage to choose June's timeline again and again, to maintain a fastidious commitment to believing that there are one hundred otherwise worlds for us to live in, that they are just around the corner, perhaps arriving already, if we listen carefully enough. That there are one hundred ways to manifest the presence of justice in the places it is most absent, one hundred modes of governance that are collective, communal. One hundred worlds for L., for Minowe, for our kids and theirs to grow old in that are free from nation-state, enclosure, private property, and all of the carceral mechanisms in place to protect it. We can be homeless together: and I hope we will continue to dream up well over one hundred ways we could live together, differently, in this place.

Robyn,

I also can't ever sleep and sometimes I watch so much *Star Trek* that I start to refer to the characters as my actual friends. Miigwech for your last letter. Sometimes I think your letters are the only good thing in the world. I've started reading Octavia Butler's *Parable of the Sower*, alongside some N. K. Jemisin. Oh you are so right. We were warned. Octavia told us.

I also love the exchange you shared between Baldwin and Lorde—her flat-out rejection of the American dream. In the days since you wrote, I've carried her rejection with me. She was never part of the American dream. Indigenous peoples were never part of the American dream—our bodies and lands were the resources for white people to build their dream on. I'm trying to think through how Nishnaabeg elders would think about that dream—a dream that from this perspective is flawed from the beginning. Why would one work hard for their own individual benefit? How is that ethical? Doesn't Nishnaabeg ethics require everyone to work hard, not for themselves but for the collective web of life? How could a people be so broken that their dream of a better life focused only on their individual wealth—at the world-ending expense of so many other living beings? This is exactly Dionne Brand's question in the face of individual or even collective recognition: *how do we change the air*? That is such a profound instruction. How do we refuse the recognition, the invitations to perform, the individual validations, the crumbs, and change the thing nearly all living things require, the air?

I come from a society that, prior to colonialism, didn't have police or the practice of policing—not because we were primitive or simple or nomadic, or because our population was too tiny to need policing, but because Nishnaabeg society was structured and practised in such a way that, for the most part, the violence of policing wasn't required to maintain social and political relations. For me, the foundations of this way of collective living are spiritual and come from a belief that the spiritual world is alive and animated and interacting with the physical world. Each living being is responsible for its own path in relation to the other living things with whom we share time and space. This means that I'm responsible for monitoring myself and my own behaviours and actions within that matrix of relationals. I'm not at liberty to interfere or judge or surveil the life paths of other living things. Nishnaabeg spiritual practices teach that everything alive also has spirit, and that these spirits are in constant interaction with each other. This means that my ancestors are always around me, as are those yet to be born. This means that I have a relationship to the plants and animals I am dependent upon in the physical world, in the spiritual world. This becomes most prominent during our harvesting practices. In Nishnaabeg society, harvesting animals or plants first requires their consent, and we believe that if the animal appears, it is giving up its physical life and returning to the spiritual world. There are a series of rituals and procedures that, when practised, ensure this transition from the physical world to the spiritual world is done with respect and honouring.

I understand this as an anti-capitalist society in a particularly Nishnaabeg formation. The practices of taking only what you need, using everything you take, sharing everything you have and giving up what you can to promote more life, created a bush economy that gave way to a very different relationship to land and water than the one dictated to us by racial capitalism. Systems of conflict resolution, repair, restorative justice, and building consensus were practised to nurture balance and peace, amongst individuals and groups of people—and not just between and amongst humans, but amongst a diversity of living beings. The idea of authoritarian control in leadership or education was relaxed and even rejected in favour of individual self-determination, consent, and non-interference. Labour, material goods, and the gifts of plants and animals were shared. Of course, things were not always perfect. Abuse, toxicity, and conflict occurred. We know because there are stories. Conflicts sometimes escalated, but the responsibility for creating safe and caring spaces didn't rest on leaders or institutions; those responsibilities were carried by individuals and families as well as the larger collective. What I learn from the way my ancestors lived life collectively is that if you build systems based on relationality, reciprocity, consent and diversity, if you refuse hierarchy and authoritarian power in both collective and intimate settings, if "laws" are practices embodied in deep relationality rather than rigid authoritarian rules, if "justice" repairs and restores and if your practice of living is also a practice of consent, you eliminate policing.

What I learn from my ancestors is that if you have a profoundly different relationship with land, with the earth— one grounded in diversity and based on consent, sharing, respect, and minimizing one's impact, instead of mass exploitation of natural resources for the benefit a small group of people willing to exercise authoritarian power— you have a profoundly different relationship to all of life, profoundly different intimate relations, and profoundly different diplomatic relations.

When I speak about Indigenous resurgence and Indigenous self-determination, my vision is to take wisdom and inspiration from my ancestors to actualize Nishnaabeg political formations outside of nation-states, economies outside of extractivism and enclosures of racial capitalism. This means deep connections to land outside of dispossession, and relationships to each other outside of heteropatriarchy. This means abolishing and reconstructing every aspect of life in North America and beyond. It is a reckoning, a complete overturning. A remaking of a Nishnaabeg world.

The vision for the future in this way of thinking is not a fixed map, but a set of ethical practices giving way to continual making and remaking processes without an ending. In my understanding of Nishnaabeg origin stories, not even Gzhe Manidoo knew how to build the world on their first try. It took many engagements in world-building to get it right. The planets in our solar system are examples of their failed prototypes for life. Of course, in our current context we have additional challenges because we are tasked with remaking a world in a place still wholly invested in world-endings. We have been both individually and collectively harmed by four centuries of oppression. There are huge losses in terms of land, knowledge, and practice, and of course not all Indigenous peoples agree, not all Nishnaabeg would share my interpretations or visions. I still find inspiration in my ancestors, and this inspiration only grows when I experience glimpses of this way of living.

How did my community and my nation get from living with very little crime and no police to being gunned down on the streets of Toronto? The short answer is colonialism. The medium-sized answer is that dispossessing Indigenous peoples of our lands and maintaining that system required and requires a complicated and multi-pronged structure of control where direct violence, the threat of direct violence, and symbolic violence, all deployed in a gendered way, are foundational to the construction and maintenance of Canada. The longer, detailed answer is more complicated, because there are variations and specificities of this circuitry in different regions in Canada; as well, the time frame is enormous, particularly for Indigenous peoples in the east and central Canada, and of course the historic record is fraught with bias, racism and the absence of Indigenous experience and perspectives. What follows here, then, is a generalized sketch of what those systems looked like and look like for First Nations in Canada, focusing on the Indian Act and how that act worked in concert with other forces to surveil, control and regulate life for First Nations people.

We need to first take a step back, though. The policing, surveillance and punishment of Indigenous bodies and our relationality actually began long before the first Indian Act. It began at contact, when explorers, missionaries, traders, and translators came into contact with Two-Spirit, queer Nishnaabeg, and those Nishnaabeg who embodied a gender identity outside of the European gender binary. In *As We Have Always Done*, in a chapter called "Queer Normativity," I wrote about how, prior to colonization, 2SQ Indigenous peoples flourished in many Indigenous nations and were highly visible to the first European colonizers. I give the example of Ozawendib, an Anishinaabe from Leech Lake who is documented in the historical record as someone whose sexuality, relationship orientation and gender was accepted into Anishinaabeg society as normal, despite it being outside of the norms of European culture. 2SQ people like Ozawendib, who were visible to the Europeans, also quickly became targets of eliminatory violence by missionaries—with Joseph-François Lafitau, a French Jesuit missionary, boasting, in 1724, nearly one hundred years before the advent of residential schools and more than one hundred years before the first Indian Act, that, after seventy-five years of missionary work, 2SQ people were "now looked upon with scorn even by the Indians." My culture had more than two genders. There was a fluidity around gender, sexual orientation, and relationship orientation. This was a direct threat to the colonizers. And so for Indigenous peoples in Canada, this was the beginning of the policing of our bodies, our sexualities, our relationship orientations, gender, and our society's queerness.

As I wrote in *As We Have Always Done*:

> [C]olonizers saw in Indigenous people's bodies—our physical bodies and our constructions of gender, sexuality, and intimate relationships—as Audra Simpson says, as a symbol of Indigenous orders of government and a direct threat to their sovereignty and governmentality. The church, the state, and broader Canadian society worked in concert to surveil and confine Indigenous bodies and intimacies to Euro-Canadian heteropatriarchal marriages, that is, singular, lifelong monogamous relationships designed to reproduce the building blocks of Canadian nationalism instead of the replication of Nishnaabeg worlds [Nishnaabewin and Nishnaabeg nationhoods], while also placing Indigenous conceptualizations and forms of intimacy and relationship as transgressive, immoral, uncivilized, and criminal.

By the time the Indian Act came into being in 1876, queer Indigenous bodies had already been policed and targeted for elimination for a century. The first Indian Act brought existing legislation regarding Indian life under one act, and it was designed to control nearly all aspects of Indian life from the cradle to the grave. I am using the term "Indian" here, although it is considered a racial slur and offensive, for the sake of accuracy because it carries legal meaning in Canada, and that meaning is confined to First Nations people. The term and the act do not include Inuit and Métis people, who have their own unique and important history with the state.

The first Indian Act entrenched the colonial gender binary into our communities by administratively eliminating genders other than male and female. It defined who was Indian and who was not, and therefore decided who was part of the reserve community and who was not. Successive Indian Acts, prior to a mass mobilization by Indigenous women in the 1980s, denied Indian status to Indian women who married white men, but granted Indian status to white women who married Indian men. The racist and sexist thinking at the time was that Indian men would not take care of white women and would need the government assistance that status provided, and that white men could take care of Indian women so they would no longer need the "benefits" Indian status provided. The Indian Act embodied a heteronormativity that rejected unchurched, queer, non-monogamous intimate relationships from reserve communities. Indigenous women who married white men, and their children, were often forced to leave the reserve and to remake their homes without support in urban centres. Queer people were also forced to leave, or to live coded and hidden lives on the reserve, obscuring the surveillance of the church and state.

Early Indian Acts (1876 to the end of World War II) did not stop here. They assisted and created the control mechanisms that enabled residential schools and the practice of state schooling. They created reserves in the southern parts of Canada. They forced people to carry European names, instead of Indigenous ones. They restricted people from leaving the reserve without permission from the Indian agent. They enforced enfranchisement (which stipulated the loss of legal and ancestral identities) of any Indian admitted to university or who served in the army, and of any Indian woman marrying a non-Indigenous man. They allowed Indian agents to lease out First Nations lands to white farmers and to relocate entire communities. They forbade political organizing, the hiring of lawyers, and fundraising to support a legal claim. They denied those who kept their Indian status the right to vote in Canadian elections, forbade some First Nations people from appearing in public wearing regalia, and had the impact of forbidding First Nations people from speaking our languages and practising ceremonies. Indian Acts from 1876 right up until today imposed (sometimes violently, as we've seen in the case of Akwesasne) the band council system of administration and "governance"—a system of government that is not founded on our political systems, but is designed so chief and councillors are enmeshed in a colonial administration with limited powers and with direct accountability to the state, not their community members.

Indian Acts placed Indian agents, representatives of the Canadian government, on reserves with the purpose of controlling Indians and enforcing the acts themselves, beginning in the late 1800s. In Canada, Indian agents administered Indian policy and the wishes of the state until the late 1960s. They exerted a tremendous amount of control over Indian people. They could recommend that a chief or councillor be deposed, and they enforced attendance at residential schools. They could dole out rations and the terms of treaty, and they could withhold those same rations and terms as punishment. They controlled Indian movements through the "pass system," a system of carding in which one needed the written permission of the Indian agent to leave the reserve. They controlled religious and cultural practices, language speaking, gender expression, intimate relationships, and sexuality. They pressured women into the roles of housewives, and men into farming or wage labour. They were to defuse any political organizing and politicization. Clergy, missionaries and the church communities (both non-Indigenous and Indigenous), white settlers, health officials, police and the military worked in concert with Indian agents to report families and individuals not adhering or conforming to colonial values or, in the case of vagrancy and prostitution laws, appearing in white spaces. The Indian Act, Indian agents and their clergy allies were a form of policing that historically had extraordinary powers in the regulation and surveillance and punishment of Indian life in order to maintain dispossession. The Indian Act was often enforced by police and the criminal justice system, and even low-level officials in the Department of Indian Affairs often had the power of life or death over Indian people.

And it wasn't just the Indian Act and Indian agents policing Indigenous life.

The dispossession of First Nations and Métis peoples from their homelands on the prairies and plains of western Canada from the early 1700s to the late 1800s provides us with a clear, well documented and horrific account of the multi-faceted violence of colonialism and of the strength and resistance of prairie Indigenous peoples. The settlement of this region was predicated on a tremendous loss of Indigenous life, and a tremendous loss of ecological life. There were a series of devastating epidemics and pandemics over this period—European infectious disease played a crucial role in weakening Indigenous nations and Indigenous resistance and eliminating Indigenous life. Racial capitalism was introduced in the form of the extractivist fur trade, at first working within the bounds of Indigenous economies, and then overwhelming those economies as enormous practices of greed took over, leading to more systems of control to secure trade. Animal populations collapsed; environmental degradation was normalized. The influx of settlers demanding land for farming, the construction of the railway, the decline of the bison, and extreme, imposed poverty and starvation were the context within which treaties and the Métis scrip system were actualized. The creation of reserves, together with the Indian Act's pass system, amounted to a form of mass incarceration for those First Nations people who were able to survive. Throughout this history, there are also many examples of First Nations and Métis resistance, sometimes large-scale and armed, sometimes in the notes of those witnessing treaty negotiations and always in the oral traditions of those peoples. Indigenous children were being kidnapped by the state and held in residential schools, which seems a lot like the state using Indigenous children as human shields, to quell Indigenous resistance while also "removing the Indian from the child."

Before police forces were established in Canada, policing was violently present in Indigenous life in administration, policy, law, social work, education, housing, religion, and health care, and that policing was there to remove, separate, and contain Indigenous peoples from land.

All of this is to say that by the time the North-West Mounted Police (NWMP) was formed in 1873 by then Prime Minister John A. Macdonald as a paramilitary organization, the practice of violently dispossessing Indigenous peoples of their lands in the prairies was already a century old. The NWMP and later the Royal Canadian Mounted Police were created to "assist with conflicts" between Indigenous peoples and settlers and facilitate a smooth transfer of Indigenous land to the colonizers; in other words, their purpose was to remove Indigenous peoples from their territories, and confine them to reserves. A full understanding of the history of policing in Canada and the United States and its current practice requires an understanding of the evolution of this system with regard to both Indigenous and Black peoples and our experiences with slavery and colonialism.

While many of the most restrictive measures in the Indian Act were removed in the 1951 amendments, the act still remains intact, particularly in terms of membership and governance, as do the attitudes and beliefs that propelled the colonial scaffolding in the first place. The legacy of these historic systems continues today, intensely, on the prairies with the murder of Colten Boushie and the acquittal of the Gerald Stanley, the white farmer who killed him, in remote and northern communities where missionaries are actively trying to convert people to fundamentalist forms of Christianity, and in cities where over-policing and over-incarceration of Indigenous peoples is an eliminator violence that has killed many Indigenous people in the recent past. The results of these historic systems continue today when police are deployed to blockades and land reclamation sites.

A cruel and enduring system of control has also been enacted on Indigenous children and their families. This won't surprise any Indigenous parents. This week, APTN News reported that in the last four months in Ontario, eleven Indigenous children have died while connected to the child welfare system. There is, and has been since the beginning of the residential school era, an epidemic of Indigenous child apprehension by the state. There are currently more Indigenous children in care than at the height of the residential school system, with 90 percent of the kids in care in Manitoba, as an example, being Indigenous. We know the outcomes of the foster care system are horrific: 60 percent of homeless youth and one-third of homeless adults have come from foster care. White middle-class social workers have wielded extreme amounts of control over Indigenous families for generations, with very little accountability. We have over twenty thousand survivors of the Sixties Scoop—a time period in which white middle-class social workers removed thousands of children from Indigenous homes, often from stable and loving families, and placed them in adopted white families. This is the direct result of social workers and the state policing Indigenous mothering and parenting, and a direct result of imposed poverty of dispossession and the intergenerational trauma caused by residential schools.

Destroying Indigenous families through sexualized violence, poverty, residential schools, the child welfare system and over-policing prevents our people from being able to launch effective resistance mobilizations to protect our lands from extractivist resource development. So much effort in colonial societies goes towards violently breaking the bond between Indigenous peoples and our homelands.

The final report of the National Inquiry into Missing and Murdered Indigenous Women and Girls talks about policing as an institution that worked in concert with other colonial institutions to exert total colonial control over Indigenous peoples. Colonial control over relationships, gender expression and sexuality was surveilled and monitored through the church, residential and day schools, and Indian agents. Nishnaabeg society, for instance, which as I've mentioned embraced many genders, relationship orientations and sexual orientations, was controlled by the imposition of a strict gender binary and hierarchy and of "churched relationships"—heterosexual, monogamous relationships. This "total control" was key in enabling sexual abuse and in the perpetuation of the racist and gendered stereotypes at the root of the crisis of missing and murdered Indigenous women and girls.

It wasn't just police forces like the RCMP that surveilled, controlled and *policed* Indigenous bodies and our homespaces. This racialized control is carried out by clergy, church communities, health care workers, teachers, social workers, companies and corporations, farmers and white people in general. Policing, in all its formations, is a foundational part of the violent system of control and subjugation that is colonialism, and it is not confined to those who wear uniforms, carry guns and murder Black and Indigenous people struggling with mental illness, poverty and substance use. It is work that white settlers willingly take on, as we witnessed in the trial of Gerald Stanley. We've also recently seen it closer to home in Orillia, Ontario, when two white people called the police when they witnessed a First Nations man fall off his bike, resulting in two Nishnaabeg brothers being attacked and assaulted by officers as a result of that call.

Several years ago, motivated by the crisis of missing and murdered Indigenous women and girls and—though this is too often overlooked, Two-Spirit and queer people—I sought out a deeper understanding of abolition through the writings of Black feminists. I sought out the writings of radical Black feminists from below because I was personally frustrated with the catastrophic loss of Indigenous life, the police and state's response, and the narrative taken up in the media and popular culture about Indigenous women in general, and those who are murdered and eliminated in particular. I found it disgusting to watch Canada consume the grief and trauma of families who had lost loved ones. I also found the gendered nature of the diagnosis, its erasure of queer bodies and reinforcement of a colonial gender binary, problematic—an impression that was bolstered by the critical analysis of the carceral state being done by so many Black abolition feminists. After immersing myself in Black abolition writing and the women of the Black Radical Tradition—writers like Angela Y. Davis, Ruth Wilson Gilmore, Mariame Kaba, and Saidiya Hartman, all of whom you have mentioned in your letters, I began to ask how it was that colonial gendered violence was disproportionately filling up prisons with Indigenous people, and that police were disproportionately murdering Indigenous peoples. I became interested in the fact that there are also alarming numbers of missing and murdered Black women, girls and queer people, and that the police are disproportionately murdering Black people. From this lens, my understandings of colonial and anti-Black violence in the afterlives of slavery became more rigorous, layered, nuanced and complete, and these broadened understandings pointed to a different organizing pathway.

Indigenous women and Two-Spirit and queer people have been organizing around the crisis of MMIWG2SQ for decades, pressing governments to take action, supporting grieving families, pressing for police reforms, and demanding justice. I am grateful to the countless Indigenous women and queer folks who have built this movement and done decades of thankless work to make the world a safer place for me and my daughter. And certainly, one of the tangible results of this work was the state's National Inquiry on MMIWG. The "Calls for Justice" in the final section of the report were also remarkable in calling for the state to engage in the wider systemic change required to lessen the violence load on Indigenous women and Two-Spirit and queer people by addressing issues around cultural regeneration, poverty, the child welfare system, health and wellness, human security, particularly in the sex industry, the role of extractivist and development industries, reforms in prisons, policing and the criminal justice system. Of course we know this work is never done with a government's final report. We know we have to go far beyond these recommendations. We know there is a huge gulf between the state's intentions and actions and the Calls for Justice. We also know from our past experiences with royal commissions and national inquiries, that these Calls for Justice will go largely ignored, particularly the ones demanding systemic change. Unless our movements are able to move our agenda forward, the murdering will continue.

The work of Andrea J. Ritchie in *Invisible No More: Police Violence Against Black Women and Women of Color* is crucial here in reminding Indigenous peoples that police and policing are never going to be a solution to the crisis of MMIWG2SQ. Ritchie emphasizes that policing is premised on punishment and authoritarian power, and was and is designed to control Black and Indigenous bodies in maintenance of racial capitalism and the settler state.

What is clear to me from the writings and actions of Black abolition feminists is that to eliminate the crisis of killing of Indigenous women and girls, and Two-Spirit and queer people, we need a shift in the focus of organizing from individual harm to collective and systemic change. From this perspective, we must eliminate, not reform the police. We must as, Ruth Wilson Gilmore says, change everything. We must eliminate the structures and conditions that created this crisis in the first place. We must go further than a government report designed on a macro-level to gut Indigenous resistance by gesturing towards change, but never implementing it. We need to reclaim Indigenous territoriality outside the nation-state, and to build an economy outside of the offerings of racial capitalism. We need to build an Indigenous movement of "feminist-inflected internationalism that highlights the value of queer theories and practices."

We need to create the conditions where the lives of Indigenous and Black women and Two-Spirit, trans, and queer people are precious; where all living things are precious.

Bringing the movement to end MMIWG2SQ in conversation with the work of Black abolition feminists creates a number of what-if questions, to my mind. What if Black and Indigenous families had safe housing, food, drinking water, education, and health care, free from anti-Indigenous racism? What if Black and Indigenous communities, both urban and reserve, had access to mental-health care from the best of both Western and Indigenous practices? What if all Black and Indigenous families had access to community-based and community-led twenty-four-hour childcare programs and programs that assist parents in developing culturally appropriate parenting skills? What if we were committed to repairing the damage caused through dispossession, residential schools, and the child welfare system and regenerating Indigenous families on Indigenous terms? What if we were committed to repairing the damage of slavery and its anti-Black afterlives? What if we did this work together, instead of begging the state?

In my own homeland as you know better than I do, movements for Black life including Black Lives Matter Toronto continue to work towards abolition with a list of demands that ranges from defunding and demilitarizing the police to decriminalizing poverty. Every single demand will make the lives of Indigenous peoples in Toronto and beyond better.

Every single demand towards defunding the police could save the lives of Indigenous Two-Spirit and queer people. Every single demand addresses the issue of MMIWG, and represents movement towards abolition. This platform does more in my mind to regenerate Indigenous communities and mitigate the trauma of colonialism than reconciliation or any state offering.

I've thought about the last section of the demands— "Create Alternatives"—the most, asking the questions, What do Indigenous peoples need in order to recreate societies that have no need for police and policing, and how do these needs drive the undoing of racial capitalism? This has become an interesting way of thinking about abolition through a Nishnaabeg lens.

We need clean drinking water in all of our communities. We need consent, sex, gender and violence education in the school curriculum, and free health care clinics. We need expanded midwifery services in homes and hospitals and remote communities so people can give birth surrounded by their loved ones and in a culturally appropriate manner. We need breast-feeding advocates and support workers. We need living income for all, and expanded parental leaves for people with all kinds of work. We need all of our parents to have access to culturally relevant parenting resources and supports, including free, twenty-four-hour childcare. We need well-funded, culturally relevant schools on reserves and in urban centres with Indigenous teachers. We need language learning opportunities, on par with French-language instruction in English Canada, for all Indigenous languages. We need food security. We need community-based programs that breathe life into bush economies and support Indigenous peoples being on the land, harvesting food and sharing those gifts with the community. We need the state and its social workers to stop apprehending Indigenous children into the child welfare system. We need an end to racial capitalism and global warming and the extermination of our plant and animal relatives.

Saidiya Hartman writes that "[t]he possessive investment in whiteness can't be rectified by learning 'how to be more antiracist.' It requires a radical divestment in the project of whiteness and a redistribution of wealth and resources. It requires abolition, the abolition of the carceral world, the abolition of capitalism. What is required is a remaking of the social order, and nothing short of that is going to make a difference."

Now, this might deal with a large chunk of practical social issues and issues of inequality stemming from colonialism, but it does not necessarily deal with the things that my people usually mobilize over—land and self-determination. Indigenous nations and communities need substantial land bases where we have the ability to say no to resource extraction. We need to be able to decide how to govern ourselves without state interference. Without resolutions to these two fundamental and related issues, the state will still need to deploy the military and police forces into our communities in order to control our governance and decision making and to protect their interests in the resources in our homelands. In the face of global climate change and its amplification of inequality, states that chose to continue on extermination courses will also need the military and police forces to protect their interests. Indigenous peoples will continue to mobilize against deforestation, environmental contamination, pipelines and the oil and gas industry, mining, fish farms, and any other industrialized development taking place on our lands without our consent.

Manu Karuka makes the argument that Black and Indigenous movements for self-determination have long critiqued the colonial/racial state and that these critiques offer sites where Indigenous and Black thought and politics can productively interact with each other, working independently and in concert towards shared ends, building capacities for futures beyond state power.

Karuka asks us to pay attention to the idea that Blackness has developed in relation to Indigenous presence. "To ignore this historical and structural relationship is one way to deny accountability across distinct claims to self-determination, in which black liberation in place is framed through the ongoing dispossession of Indigenous peoples." Karuka then quotes Audra Simpson, making the point that colonialism has not been successful in that Indigenous peoples still exist and we have not been absorbed into a "white, property-owning body politic." Karuka suggests that settler colonialism's failure, then, "might potentially be a fulcrum for Black liberation."

Our movements and our communities come from different experiences and histories with genocide. They are informed by different theoretical positions and meaning-making practices, and while the results of colonialism and transatlantic slavery might place our peoples' struggles—with poverty, with mental health and substance-use issues, with insecure housing and food systems—in a linked formation, our political struggles and historic resistances are different.

This difference is a strength.

Certain formations of Nishnaabeg nationhood and self-determination have the potential to be a mechanism that supports, philosophically, ethically, and materially, radical Black freedom through mutual accountability and deep reciprocity. I believe that we are best served with movements and theoretical foundations and bodies of knowledge that centre anti-colonial struggle in the global theatre. I know that real change takes tremendous amounts of work and successive mobilizations by waves of peoples. Defunding the police and the policing of Indigenous and Black people, then, is a huge part of undoing the system of colonialism in Canada. It must be part of the calculus of our anti-colonial organizing.

I want to build societies where we take care of the land and the waters and live in a way that promotes more life. I want to live in a way that doesn't cause the extinction of vast numbers of plants and animals, where environmental desecration isn't inevitable. Where extractivist economies are not the norm and where capitalism is not assumed to be permanent. Where there are communal and embodied ethics and practices that make slavery and colonialism unthinkable, where one hundred musicians show up at busy intersections and no one is surprised.

Where we literally change the air, and it saves the planet.

PART FIVE

───────────

"We Are Peoples of the Lands,
of More Lands Than Could
Ever Be Counted"

Dear Leanne,

I've been delaying this letter because I was waiting for the right words to come my way. A few days ago, I finally heard the words that helped me to articulate my response to you. This happened while I was roasting a chicken, of all the things, which I had soaked in a seasoned brine overnight.

As a sidebar, this is an absurd amount of food, really, for one person. But given my newly single status since the pandemic began, I was proud of myself. Was feeling like a butch and a boss in the kitchen, in life. (I take great satisfaction in making small parts of my life symbolic.) But this is otherwise beside the point. Because what is more important than *what* I was cooking is that *while* I was cooking, I was watching a documentary about Ousmane Sembène, the Senegalese anti-colonial novelist and filmmaker. It was grainy and slightly difficult to follow, as the film had been pirated onto YouTube, but brilliant, nonetheless. Something that he said jumped out at me, made me interrupt the cooking process, wash and dry my hands so that I could scroll the film backwards and take note. In this particular scene Sembène is sitting at a table, wearing dark sunglasses, at what appears to be an outdoor café. In response to a question about Europe's colonization of Africa, he answers this, about the colonizers: "They've never invented anything to make earth habitable. Everything they do is to destroy the land." After this, he gestures, silently. The interviewer, in turn, gestures silently. After a long pause, the scene closes. What more needed to be said, anyways?

Everything they do is to destroy the land.

I've leaned in for a few days now to your gentle but firm insistence that the abolition of police and prisons must be a pillar of decolonization, *and* that Indigenous land-based struggles could/should/must be considered within what abolition demands of us. #LandBack. Land. Back. In this crisis of the earth's habitability, your words are pushing me to think more extensively about abolition and land. About my own responsibility to you, to the place that I live. Your words are a necessary reminder that, in addition to the role of policing in enforcing Black people's unfreedom (and perpetuating an economy that relies on a multitude of unfreedoms), policing has always served, and serves, still, to sever Indigenous peoples from their lands, from non-capitalist ways of relating to land and to all other non-human relations. That policing functions in the service of those who destroy the land. That one opposite of policing is Land Back, which is, after all, an end to the imposition of private property regimes and the carceral technologies developed to enforce them.

Everything they do is to destroy the land. Indeed: aren't *all* carceral sites and technologies, at some level, really, about cementing the theft of the land, to cement its (purported) transformation into capital, for some colonizer somewhere? Ingrid Waldron's work details the twin criminalization of African Nova Scotian and Mi'kmaw peoples on the east coast, alongside and in parallel to the environmental devastation of their communities. Africville, Lincolnville, North and East Preston, alongside Eskasoni First Nation, Millbrook First Nation, and Acadia First Nation, as she highlights, are places where the state targets our communities for incarceration, and where large companies facilitate our ongoing economic plunder. And so, as we enter a crisis of the earth's vulnerability, I do not see a contradiction between Black-led abolitionist struggles against carcerality and the Indigenous struggle for white settlers to rescind their purported ownership of land. Instead, I see a site where struggles can/should/must/do overlap.

This is partly because within Turtle Island and across the Black global south, prison serves, everywhere, among other things, toward the destruction of the land. For the colonizer, for the multinational corporation (these are not necessarily distinct in a meaningful way.) Because not just settler colonialism, but all colonization was itself a project of land theft. As written in 1900 in the *Lagos Observer*, "Forcible concessions of land in places where there are any prospects of vegetable or mineral wealth, and oppressive Lands Bills have left the Natives of the soil hardly any control over their ancestral possessions." To hold and keep African territories and peoples under European control, colonizers built substantial networks of prisons, with technologies perfected in the coastal forts built for the slave trade, and with technologies of forcible confinement and constraint that were developed over centuries of Black enslavement. In Kenya, the settler colonial government, as part of a broader program of brutal and spectacular forms of violence, used detention to cement the process of massive land grabs that extended from 1890 onward. (And if you were wondering: this violence was tacitly and at times formally supported, as most global violences are, by Canada: former RCMP officer John Timmerman was the assistant to the chief of police during the anti-colonial uprisings.) This land theft continued into the so-called independence era, now at the behest of the neo-colonial rulers. This practice was satirized in a play (that took to task, as well, other neo-colonial hypocrisies) by Ngugi wa Thiong'o. And prison continued to serve its same purpose: for levelling this critique, Thiong'o was duly placed in detention in the nation's Kamiti Maximum Security Prison. They could not, however, hold his mind captive: he published a series of prison writings that would have him join the ranks of Wole Soyinka, George Simeon Mwase, and J. M. Kariuki, entering a tradition of incarcerated African radicals who would write freedom from spaces of captivity. Who were punished for dreaming, among other freedom dreams, of how land could be held, lived, owned, shared, otherwise.

Everything they do is to destroy the land. In Haiti, the Lavalas movement undertook educational and labour reforms and a radical project of land redistribution for the mass of Haiti's landless peasants, with broad popular support. And, of course, was overthrown by a *coup d'état* orchestrated by the governments of Canada, the US, and France in 2003. The land program, and all the other moves toward ending privatization and mass impoverishment, was thrown out by the brutal puppet government of Gérard Latortue, installed by the coup leaders. This government would go on to police and incarcerate those who had deigned to organize land and life otherwise, with Canadian "aid" money funding, and providing training for, Haitian police and prisons. I think that few Canadians realize just how substantively their country's carceral practices extend beyond its national borders. In so many instances the same police forces that we are protesting here are used to uphold a *global* economy of racial and gendered subordination (headlines like this one: "Quebec police officers engaged in sexual misconduct in Haiti," have not made waves in the broader discourse). And yet the RCMP, the Montreal Police Services, and the Correctional Service of Canada are all Canadian exports which serve to contain and confine much of the Haitian population, preventing Haitian peoples from adopting less oppressive forms of land ownership and less exploitative labour practices.

Everything they do is to destroy the land.

Of course, they also destroy much more than this. Western imperialism in the global Black world, anti-Black violence past and present—these are not only matters of the land. Black peoples' bodily and ontological sovereignty matters; who "owns" our labour and the products of our labour matters. And, land matters. These are not unrelated matterings.

Robin D. G. Kelley writes, speaking to the context of settler colonialism on the African continent, "they wanted the land *and* the labor, but not the *people*—that is to say, they sought to eliminate stable communities and their cultures of resistance." This includes, he notes, the "metaphysical and material relations of people to land, culture, spirit, and each other." *All* forms of life are homogenized for transformation into capital, into surplus value. Particularly those for whom life is lived in/as the afterlife of property. And still, other ways of knowing and relating to land, to all living things outside of capital, are subject to policing and criminalization, from Wet'suwet'en to Port-au-Prince to Soweto. And all of this, so often funded by Canadian tax dollars.

Abolition and the land, these are issues that we cannot separate here or anywhere.

Everything they do is to destroy the land. And so ongoing Black radical struggle forges and maintains a multitude of alternative, non-exploitative relationships to the land, beyond and outside and against the brutalities of capital. The protection of ecosystems and the earth is at the forefront of many Black struggles: in North Preston, Nova Scotia; on the Honduran North Coast; in the Niger Delta of Nigeria, where the Ijaw Youth Council worked, in 1999, to forward an environmental awareness campaign called "Operation Climate Change." Tanzanian independence leader and anti-colonial nationalist Julius Nyerere stated that "the foreigners introduced . . . the concept of land as a marketable commodity" to Indigenous African societies in the lands that came to be deemed Tanzania. Decolonization wrote new relationships to land. Burkinabé revolutionary Thomas Sankara made this link explicit, tying African revolutionary struggle to care for the land. At the Silva Forest Foundation's first international conference in Paris, in 1986, speaking to the encroachment of the Sahel desert in Burkina Faso, itself the result of mass colonial plunder and deforestation, Sankara spoke these words: "This struggle to defend the trees and the forest is first and foremost a struggle against imperialism. Because imperialism is the arsonist of our forests and savannahs." Black women, especially, have been at the forefront of land defence. Black women in South Africa, organizing under the name Sikhala Sonke, for example, led support for the 2012 miners against the British-owned platinum mines in South Africa's minerals-energy complex at Marikana. They took aim, not only at the Lonmin company, but at the World Bank, fighting against both intolerable labour conditions as well as the massive ecological destruction wrought by finance capital and extractive industry. And for this, of course, as always, they faced carceral retribution. As Winona LaDuke writes, though: "In a time when the rights of corporations override the rights of humans, *stay human*, and remember that the law must be changed."

Everything they do is to destroy the land. And still, Black peoples, if continually made homeless by capital, forge and have forged relationships with land, despite and against ongoing displacement.

After sitting with the works of the late Caribbean surrealist and Negritude writer Suzanne Césaire, I scribbled this note in the margin my writing book: "We are peoples of the

lands, of more lands than could ever be counted." I read
these words out loud to L. sometimes, because I like the way
that they feel, because they feel comfortable on my tongue.
"We are people of the lands, of more lands than could ever
be counted." I want him to know the multiple lands he can
trace his ancestry to, and hold a connection with, and I want
him to understand the histories of the lands that he resides
on. To me, that involves teaching him about the soil, about
the plants, about the snails, about how we respect living
things, how we are part of this world that we inhabit.

Some of this is small things, the day-to-day. Many of
these small things, as it turns out, involve me pretending
that I'm not a wimp. Me holding back my urge to scream
when we pull from the soil a cabbage that is filled with massive grey slugs. Me, resisting all of the forces inside me that
are driving me to kill the massive (and honestly, terrifying)
spider at the bottom of the staircase. Me, instead, naming
the spider Winston, and casually—or so it would seem—
saying, "What's up, Winston?" every time we saunter down
there for bath time.

And yet the bigger picture, too, of a more serious nature,
has its own simplicity. It is part of my work to help him
connect to living things, to land, to the place we call our
home. To do so, I teach L. how white settlers only *purport*
to own all of these lands. How these lands were in fact violently stolen from peoples who had lived here for thousands
of years. Were stolen from people who are here, still. I teach
him, too, that many of these same peoples purported to
own *us*, too. That many would purport to own us, still.
That our lives are governed, in fact, by many logics that

mean nothing to us but nonetheless have deadly repercussions for us when ignored. That there are other ways that this land has been held, loved, and tended. That we, too, are people of lands, more lands than could ever be counted, even if our family has only spent two generations on these ones. That our peoples—Black peoples here—have loved and tended and held kinship relationships to the lands beneath our feet. And that the homespace we inhabit is a land of water protectors, land protectors, whose struggle is in more ways than one our own. And this is how #LandBack is part of my COVID-19 home-school, part of our gardening lesson, however clumsily I may impart it.

And so, yes, to make a short story long, I agree with you, that abolition and Land Back are interlocking projects. They are transnational projects, too, in service of the liberation of earth and its peoples from the throes of capital, toward the end of all forms of captivity.

Because that is what is happening here: they are holding captive an ailing planet. They are ramping up extraction even as the earth is fighting back, and they are criminalizing all of those who would deign to take the side of the earth. The side of the living.

Everything they do is to destroy the land.

It is not only us who see these connections, but those who deign to rule us. As our communities map, more clearly every day, the connections in our struggles to build a world free from land dispossession, environmental degradation, police, prisons, and national borders, Western leaders appear to be committed to intensifying this devastation at every turn, on every front!

They forge their own solidarities. Since the pandemic began, Doug Ford has not only vowed more spending on jails and police. He also used the public health State of Emergency to suspend, between April and June of 2020, environmental protections including Ontario's Environmental Bill of Rights, and by July had passed law that further weakened the already-too-fragile protections in the Environmental Assessment Act. And the carceral state upholds the earth's devastation: Haldimand-Norfolk MPP Toby Barrett tweeted that protestors could face mischief charges for occupying the site of a proposed land development on Six Nations territory, where protestors have renamed a site of an intended housing construction, aptly, 1492 Land Back Lane.

If we do not explicitly link our struggles to end carceral controls and our struggles in the service of the earth, they will cage us and call it "climate action."

Of course, this is already occurring. As the Prison Ecology Project has documented, prisons and detention centres are themselves sites of mass environmental toxicity. And yet the state response is a perverse co-option of habitability, which excludes the protection of *human* life and suggests that the solution is to build a greener cage. Justin Piché, a prof at the University of Ottawa and a dear comrade in anti-prison struggle, has written about how prison expansion in Canada is increasingly marketed as "green" and sustainable: "Designing a prison to be more sustainable," he writes, "reinforces the belief that imprisonment is a sustainable solution to criminalized harms." According to a 2017 schematic report, a new immigration detention centre being built at the behest of the federal government is slated to be built to LEED standards, employing low-voltage lighting and made of recycled materials and wood sourced from Forest Stewardship Council–certified forests. The iron bars of the windows are designed to be covered—on the outside, mind you—in foliage.

And here, even with our communities on the forefront of a global struggle against environmental devastation, we are disappeared, in the greening of captivity. And here the state rebrands carceral tactics as "green" while recycling the practice of racial punishment and captivity, all the while extracting ceaselessly and by any means necessary. And at the same time, of course, it is prisoners who are most vulnerable to the impacts of the climate crisis. During the massive heat waves of July 2018 in Canada's Atlantic provinces, the women's wing of Nova Scotia's largest jail was not equipped with air conditioning, leading to horrific conditions inside. In a prison strike that occurred a month later as part of the Black August uprisings, Black prisoners denounced the health threats of that summer's heat waves, and tied their protest to broader crises at hand. In their statement, dictated to El Jones, they wrote: "we recognize that the injustices we face in prison are rooted in colonialism, racism and capitalism." This is what is at stake in our struggles, which are necessarily overlapping, as they try to shove these so-called green initiatives down our throats.

And so, in a crisis of the earth's viability, to struggle in support of living things, rather than to side with death—is there any other option? The ethical imperative of abolition asks us, too, as Black folks, to think about land, we people of more lands than can ever be counted, to fight against both dispossession from land *and* the destruction of land, wherever it appears, and from wherever we stand.

To me this means that as we struggle against the environmental racism faced by our own communities across these lands, we must, too, uphold the land-based struggle of the Wet'suwet'en. Of 1492 Land Back Lane at Six Nations. Of the Sikhala Sonke, and the Garifuna peoples. And, too, the Palestinians under siege in the West Bank and Gaza; the landless farmer under Modi's rule in India.

There are better ways to be in relation with one another and with the land.

I find it helpful to remember that Europeans, too, had their own relationships to lands. They colonized themselves, of course, before they ventured out to the rest of us. And they were not unified; they had created their own n*ggers and Indians on the continent before they left and projected those features onto us. Their expropriation of European peasants from the land, its subsequent devastation: the destruction of the commons is their own ghost, from whose haunting they have not yet emerged.

I'm not sure if I've mentioned this to you, but I have been gardening for the first time. I have the great fortune of renting the first floor of an affordable (for Toronto), if run-down and slightly mouldy, house with a backyard—a rarity in Toronto these days. In late spring, I planted squash, corn, and beans. I was taught to plant this combination of vegetables by Candace Esquimaux, who every year, near the Humber River, teaches the land-based programming for Black and Afro-Indigenous Freedom School kids (and, by proxy, their parents). I still had no idea what I was doing as I covered the planting area with compost and embedded the seeds, supplementing my learnings with wikiHow, one centimetre deep into the soil. The corn was immediately eaten by squirrels, despite my best efforts.

Yet now that the full heat and humidity of summer is here, the massive leaves of the squash plant have climbed up and around the yard, have taken over the spaces I had tentatively allotted to flowers. They have climbed up my small square of patio and captured my bike, have woven into my rusty barbeque, rendering it, for now, unusable—but I don't mind. I would never have imagined that so much lush, leafy greenery was part of producing these dense and chubby root vegetables. The vines from the bean plants climbed up the walls of the house; it took me a while to catch on that actual beans were growing, hidden as they were behind the leaves. They were mysterious to me for the first few weeks when they started coming in, until my son pointed out their presence to me. Despite my elderly Portuguese neighbours inexplicably burning their garbage in their barbeque twice a week, making the outdoor space less than palatable at times, this unexpected urban savannah that I've somehow facilitated serves as a reminder that I am part of and reside not only in a city, but on living planet. In a mini-ecosystem of me, L., these plants, and the skunks and racoons that live in the landlord's shed behind my house. This has helped remind me, too, that I am people of lands, that if *everything they do is to destroy the land*, I can choose, still, an alternate path: to support a return to forms of land stewardship that are amenable to a habitable earth. To render things habitable once again, in the human sense, as well—no settlers or cages. #LandBack.

It is, anyways, in looking into this swath of unchecked and improvised plant life that has exploded across my small square of yard, that I can listen to the vegetation. The curling vines seem to whisper quietly that we can shake off these brutal, if enduring forms of land valuation. That the land's value has, can, and will again be divorced from the violence of surplus value and the other ignoble measures of our times. As I carefully remove the aphids from the leaves of the green beans pressed against my crumbling red brick walls, they murmur, with words barely audible under the sounds of the traffic on Bloor: For the earth to live, capitalism must die.

It is getting to be harvesting time. If I thought there was a realistic chance of us seeing one another face to face anytime soon, I would set aside one of the squash for you. I would offer this small gesture of the earth's gifts so that we could feed our families together with some of the products of the summer of revolt, and let this nourish us for the difficult months ahead.

Robyn,

In the beginning of the pandemic, I travelled to Cleveland, Ohio to an event at the Museum of Contemporary Art. I was participating in a group exhibition called *Temporary Spaces of Joy and Freedom*, curated by La Tanya S. Autry, the Gund Curatorial Fellow at moCa, featuring works by me and Amanda Strong, Vaimoana Niumeitolu and Kyle Goen, John Edmonds and Tricia Hersey. The show was to honour the discussion that I had with writer and scholar Dionne Brand, and it was a reflection on colonialism, anti-Blackness, Indigenous and Black liberation struggles and "the importance of ephemeral expressions and the arts in creation of freedom."

I did not realize the significance of the exhibit until I arrived and met La Tanya. She introduced me to Black Cleveland, or just Cleveland as she called it, and the rich history of resistance, revolution and revolt. She laid bare the

anti-Blackness of art institutions like moCa in Canada and
the United States and told me that she was the first Black
curator at moCa, despite Cleveland being a Black majority
city and home to a brilliant Black artistic community. La
Tanya told me of some of the many sites of resistance she
had taken up inside the institution: everything from the
conception of *Temporary Spaces of Joy and Freedom* to
insisting that surveillance cameras not be part of the exhibition. When La Tanya arrived at moCa it was already free of
charge for the community and free of security guards.

Looking back now, La Tanya took the institution, made
it a Black homespace and then invoked Moten's idea of
homelessness in the space. She invited us all in.

That work cannot have been easy. I know because at the
opening, the white folks from moCa were visibly nervous,
in the best way.

The day of the opening, I thought of Tamir Rice and
his family. La Tanya had arranged a luncheon for the exhibition artists with Black artists, community organizers,
arts administrators and activists. I sat with two young and
amazing Black artists and community organizers from the
organization Shooting Without Bullets. We talked about
our experiences working with Indigenous youth, for me,
and Black youth, for them. Shooting Without Bullets is a
Black, youth-led organization that uses artistic activism to
elevate youth voices to shift policy, perspective and culture.
I thought of the potential of LeRoi Newbold and Nauoda
Robinson's Freedom School in Toronto, Dechinta, and
Tasha Spillet-Sumner's Red Rising Freedom School in

Winnipeg for Indigenous youth collaborating and visiting and making art with Shooting Without Bullets.

The night of the opening, I witnessed the gallery full of Black people from Cleveland, Ohio. Overflowing. This was honestly my first time in a large institutional art gallery where the vast majority of people were Black youth, families, artists and organizers. La Tanya had facilitated Black life inside the gallery, outside the gallery and in every space in between.

The piece in the exhibit I've thought most of since then was Tricia Hersey's. Tricia lives and works in Atlanta, Georgia, and she is the creator of The Nap Ministry. The Nap Ministry is "an organization that examines the liberating power of naps and rest as a form of resistance through communal installations of sacred and safe spaces for the community to rest together." Tricia explained during the artist talk that night that, during slavery, Black people were not allowed to rest or to sleep, and that this lack of rest had continued on into formations of anti-Blackness. Tricia explains:

> I was inspired by the idea when I was in divinity school and I was dealing with all of the—Black Lives Matter was actually just heating up at the moment. It was, like, 2013, and a lot of the lynchings were back-to-back online and being shared. And I was a graduate student in a predominately white institution. I was just really exhausted from living as a black woman in America—you know, poverty and crime. I was robbed once when I was in school. And just all of the things around me were coming on me at

once, and I just decided to rest. I decided to take naps wherever I could, and it started to combine my research. I was researching black liberation theology, somatics, cultural trauma. I was doing a lot of research around slavery and historic—looking at the historic documents around the commodification of black people in America.

Tricia installs big, beautiful beds and napping areas in galleries and public spaces because, as the insert in the exhibition catalogue states, "Naps help you wake up"—and I'd say, from watching the conversation that night and watching people move through the gallery space, that her napping area, which was a gorgeous, tranquil space with a couch and a bed, had the best impact. Watching people find home and comfort inside this big cement building that was built to house and celebrate white artists was a precious thing to witness. Seeing Black children climb into the bed and relax for a second, touching the art, being impressed in the installation because they were supposed to be there, was a profound disruption of anti-Black institutional space. One of your letters in this project of ours, started at 4:30 a.m., reminded me of the Nap Ministry. You wrote the letter the night you were doing solidarity support work for your comrades in jail, arrested for having thrown paint on racist and colonial statues in downtown Toronto.

My sister Ansley, a singer-songwriter in Toronto, wrote a song called "The Fix" a few years back, which will appear on her new record *She Fell From the Sky*. It has the line "Wrap their ankles pull them down, Lie by lie and town by town,

Heat their bodies molten red, Turn them into arrowheads."
I remember the first time I heard the line, experiencing it as
a futuristic vision, one that I never thought I'd like to see. It
reminds me of a blog post by NourbeSe Philip:

> when i began this blog the idea that police forces should be
> defunded or abolished was unheard of—
>
> when i began this blog Aunt Jemima still appeared on pan-
> cake syrup bottles—
>
> when i began this blog the statue of the former slave owner
> Edward Colston had not yet been thrown into the Bristol
> Harbour—
>
> when i began this blog three young Black girls had not yet
> danced on the plinth on which Colston's statue stood—
>
> when i began this blog I had no idea what deep and vis-
> ceral satisfaction I would get from watching statues topple—
>
> when i began this blog no statues of Robert E. Lee had
> been removed or pulled down—
>
> when i began this blog all the statues of King Leopold
> were intact in Belgium—
>
> when i began this blog the statue of Christopher Columbus
> in Baltimore had not yet reached its expiry date—

Ansley's song was written at a time before the summer of
revolt in 2020, the time in which actual statues were torn

down. I feel grateful. Black Lives Matter is so generous. It has carried our movement forward, and achieved things we couldn't achieve during our previous mobilizations. A few months ago, despite decades of Indigenous resistance, sports organizations like the Edmonton Eskimos, the Cleveland Indians and the Washington Redskins had no intention of ever changing their names. Statistics regarding police shootings of Indigenous peoples were not on the radar of white Canadians despite decades of organizing around the Missing and Murdered. Black Lives Matter has included Indigenous peoples in a way that I haven't witnessed in a very long time. I am so very grateful.

In January 2018, x University in Toronto unveiled a plaque at the site of the Egerton Ryerson statue on campus, a result of the recommendations from X's community consultations in response to the Truth and Reconciliation Commission of Canada. The plaque reads:

> This plaque serves as a reminder of Ryerson University's commitment to moving forward in the spirit of truth and reconciliation. Egerton Ryerson is widely known for his contributions to Ontario's public educational system. As Chief Superintendent of Education, Ryerson's recommendations were instrumental in the design and implementation of the Indian Residential School System. In 2015, the Truth and Reconciliation Commission reported that children in the schools were subjected to unthinkable abuse and neglect, to medical experimentation, punishment for the practice of cultures or languages and death. The aim of the Residential School System was cultural genocide.

The plaque blurb ends with two quotes, one by Chief Sitting Bull ("Let us put our minds together to see what kind of lives we can create for our children"), the other from the Truth and Reconciliation Commission of Canada ("For the child taken, for the parent left behind").

The administration at X University could have taken the statue down—years ago, in fact, and certainly after the release of the TRC's final report. They could have changed their name and branding. They could still do those things. I was not present or a part of the discussions that led to the plaque. I suspect that the university presented the removal of the statue as impossible because of costs and because we should not erase our history, but contextualize and explain it, as the thinking goes. The plaque is an attempt at contextualization, I suppose, and yes, Black and Indigenous activist communities in Toronto have taken over this space as a site of resistance.

I was thinking about this statue and the plaque a few months earlier when I visited the Tate Modern in London, UK on my way to give a talk at Cambridge. I was at the Tate to see Kara Walker's installation, *Fons Americanus*, in the Turbine Hall. *Fons Americanus* is a thirteen-metre-tall fountain that is a play on the memorial to Queen Victoria located outside of Buckingham Palace. Walker's statue is in the style of that memorial and it is a code. Her figures reference the history of empire, transatlantic slavery, and resistance. Her installation takes modernism's references and remakes the language of public monuments as one that centres Black knowledge, a language that affirms me as a Nishnaabekwe. *Fons Americanus* is a satirical and exuberant rebuke to British tellings of history and nation, and in that refusal, I felt seen, more than any other place in my visit to England.

In contrast, when I stand beside the statue of Egerton Ryerson in my territory, I feel deflated. I feel the horror and the trauma he caused five generations of Indigenous families. I feel the obtuseness of the institution for adopting him as its namesake in the first place, and I feel its refusal to make it right. I feel ashamed, even though I know I shouldn't. Ashamed for what happened to my people and for our inability to remove this thing and tell a different story, and tell the truth. (I also feel a little bit of pride and respect for the Indigenous peoples who were in the room when the TRC recommendations and the statue were discussed: I suspect they fought very hard for that plaque and the words on it.) The plaque, then, doesn't make it better. It doesn't complicate Ryerson for me—the man, and what he represents, isn't actually that complicated. Sure, Egerton Ryerson is part of Canadian history, as is the legacy of residential schools. But what would it be like if this statue was taken down and thrown into Lake Ontario, and a statue of a young, queer Indigenous and Black activist was put on the plinth in its place? How would this action, even though it was largely symbolic, change the narrative, complicate our history, make visible a different history that is equally relevant and influential, and also equally related to residential schools and Canadian history? How would this statue make me feel/think?

I get a glimpse of this possibility from the gorgeous actions of Black Lives Matter on July 18, 2020, which covered the statue of Egerton Ryerson with pink paint and the words "Tear down monuments that represent slavery, colonialism and violence."

Toronto police arrested three of your comrades in connection with the action, and that is why you were up at 4:30 a.m. writing to me as you worked to get your comrades freed from jail. Forced up and denied sleep, because capitalism values statues and property more than it values Black people and Black lives. Up writing, again, instead of at the Nap Ministry.

I'm glad that you are holding on to optimism through all of this. I like that you and your comrades are writing the movement as the movement is happening. The first time I was a part of the idea of writing the movement was during Idle No More. I really appreciate you seeing the seeds that were planted during the mobilization and those that followed. It was lovely to read your words affirming the Wet'suwet'en mobilization as a midwife of this current movement. I regret not doing more to reach out to Black activists and the Black community during Idle No More. I regret not doing the work that would have affirmed Black presence during that mobilization. I am happy to see our communities reaching out to each other more and more as we move out of our organizing silos and into a more reciprocal meeting place.

I miss the energy I felt at the height of Idle No More. I felt the feeling of belonging, that my community was working together, doing different things together towards some broad political goals in spite of differences within the Indigenous community. Indigenous peoples, and therefore our movements and mobilizations, are so entangled with the state through legislation, law, and policy. I have no faith in the state to value Indigenous life or Black life or to make any of the issues we mobilize around better. For me this comes both from decades of study, and my lived experience. I don't believe in Canada. I don't believe federal and provincial governments have the skills, knowledge, and resources to build the kind of society I'm interested in living in. I think that at this point in my life, I am most interested in building systems that address conflict, harm, poverty, substance use, health, education, politics, economy, and our relationship to the land and waters.

There is always a cost to large-scale mobilizations in Canada, whether they are Oka or Idle No More or movements for Black life. There is an emotional and physical cost to individuals on the front lines, much like there is an emotional and physical cost to individuals that are forced to live on the front lines of poverty or the overdose crisis, much like there is a physical and emotional cost to anti-Blackness and colonialism. It is difficult to maintain large-scale mobilizations—they aren't, at the core, sustainable for communities already struggling, and that's why they are so vital and so important. There is always a backlash in mobilizing against racial capitalism, and the white liberal "allyship" primarily motivated by guilt is fickle and unreliable and disingenuous at the best of times. The state has a myriad of tried and true ways of intervening in our uprising. Some are violent and overt. Others, like elections and false hope, are trickier. They like to study themselves in royal commissions and inquiries as a way of moving us out of the streets and into the boardroom. They like to find Indigenous folks to run for their political parties, promising to do better if they are elected to power. They like to include us by offering us slight shifts in policy or new agreements, by showering us with recognition—like giving us publishing contracts, book awards, music prizes and faculty positions—all the while refusing structural change. They like to divide and conquer and stir conflict until the lateral violence within movements and communities is so virulent that all they have to do is stand back and watch while we tear each other down for sometimes legitimate reasons, and other times for not. They like to make sure we take down our own.

Today is Emancipation Day. And a lot of activists were up through the night working to secure the release of Moka Dawkins. Moka Dawkins is a Black and Indigenous woman, activist, frontline worker, and valued community member. Members of Not Another Black Life were up all night sitting outside of 55 Division, and greeted Dawkins when she was released this morning. I know they must be getting exhausted. I know they must need the Nap Ministry.

Slavery was legally abolished in the British empire on this day in 1833 by the Slavery Abolition Act (after the British had outlawed the slave trade in 1807); unfortunately, white supremacy was not. There is more visibility for Emancipation Day this year in the mainstream media, yet most of the coverage has been from the perspective of Canadians as rescuers, what art history professor Charmaine Nelson calls "good abolitionists," and the idea that 1833 was the end of Canada as a slave holding nation. We know, of course, that slavery just changed form, and morphed into the anti-Black system we have today. "I've never yet had one Canadian student enter [my] class knowing that slavery transpired in Canada," Nelson told the CBC in 2017, "but they have all been schooled in the fact that, 'Listen, we as Canadians were good abolitionists. We helped to liberate African-American slaves who fled north.' That is what they've been, you know, inculcated with, that's been ingrained in them since elementary school." She goes on to say what scholars Afua Cooper, Delice Mugabo, and many, many others also say repeatedly whenever they are asked: that slavery was pervasive in Canada, and not just among white elites. It was pervasive in all levels of society.

Without this critical Black truth-telling, then, the Canadian education system is teaching that slavery and its legacy do not exist here, that anti-Blackness does not exist here. And yet it is the belief in Black inferiority that perpetuates the abject violence against Black people that you describe in *Policing Black Lives*, and that underpins the current revolution in the streets. What I find myself thinking, days after writing that last sentence, is that this is also the history, the whitewashed untruthful history, that Indigenous peoples are taught in provincial curriculums on reserves and in urban settings across Canada.

Many of my peoples do not know your history and therefore your present. Part of why this project with you, Robyn, is so important to me is because I believe, like Angela Davis, that our movements need to pay as much attention to popular education as we pay to mobilization. Indigenous peoples know that state education is calculated and designed to reproduce the colonial and anti-Black systems of oppression Canada was founded upon. If we don't do the popular education piece within our communities, our movements, and between our communities, our movements become vulnerable to the "seductions of assimilation and replicating the logics of colonialism and anti-Blackness."

Colonialism is invested in us not knowing Black and Indigenous histories. Our truths are not included in state curriculum, and, when we are present, we are a whitewashed, watered-down version of dream catchers and the underground railroad instead of four centuries of brilliant and radical Black and Indigenous resistance.

As an Indigenous educator, I have responsibility to bring the history of transatlantic slavery and the current legacy and reality of anti-Blackness into everything I do.

At the end of *Policing Black Lives*, you write that "In Canada, any struggle for economic, racial and social justice must necessarily address ongoing settler colonialism. In a white settler colony like Canada, it's not possible to talk about abolition—not only of prisons but also of the enduring legacy of slavery in all state institutions—without simultaneously supporting Indigenous decolonization movements." In Canada, any struggle against colonialism must necessarily address the ongoing Canadian practice and ethic of anti-Blackness. In an anti-Black colony like Canada, it's not possible to talk about decolonization or to organize and mobilize around decolonization without simultaneously supporting abolition and the total annihilation of the enduring legacy of slavery in all state institutions.

To only focus on the Indigenous in North America is to be thinking through things and theorizing with incomplete knowledge. We cannot afford to build incomplete worlds on incomplete knowledge; if we do, we risk replicating the very oppressions we are trying to liberate ourselves from.

A few months ago, you texted me a photo of the Freedom School Toronto with a solidarity banner for the Wet'suwet'en. A few months later, my kids, who are teenagers, invited me to a Black Lives Matter protest. It was the first protest during the pandemic. At the meeting spot, organizers greeted and welcomed us, handed out masks, and reminded us about physical distancing. My family has been to lots and lots of protests, but this one felt different to me. There were DJs and music. There was dancing and joy. There was a level of organizing that made everything smooth, and I'm sure this was in part motivated by the increased policing of Black protest in southern Ontario and beyond. On the way to the protest, ten minutes before it started, the local rock radio station read an announcement that the local police were in support of the protest. This never happened during Idle No More or the countless Indigenous protests that I've participated in here. This protest was against the police and policing, and they attempted to appropriate it.

Seeing the chief of police take a knee at the protest reminded me of every single part of reconciliation.

Now it is mid-August, and attention is turning towards back to school and back to teaching. While the universities are online, public schools, driven by economic concerns, are heading back. Black people and people of colour comprise 83 percent of the COVID-19 cases in Toronto. We know that Black children and families will take on more risk than white families in the return to school. Still, in spite of this global pandemic, Black movements have organized through it and have changed the city, the province, and the country by moving us a giant step closer to the worlds we imagine. And, I know it isn't over. I'm grateful. I'm grateful for the care and attentiveness you've paid towards my community. Organizings for Black life are regularly affirming Indigenous peoples. We both know these moments don't come along often, maybe only once in a lifetime, and so we know to push through exhaustion. We know that our work will never be done. That these are seeds our children will have to nurture and grow and then take to the streets once again.

The pandemic confirms this.

In a few short weeks the minomiin, or wild rice, will be ready for harvesting in my territory. Michi Saagiig Nishnaabe families will sneak our canoes across leaf-blown, white-cottaged lawns and launch into contested waters. Some of our rice beds will have been destroyed by cottagers who desire pristine beaches. Our Elders will point to sites of monster cottages and tell stories of camping on those very spots when they were kids. There will be sadness and loss in our canoes and also hope because we are still here, harvesting our good seed. Minomiin will get gently knocked into the bottoms of our boats, on tarps and bedsheets, and much more will get knocked into the lake, fall to the sediments and get planted for next year. Still other grains will end up in the stomachs of geese and ducks, who will use minomiin's energy and spirit to propel them south on their migration. The harvest will look different this year. We won't be able to do it together, but rather in small family units. This is fine for the harvesting part, but it will make the processing of the grain more difficult. The roasting and parching, breaking the shell off and winnowing will be more labour-intensive. There will be more fear and less safety when we are out on the water in smaller groups, inevitably confronted by angry white cottagers who wish we were dead, so they could enjoy our land in peace. This year there will be no angry town hall meetings where the racism of white people is on full display without consequence. Ricing, and the rice wars, will look different this year.

The wind on the lake sometimes works with us in the harvest, and sometimes the coldness, the strength, make it harder to collect rice. The wind has its own work to do, but it reminds me of breath and breathing. It reminds me that at some point, someone else breathed for us.

Again, I return to "Ga(s)p." NourbeSe sings:

We all begin life in water
We all begin life because someone once breathed for us
Until we breathe for ourselves
Someone breathes for us
Everyone has had someone—a woman—breathe for them
Until that first ga(s)p
For air

And, later in the piece:

Each of us has had someone, a woman, breathe for us. To keep us alive. Each of us has allowed someone, a woman, to breathe for us, our coming-to-life dependent on an Other breathing for us—a form of circular breathing this:
    Circle breathing

Circle breath
Circling breaths
Breathing for the other
Could we, perhaps, describe this process as an example
and expression of radical hospitality?

Radical hospitality. Radical sharing. Radical generosity.
Homelessness. Homespace. Doing. Making. Being. Expand-
ing. Building up. Wayward expansion. Black Land. Indigenous
Land. Circle breathing. Queering. Mino-bimaadiziwin.

PART SIX

Rehearsals for Living /
areyousurethatyoureallywanttobewell

Dear Leanne,

In taking in your words and NourbeSe's—*breathing for another*—I am also thinking about the state of your lungs. I've been wondering if the smoke of the forest fires has made its way up to your bush school, and am thinking about your respiratory cilia.

The world is on fire, again. The *Los Angeles Times* is reporting that as of today (September 15), this year's wildfires have burned over 3.2 million acres in California—a land mass equivalent to the state of Connecticut. The smoke has extended through to the west coast of Canada, has made it as far as Northern Europe.

The Department of Psychiatry and Behavioral Science at the University of California in San Francisco recently put out a guide called "Coping With Wildfires and Climate Change Crises." Under a section called "How does smoke affect our health?" they describe the way that the smoke

237

from the wildfires causes the respiratory cilia to become inflamed, because they are the first line of defence to prevent dust and smog from entering our airways and lungs. This, in turn, they note, may itself increase the risk of COVID-19 infection. Because, as described by a pulmonologist, the cilia are also among the first to succumb to the attack launched by the COVID-19 virus: ". . . COVID-19 first attacks the upper respiratory tract, entering through the nose or mouth. It then zeroes in on the cilia," setting up a chain of events that fill a person's lungs with fluid.

This is weighing heavily on me today. Although I'm in Toronto, my best friend A. is an ER nurse in Vancouver, where the smoke from the fires is so concentrated that each hour spent outdoors is the health equivalent of smoking one to two packs of cigarettes. I am worried about her respiratory cilia, too.

A. has been texting with me during her breaks. We often check in during the off-times of her twelve-hour shifts—shifts which, these days, as she describes them, consist largely of intubating patients brought into the ER. She is as usual using her break to escape from the suffocating sensation wrought by the intensive PPE gear that must be worn at all times because of COVID-19 (she described this once to me in these words: "Imagine your face is in a potato sack. Like, you are suffocating in a potato sack. But kind of also suffocating in a Ziploc bag?"). As usual, too, we are sending voice texts to one another, about the serious as well as the inane: she has made a comically and tragically disastrous decision to adopt a rescue dog—a massive Rottweiler that she has named Baby Lulu—in an ill-fated attempt to help her take her mind off things. Baby Lulu has, instead, been destroying her house, barking and crying and urinating continuously. A. is rolling with it; she has a dark sense of humour. She's messaging me from her usual place outside the hospital, where she normally takes her break. But because of the smoke, her breathing is encumbered even with the PPE gear removed. My eyelids feel heavy today—I've stayed up many nights this week several hours past my bedtime, lulled by her voice, our laughter, the "ding" of my phone lighting up the darkness in my room, holding a temporary intimacy of shared worry and friendship into the near morning.

I've just turned off the radio, but talk of the fires is on every medium and being broadcast over every medium.

I suppose it's fitting, given how we started out, that what I imagine to be my last letter to you finds me in *almost* the same position as the first: doom-scrolling the climate crisis, worrying about those of us who are collectively poised to die first, and those who are already dead or dying. The shared images haunt: unfiltered shots of skyline that are blood-orange, green, yellow, looking more like an alien, *Blade Runner* sort of landscape than any earthly vision. (According to NASA, this discoloration is occurring because smoke particles are blocking certain wavelengths from the sun.)

The multiple emergencies confronting our respiratory cilia represent an emergency born of violence that "we" (this term is too loaded to use un-self-consciously) refuse to break with, let alone acknowledge. It is the collapse of linear time, of colonizer and capitalist time, in a sense. The wildfires are raging out of control, in part, because the long-standing *human* crisis of the state's reliance on the unfree labour—modified slave labour—of incarcerated fire fighters (who are disproportionately, yet not entirely Black) has merged more fully with the ecological and public health crisis of the present. COVID-19 outbreaks have ravaged North America's incarcerated populations: over twelve thousand prisoners and guards have contracted the novel coronavirus in US state prisons. Quarantines, lockdowns, and (grossly limited) early release, all have limited California's ability to put out the fires. In this sense, the pandemic has put a wrench in the careful logics of human sacrifice that are embedded into the state's, country's, and continent's economy. And, thus, has interrupted the brutal efficacy of the political choice to place Black aunties and sisters-in-law and parents and little brothers paid one to five dollars per day—captives of the state—as "the first line of defense against wildfires" in an effort to minimize state spending. They have been described by the state's main firefighting agency, Cal Fire, as "a tremendous resource" (the latter a word all too pregnant with its own history). And as well, the wildfires are raging in the same purposeful and malevolent ignorance that was a requirement and a product of the US government–orchestrated Indigenous genocide. Robin Kimmerer, Potawatomi plant ecologist, has consistently demonstrated that Euro–North Americans' refusal to understand Indigenous people's relationships to land, particularly the complex forms of fire management that predated colonialism, have contributed enormously to the increasingly catastrophic burning on the west coast. She has described for decades now how the crisis of forest fires—of course massively expanded as the climate

emergency intensifies—stems neatly from US federal policies that purposefully attempted to destroy both Indigenous
peoples and their relationships with the land. Including, she
notes, the eradication of the sophisticated use of controlled
burns for pest control, for fireproofing, and the maintenance of food security and biodiversity, practices that had
derived from "millennia of experimentation and detailed
observations." Uncontrollable fires, then, the end result of
the violent ejection of Indigenous peoples from the index
of civilization.

And so today the landscape—the unrecognizable skylines and unbreathable air in this moment—stands as an
indictment of Western civilization writ large. Even the most
purposefully ignorant must know now, at some level, that
in damning the wretched of the earth, and the earth itself,
they were also damning themselves (even if they would kill
to avoid admitting this). There is no innocence in a society
which refuses at every turn to make a decisive break with its
history, and which now finds its own house on fire. These
forest fires, like the pandemic, are not tragedies with no
author. James Baldwin wrote in a 1963 letter to his nephew
words which remain, nearly sixty years later, precisely as
relevant: ". . . they have destroyed and are destroying hundreds of thousands of lives and do not know it and do not
want to know it . . . it is not permissible that the authors of
devastation should also be innocent. It is the innocence
which constitutes the crime."

In today's skylines, we are witnessing the unfinished
catastrophes of ecocide and genocide. All of this organized
violence laid bare in the landscape, erupting into the frame,

and impossible to disavow. The wildfires in California, British Columbia, and in Pará, Brazil are telling a story that is increasingly difficult to ignore, even for those who are most practised in denial. And though I don't want to be naïve, or to underestimate this society's commitment to evading reality at any cost, I am still holding within myself that nascent shimmering of possibility. As those in the imperial centre come face to face with the product of their society's choices, there is the opportunity to face reality, and thus to break with five hundred years of organized destruction. Perhaps this moment could be, in Arundhati Roy's terms, "a portal, a gateway between one world and the next."

During my twenties, as I went back and forth between smoking and not smoking, I used to keep a photo of a cluster of cilia, magnified in close range, on my phone. It served as an anti-smoking aid, albeit an unconventional one. The respiratory cilia allow us, under normal conditions, to breathe clearly. They are the tiny, tentacle-like structures, one thousand times smaller than a human hair, that cover our respiratory tract. They are in constant motion, and when they are working as they should, they "propel mucus cephalad at 4 to 20 mm/min"! They move synchronously, fifteen cycles every second. They are bathed in water-like fluid and, as the mucus layer on top of them traps debris, their rhythmic movements thrust it forward, away from the places where it could do damage. And from a visual perspective, the respiratory cilia are stunning! This is what first drew me in. I would close my eyes and visualize this movement that is constantly taking place in my body, so essential to my health and survival yet outside of my conscious awareness or control. How could one knowingly damage something this beautiful, this essential? There are times where I forget to connect, otherwise, with the fact that I inhabit a body, that I am not separate from my own flesh. Yet through my desire to protect the respiratory cilia in all of their complexity and fragility, I discovered a renewed ability to reconnect with the corporeal sides of life, if vicariously, and thus began to truly examine what it meant to care for myself.

This reconnection is fleeting; care for the self remains an ongoing struggle. But it matters: it's a choice that needs to be made and remade. The first time that I opened Toni Cade Bambara's *The Salt Eaters*, I experienced her words like a line of bullets that had been moulded specifically for the soft places inside of me as I read the first line of the book: "Are you sure, sweetheart, that you want to be well?" There is something in the words, however gentle the phrasing of the question, that forces an exposure of one's relationship to oneself.

Because of course I am a product not only of my chosen political community. I am also, to some extent, a product of my society, and I live in a society that has committed itself to evading wellness at any cost, and in doing so has damned the vast majority of the world's population to being subject to the same fate. Shirking wellness, for the self, for the collective, is a national pastime, which has colonized all of our minds to some level.

There is nothing simple, then, about the generative rupture, the portal, the new possible worlds that emerge over and against the overlapping crises of this moment. The possibility of a world governed around wellness has been presented, often by those with least access to it, only to be violently refused by those whose needs are already met. We have been conditioned to accept and to tolerate the ugliness of the present, to accept cruelty as normal. It is a barbarism that is familiar to us, and this is the sickness, of course, that must be overcome, which afflicts all of us, even if it differs in matters of degrees, scale.

We have been trained to hold an attachment to the murderous familiar.

And while it would be easy to relegate this "we" to those who wield the concept like a knife to keep us out of it, who would never include us within the *we*, I mean *us*, too: that is, you and I, our communities. Even those of us who have little to gain from this status quo, for whom the "wages of whiteness" do not or hardly apply, can become invested, psychologically, materially, into this way of life, and the denials and repression required to uphold it. We are, continually, hailed to uphold and even defend it, over and against our own communities. We are rewarded (with symbolism, with tokens, with a pat on the head, with a well-paid position) if and when we choose to do so. We are continually proffered the promise of inclusion, even if our acceptance would be, at best, contingent. I know you've witnessed, as I have, the way this promise captures even those we thought immune to its call. The community leaders, the former grassroots activists who, for one reason or another—for personal ambition, out of sheer fatigue and exhaustion at coming up against the same barrel of the gun—begin to believe, or at least perform, a renunciation of past radicalism, a new embrace of *the way things arrange*. Who try, now, to sell to us on the notion that tinkering with and making cosmetic improvements to this machine will somehow offer *all of us*—and not just them—"a way out of the prison." Such is the danger of the falsely benign promises of inclusion: while often going unrecognized, they are malignancies that threaten to poison the entire organism.

And yet. There is knowledge in us that runs deeper, even if some of us are more practised at ignoring it. It is less recognizable, yet it flows as a continuous stream, if only we will hear it. I would forward that this is so particularly, though not exclusively, among those who have not, ever, been numbered among the "we" of this society. We have never had the privilege of imagining our presents as magically divorced from the past. Parts inside of us are attuned to the deeper knowledge, that which Audre Lorde has named *the erotic*, that senses a whisper, a glimmer, that exposes one's failures to live authentically and honestly with oneself and the world outside of us, and suggests, and extends, the possibility of a rich, fleshy wellness.

Because of course the portal has been there all along.

And this is true at an atomistic level: we encounter smaller versions of this portal in our own lives, whether we choose to jump through the gateway or not.

there are times that this whisper areyousuresweetheart thatyouwanttobewellareyousuresweetheartthatyouwant tobewell

that is constantly beneath the surface of our lives turns into a scream, until there is nothing but a cacophony, chorus upon chorus of love and rage and despair from the collective wisdom of the ancestors and sometimes you work up the courage to see that it is not an accusation to be evaded but a gift and you.

say.

yes.

I am sharing with you the following passage because we are near the end of this version, at least, of our correspondence, and I want you to know me:

> Perhaps everyone had his tomb: the mother hunched over the table all night might be locked in hers, her father, stretched on the cot, might have been sealed in his, just as she was shut within the lonely region of herself. She might never find a way out, but like Miss Mary, move from one death to another . . . She wanted something else . . . She heard noises from the street, the brash, surging, alive sound of children playing. It rushed in to fill the emptiness, and caught between that clamorous call and Miss Mary's fixed silence, she knew what she wanted. It was not so much a thought as something deeply felt. To flow out of herself into life, to touch and know it fully and, in turn, to be touched by it. And then, sometimes, to withdraw and be quiet within herself . . . But how? How even to begin? She did not know.

I'm sharing with you the above passage, which comes near the end of Paule Marshall's *Brown Girl, Brownstones*, and in doing so, I'm sharing something intimate about myself, too. When I first encountered this passage, I was in the midst of making a choice that would be difficult and massively disruptive, that would undo me in ways and that scared me half to death. I knew this choice to be necessary if I wanted to really become myself, the self whose emergence I had been carefully shunting into a box, even as I became increasingly afraid that by the time I allowed her to emerge I would discover she had, in fact, been suffocated long ago. I suppose in some sense, it can feel simpler to allow contradictions and suffering to remain in our lives because they are familiar, because they are *ours*. I was backsliding again into the stasis of indecision, lulled back into the easy, if increasingly painful status quo when I stumbled upon Marshall's book.

Marshall's words spoke directly to me. I underlined them, set them to memory, scrawled them in my notebook, and dictated them to friends. As much as I could, I fastened them inside of myself and made them a part of me. I, too, wanted something other than *the way things arrange*, to use the words of Silla, the protagonist. Like Silla, I wanted, too, to touch and be touched by life, even if I didn't quite know what this looked like, and I knew that this meant walking away from the life that I knew. I made my choice, and exploded my life.

———

I HAVE SINCE LEARNED THAT I have to *choose* to lean into the feeling of sun against my skin, the warmth of another's breath, the glorious aching of my muscles, sore and strained after being pushed to their near-limits. I have learned that we hold sanctuaries inside of ourselves if we know where to look for them.

It has been increasingly clear to me that we cannot live in community or move toward political transformation if we are not able to commit, in the most intimate part of our lives, to authenticity within ourselves and to wellness. We individually and societally continue to evade wellness, and so we continue to evade something that could approximate freedom. To return to Baldwin, who highlights the confluences—and consequences—of these evasions: "Privately, we cannot stand our lives and dare not examine them; domestically, we take no responsibility for . . . what goes on in our country; and, internationally, for many millions of people, we are an unmitigated disaster." We cannot break away from that which we refuse to see.

To break away: this does not mean that we abdicate pleasure, individually or collectively; only that we cull that which we know to be harmful. It asks that we affirm the necessity of pleasure, too, for the collective. While it is mistaken to romanticize the past and to long, uncritically, for a return to normal, of course there were *some* parts of normal we long for. We all want to touch life, and to do so beyond the constraints of quarantine and physical distance. I miss some parts of living. Not the apocalyptic horrors that governed and govern this world, the constant dangers imposed on Black, Indigenous, queer, trans, mad, and homeless peoples' lives (and anyways, these are still with us, more acutely than ever). But I miss the levity, and the texture, of the day-to-day. I miss spending money I don't have on buying massive crabs from Chinatown to share with my family, so that Leroi can slice them up while the kids dart in and out of the kitchen, equal parts fear and excitement at live crabs scuttling around in a box of newspapers, all of us, later on, dipping the food into shared butter dishes, drinking cheap wine and staying up past our bedtimes. Touching hands with a beautiful stranger, wild unexpected love, hearing music that transports to another plane, ballroom, whispered conversations in crowded book events. And I know that these are small things, they feel like foolish things to long for when the world is on fire, and hundreds of thousands—more!—are dying. And yet it is not foolish to want to live, to experience pleasure, in this life. I want this, it's just that I want it—want a way to live, to truly live—without all of the extenuated violence of the governance of this world.

There is no *wellness* here, on the path where we are headed, collectively. Only more corpses piled on top of the remains of Lumumba and Sitting Bull and Fred Hampton and more than I can name without becoming hoarse.

Because isn't this a grave of sorts for all of us, when some must die or live in deprivation in death's proximity so that others may live in an excess of luxury? The comforts of life, here in the imperial core, also denote a shared culpability, or perhaps, a shared responsibility, even if I would never presume to say that we share in the comforts nor the responsibility evenly, those of us in internal colonies. If we refuse to accept that *the way things arrange* is based, in these times, on a series of unmitigated disasters meted out on the world's expanding population of dispossessed, we will never, any of us, escape the passage from one death to another. We will never understand, either, that we deserve, all of us, so much more.

We do not have the road map for this. And yet. There are glimpses.

The scientific community has not yet reached consensus on the precise way that the respiratory cilia manage to move the mucus layer that lies over top of them. It is still subject to intensive research. In the videos I have seen, where the cilia are magnified and their movements slowed down, they appear almost sentient as they gently pulse backward and forward. Millions of tiny parts working together with what can only be described as graceful movements, all geared toward a singular and admirable task of preventing harmful substances from entering the lung. A practice of collective care, toward the protection and the safety of the broader organism.

To value collective livingness, to touch and know life fully, to know a life that is not in some way predicated on and subsidized by the suffering of another: I suspect that this is what liberation is. I suppose we will find out, or maybe our children or theirs, if we do enough with this moment.

If the fires, the floods, are speaking to us, forcing all of us to take note of the wreckage that the last five hundred years have wrought, we, too, have been working on ruptures of our own. Insisting, too, that we will not let the dead victors sleep!

I suspect that we are encountering, not a single portal, but a kaleidoscope of portals spanning our most intimate lives, our communities, the broader terrain of struggle.

The battle waged over the naming of Quebec's "N*gger rock," a mass grave so named to ostensibly commemorate the enslaved Africans who were buried there; the struggle to rename Ryerson University after someone who did not create the genocidal residential school systems: these are precisely battles over the dead. Over their dead and ours, too! As Saidiya Hartman states, "History is a battle royal, a contest between the powerful and the powerless over 'what happened'"—and our peoples have not given up that fight. The struggle over the representation of the past—to expose its monstrosities—is also a struggle to put to rest some forms of the past that we wish, for fuck's sake, to be done with. That slavery and colonialism could be past, truly past, is a dream to hold tightly to. We are continually engaged in a struggle over history because this is a struggle, too, for our futures.

Perhaps, then, it should come as no surprise that we are witnessing a quite intentional struggle over monuments and public memory. Some may dismiss this as a struggle over mere symbolism, as attending solely to the superstructure, if you will. I see it instead as part of a multi-pronged attack on History (not history) and all of its attendant human and ecological devastation. It is a rejection of the episteme of the settler-master. It is part of the defence of our respiratory cilia. Because a struggle over how we memorialize the dead is also a struggle over how we care for the living.

And perhaps some of the forms of struggle that we have long waged are coming, now, into their season.

As I wrote to you in my first letter, there are some world-endings I am comfortable with. Some feel easy. A few weeks ago, while riding in the car with my three nieces, beautiful children of seven, nine, and eleven, I receive a text. A friend has forwarded over what has now become the infamous video of the John A. Macdonald statue being brought down in Montreal following the Defund Police rally. Knowing this will likely be a gem for us all, I raise my voice over the din of the three kids and three adults squeezed into the car: Who wants to see a statue of John A. Macdonald get knocked down? *Who's that?*—this from N., the youngest of the nieces. This question, as you can imagine, already warms the heart. Our family is well-educated, you see. You don't have me as your auntie and L. N., director of Freedom School, as your parent without knowing the important names: Assata Shakur, Nanny Maroon, Sherona Hall. In response to "Who's that?" I give them the Cliffs Notes of all that really matters about John A. in this instant: *He killed Louis Riel and his family owned slaves.* They stretch their seatbelts and lean closer to the screen of my phone.

We are gassed up, revelling, truly, in the theatre of it all. As John A. falls, the head has somehow popped off, it is rolling, quite indecorously, several feet away from the body, at a surprising velocity. Elsewhere, on some ranch, I assume, Kenney and O'Toole are fuming and posturing: they are on some shit or another, tweeting about the sanctity of Canada being desecrated. But here, the kids are in hysterics. Me ignoring their sticky fingers on my screen because I want to savour their easy acceptance of this occasion: "bye, mister macdonald," they squeal. Cackles, gorgeous Black children pressed firmly against life as the supposedly mighty fall— their violent legacies, we hope, along with them. Though I've had the honour of guest-teaching the Freedom School kids many times, this has been easily my favourite history lesson. It's these small wins, somehow, that are everything.

Because this new generation, especially, has seen other possibilities. Not only do they not give a shit about John A. Macdonald, they know that police, prisons, and borders do not keep us safe and do not need to be permanent fixtures of this, or any society. The possibilities for what is available, with this as your base, seem endless.

I know that it will all not feel easy like this. But we need these moments of reprieve. Every small breach with the status quo counts, is its own portal. *Lie by lie and town by town.* Even if we may not live to see the outcome.

And of course, jumping through the portal, the portals, asks of us that we assume an element of risk. It demands a certain sacrifice, that we cannot know in advance. It demands the end of the safety that some of us have come to know. But safety is already over. And for some of us, it never arrived.

I am not naively optimistic. I know that even major wins are always accompanied by blowback. I can already see the tide shifting somewhat, as the BLM signs are coming down from windows and shops, already, part of the reconsolidation of capitalist and carceral controls over the fabric of daily life. The reality of the forces working to maintain brutality are at work, as ever. This cannot be wished away, dreamed away, or underestimated. But I also believe that even amidst the truly apocalyptic landscapes of this moment, the energy that is holding us close right now will remain with us, at least for a while, and that we can do with it what we will. What we must.

There is work to be done. The long work of choosing life, wellness, of rebuilding the world. It will take all of us, and so many more.

So I am making a toast to you:
To the end of (this) world.

I will breathe for you, too. I am ready to grab your hand and jump through the portal.

Robyn,

It's November now. The US election is over, and there is a new president or, as the Haudenosaunee say, a new Hana-dagá:yas, or Town Destroyer. We are in the second wave of COVID-19, and our politicians are busy calculating how much white death is acceptable to keep the stores open, while Black and Brown people continue to die at much higher rates. The opioid crisis still wears on, with more deaths from overdoses, in the city where I live, than from the virus. Black people are still being deported. Police still end well-ness checks with death for Black and Indigenous peoples. We aren't dropping off care packages on our neighbours' porches anymore. We aren't banging pots and pans every afternoon in support of health care workers. No one is baking sourdough.

Nearly everything we wrote about in those first few let-ters has come to fruition. Our analysis and predictions were true. And while it does not take much to see the end of this world, it is also so clear to me that this world will not go quietly or easily. This world will ignore the piles of evidence, it will be immune to the mounds of Black, Brown and Indigenous bodies, it will destroy every species and contaminate every molecule of this world, and it will live in denial until the very end. In each new crisis, white people will be surprised, as if they just heard of MMIWG in 2019 and police violence ending Black life in the summer of 2020. The liberal ones will be enraged, as if their lives are built upon Black and Indigenous suffering. Their guilt will book us for talks, give us book contracts and awards our aunties could have only dreamed of. They'll hire us into tenure-track positions, and donate their proceeds. They will take our organizing and our work and make it their own, watering it down, washing it in white, so that our radical imaginings become window dressings on the status quo of this world. They will beg us to vote for the next Town Destroyer. The system will remain intact and at the end of every event, they will ask us where we see hope.

Robyn, sometimes I write a paragraph and it puts a smile on my face and I wonder if that paragraph will make it to print. Sometimes they do, and when that happens, inevitably a white interviewer will read out the paragraph because it is something they've never thought about, and it changed the way they think. Which is of course a good thing. I imagine this will be the case if that last paragraph makes it into print. In this case, I imagine the interviewer will add, after reading it out loud, "Do you really have no hope?"

We both know hope is a luxury; my ancestors have taught me that. My people got up and worked really hard all day with or without hope. My ancestors didn't need hope to build resistance, to build Nishnaabeg life and imaginings beyond regulation. Our movements and mobilizations do not have the privilege of resting upon a fleeting emotion. The absence of hope is a beautiful catalyst. Tenacity, persistence, stubbornness, rage, resentment, pessimism and despair are all motivators. So are joy, love, attachment, care, truth, optimism, respect and reciprocity. So is the delicious soup in which all those exist at once. The tentacles of racial capitalism do not get to demand hope or optimism, or celebrate rage and pessimism or consume our trauma and tragedy, or transform me into "uplift"—what Saidiya Hartman calls "a translation of Black suffering into white pedagogy."

What I can learn from my ancestors about "Armageddon in effect," as Public Enemy says, is that we world-build anyway, as a practice, as a way of life. In the bush, my ancestors got up and built life, every day, no matter what. They built life even if it only lasted for a fraction of a second at the hands of the colonial death machine. They built it anyway. Over and over—because they believed the practice of life-building to be the essence of life, and crucial for the generation of more life, or mino-bimaadiziwin. They knew that, even if life was taken away from them, this practice of world-building might still plants seeds for others, both human and non-human. This practice of collective world-building might unlock knowledge that has the potential to nurture more life-giving beginnings. This wisdom comes from the land.

In Nishnaabeg practice, water, Nibi, is commonly thought to be in the realm of responsibilities of women. Often in our ceremonies, women will pray and sing to the water. These songs focus on thanksgiving to the water for giving us life. It is common to explicitly express love for the water, and our utter dependence upon Nibi. We've seen Nishnaabeg women, notably Elder Josephine Mandamin, walk around the Great Lakes as a way of drawing attention to the health and well-being of the water. We've seen Autumn Peltier from Wikwemikong fight for access to clean drinking water and the protection of water since she was a mere twelve years old. I've always assumed this responsibility falls to women because we carry water in pregnancy, because our mothers carry us, carry us first, in water. Water is our first environment, as Mohawk midwife Katsi Cook says. And in this way, the gendered nature of this responsibility dissolves. We are all made of water, we are all responsible for water. All genders carry water inside our bodies, breathe in and out water droplets even into our cilia, and rely on clean water for our health and well-being. All genders have a deep relationality to water and therefore carry responsibilities to Nibi because without Nibi, life on planet Earth isn't possible.

Nibi is interesting to me because it is something all humans have a relationship with, and because it has the ability to both travel and change form. It is an entity that is in continual movement, cycling through the atmosphere in clouds, and through ground in underwater streams and aquifers. The cycle of water is global, and it connects us to all of life on planet Earth. Nishnaabeg know the creeks, rivers, streams, and lakes in our territory as the lifeblood of the earth. We think of the Great Lakes as the internal organs of the earth, filtering and cleaning water and then sending it out to the Atlantic Ocean through Gichi Ziibi (big river), or the St. Lawrence River. We rely on coastal First Nations to take care of the parts of the Arctic, Pacific and Atlantic oceans they belong to. We rely on northern Indigenous peoples to take care of the northern oceans, the permafrost, the snow, and the sea ice. We rely on Indigenous peoples that live in the deserts and arid regions of the globe to remind us of the power even a little bit of Nibi holds. We rely on oceanic peoples to know the currents and the movements and to monitor the health of the systems. We rely on the mountain peoples to take care of the headwaters and the glaciers. I rely on Black feminists like Christina Sharpe and Alexis Pauline Gumbs to teach me what Black intellectual traditions theorize about the Atlantic and the middle passage.

We know that water changes forms and transforms depending upon environmental conditions. Cold temperatures mean ice. High temperatures mean humidity. Evaporation. Condensation. Precipitation. Collection. Into the bodies of plants and animals, out of the bodies of plants and animals. Breathed into my body, breathed out of my body, and then into someone else.

In our fasting ceremony, we choose to go without water, often for four days, as do so many others in different cultures and religious traditions. Going without water for an extended period of time has demonstrated to me, in a physical way, how dependent upon water I am: a teaching that, in modern life, I rarely have to think about. This isn't true for many First Nations communities. It isn't true for Black communities in places like Detroit. This isn't true for many Black, Brown, and Indigenous peoples in the global south. As we all put our masks on during the pandemic, we become quickly aware of how much of our breath is water, and of how much our breathing connects us to others, to the point where, in the time of the out-of-control virus, breath connection is dangerous.

Nibi is very much an inseparable part of land, and although Indigeneity is most commonly associated with land, within/inside Nishnaabeg thought, land and water are one in the same. Nibi is very much an inseparable part of me and my body, and although I am most associated with flesh, within/inside Nishnaabeg thought, my body and water and land are one in the same. What happens outside my body, also happens inside my body.

In my language, the word for November is based on the word gaskadin, "it freezes over," referencing the time when the lakes freeze over. For me, this has become a time to think about the apocalypse of climate change, because our lakes don't freeze over now until January. If we are lucky. The ice road that used to go across Rice Lake is no more. The clear, dense ice, the kind that forms before snow comes, is something I've only seen in Denendeh. We know that the violence of racial capitalism has hurt Gabiboona'kan, Winter Maker—the spirit and being responsible for the cold—and that they are struggling and suffering right now and out of balance with Niibin, the summer, and Zhawanong, the south wind—the spirits that bring us summer light and warmth. November is also the time where I wish and yearn for the brightness of snow to break the grey monotony of the month.

I like snow, because it makes visible another power of water. Starting out as a single nucleus of desert dust, falling 3.5 feet per second, enfolding, one crystal at a time, forming a nation of stunning difference, propagating arms of crystal, offering the full spectrum of possibility, reflecting the full spectrum of light. I like the idea of one molecule practising world-building, combining with other molecules, falling in formation with others until the world is blanketed with snow carrying light, and the world is transformed to our winter lodge.

I like the idea of those same molecules reaching your cilia.

Nibi insists on internationalism. Nibi insists on us seeing ourselves outside of our own perspectives.

While the work we've done together in this book has focused on Black and Indigenous relationality, Nibi reminds me that radical imaginings and world-building must be international in orientation, reaching beyond Canada, beyond North America and beyond the Atlantic—not as an afterthought at the height of mobilizations, but as a foundational practice. This, of course, is something that the Black radical tradition, Black feminists, and Indigenous liberation collectives have been doing for decades. I am reminded of the delegation of Indigenous, Black and women of colour feminist scholars who visited the West Bank in 2011. They were shocked by the quotidian violence of the occupation, and upon their return committed to the Boycott, Divestment and Sanctions (BDS) movement and to strengthening relations between their own organizations and circles of influence and the freedom fighters they had met in Palestine. Dakota scholar, activist and writer Waziyatawin was part of that delegation, and she writes, "Sometimes it takes seeing the suffering of others to realize the full magnitude of our own suffering. As a Dakota woman in Palestine, I had the painful experience of witnessing the monstrous destructiveness of settler colonialism's war against a People and a land base. I told one friend that it was like witnessing a high-speed and high-tech version of the colonization of our Indigenous homelands." Both Davis and Waziyatawin write about their knowledge of self, Indigenous anti-colonial movements and abolition deepening through their experiences with Palestinian resistance. More recently, Steven Salaita has argued for Palestinian struggles to take up a more central position in critical Indigenous Studies by laying the conceptual groundwork to link our struggles through settler colonialism, state violence, occupation, and Indigeneity. In Indigenous mobilizations in Canada it is common to see Palestinian solidarity, most recently with local Palestinian support of 1492 Land Back Lane and the support of the BDS movement for the Wet'suwet'en mobilization. Smaller grassroots organizations, including Families of Sisters in Spirit (FSIS)—a volunteer collective of family members of murdered and missing Indigenous women—have issued solidarity statements for Palestinian freedom. These families know that freedom is a place, as Ruth Wilson Gilmore says, and that place-making is a global practice.

We are remaking the whole world—at once in our most intimate and local places, and through our matrix of relationality with all living things and anti-colonial movements on the planet. A never-ending project, a practice, a way of living. In this sense, our work will never be "done." Still, I'm sad that this shared writing and thinking space is coming to an end. This place is one where we've been vulnerable and caring with each other. Where we've spoken hard truths. Regrouped. Rethought. This is my favourite part of writing, where every morning I get up and give myself over to a creative space that exists only in my head. Where I can say or imagine or write whatever I feel and think. This is the first time I've shared this space with someone. This is a beautiful, productive, and challenging homespace we've made together, out of nothing. Of course, we're not done; in these next parts we'll bring our critical minds into the project, we'll bring our communities of thinkers together to point out the flaws we already know exist, and to make our thinking and our work more robust. This will require a different kind of brave. Eventually, if we are lucky, we will release this work from the past, through the present and into the future, as a record of how we thought and interacted at one point in time. We'll be critiqued and there will be correctives. We'll also be loved and, with luck, the work will travel and inspire more life. We'll both be awkward and uncomfortable. Our ethics and our humility will frustrate and irritate the publicist. Our answers will baffle the interviewers. And to me, none of that matters.

Miigwech, my friend. In my language that is often translated as "thank you." Miigwech comes from the verb miigiwe, which means "to give." For Nishnaabeg, miigwech isn't a thank-you; it is a start to gift-giving. It is a commitment to give to others what has been gifted to you—whether that is presence and time, physical or emotional labour, material goods, spiritual energy, care, or kindness and solidarity. Miigiwe is relational. To me, that means that I see the gifts you've given me, through your thinking through with me in this project and through your example of how to live at the end of the world, and I hope that my thinking through and living at the end of the world is in keeping with our practice of living with reciprocity.

Miigwech, my friend, and, as Mariame Kaba says, hope is a discipline, hope is a practice. So is our continuous rebirth.

AN AFTERWOR(L)D

Robin D. G. Kelley

> Too bad for those who consider us mere dreamers.
> The most unsettling reality is our own.
> We shall act.
> This land, ours, can only be what we want it to be.
>
> —SUZANNE CÉSAIRE

The story of the Ghost Dance, no matter how skewed, is the one bit of Indigenous history taught to settlers in the lower half of Turtle Island. The basic outlines are familiar. In 1889, a Northern Paiute spiritual leader named Wovoka prophesied the end of the (settler) world. According to the Lakota version of the prophesy, Wovoka predicted the imminent rising of Native ancestors to cleanse the land of whites and restore balance, wellness, and Indigenous sovereignty. He and his followers performed what became known as the Ghost Dance to help prepare for the coming world. We know what happened next: President Benjamin Harrison dispatched the Seventh Cavalry to Wounded Knee, South Dakota, in 1890, where they killed Lakota spiritual leader Sitting Bull and massacred some three hundred unarmed members of his nation, including women and children.

Liberal historians, who don't actually believe the prophecy, continually remind us that the Ghost Dance was not a violent rebellion but a peaceful assembly—they were the unfortunate victims of excessive, racist military force. But clearly the president and his people believed Wovoka because they waged a genocidal war to forestall the end of the settler world, as they always had.

Even in US settler discourse, the Ghost Dance and the Wounded Knee massacre are presented as a kind of "end of the world" trope that marks the end of the frontier, the triumph of continental Manifest Destiny, and the opening for US expansion into the Pacific and the Caribbean. From a Native perspective, however, the Ghost Dance is about Indigenous futurities. Wovoka prophesied what *must* be, what is required to restore life balance—not just in the lands of the Paiute and the Lakota but across all lands. It was a call to *wage love*, not to hold hands with settlers but to push back their pestilence and protect the water and defend the land and their animal and plant relations from enclosure, "homesteads," dams, mining companies, steamboats, railroads, commercial agriculture—that is, from the ongoing violence of dispossession and racial capitalism. Wovoka was right all along. Indigenous people—living, spirits, ancestors—spent the next century plus resisting the settler state, just as the United States and European nations extended their colonial wars to the rest of the planet.

Two years after Wounded Knee, in November 1892, Black workers employed at the granite quarries at Stone Mountain, Georgia, stopped coming to work. The recent discovery of a distant comet, followed by rumors that it was barrelling toward earth, convinced a number of Black folks that the world was ending. The quarrymen had no intention of returning to Stone Mountain. "The negroes have become so wrought up over the end of the world, as they call it," observed an incredulous white reporter, "that they devote themselves to the wildest religious orgies. Their houses are left open, and everything is in common, but so intense is the belief in the coming of judgment day that nothing is disturbed." Everything is in common, nothing is disturbed. Their religious orgies likely involved singing, moaning, praying, and dancing the "ring shout," a sacred dance carried from West and Central Africa, where worshippers bent toward the ground and shuffled in a counterclockwise circle. They probably believed the comet was going to take out all the "crackers" who once claimed them as property and now ruled the South, which Black folks fought so hard to democratize after the Civil War. This was the beginning of the Jim Crow regime of lynching, disfranchisement, and segregation, which itself was a response to Black-led multiracial insurgencies to preserve and expand democracy, protect the rights of working people, redistribute land, and dismantle the plantation oligarchy. It is no small irony that Stone Mountain became the site for the rebirth of the Ku Klux Klan in 1915.

These Indigenous and Black "end of the world" scenarios echo what Robyn Maynard and Leanne Betasamosake Simpson express throughout their extraordinary epistolary exchanges: the end of the world promises nothing except a chance to make the world anew. The world we now inhabit is unsustainable, and not simply because of accumulating greenhouse gases and rising sea temperatures, but also because people are rising and the self-proclaimed rulers of this earth can no longer continue as they have in the past. "Black and Indigenous communities," they write, "are collectively positioned on the very forefront of the unfolding catastrophe." It is a position we've held for five centuries.

A change is gonna come, but it could just as easily take the form of more fascism and more violence, accelerating the inexorable descent into planetary extinction. Yet we are saddled with a "woke" white liberal belief that this world is worth saving, and the very communities on the front lines of the catastrophe will save the planet. The promise of Canadian multicultural inclusion and the redemption of the "American" soul through a racial reckoning will bring all of us together to fight the depredation of the Anthropocene in a united front—this is how every big budget Hollywood apocalypse film ends. The people join together to beat back the invader, and now the shopping malls can reopen: mission accomplished. Maynard and Simpson obliterate this fantasy, reminding us that there is no Anthropocene, only a racial capitalocene, a crisis created by a parasitic class whose power was built on genocide, land theft, slavery, white supremacy, heteropatriarchy, prisons, state violence, racially differentiated labour exploitation, and unbridled resource extraction. Hence Indigenous and Black people have been in the folds of the catastrophe from its inception. Maynard and Simpson knew way before the first letters between them—before they had even met—that this world is irredeemable. They have been at the forefront of the struggle to birth a new world, to abolish racial capitalism, all carceral institutions and logics, and the police and military, and to decolonize the land, our bodies, and our minds.

"Abolition now!" "Decolonization now!" These are popular, irresistible slogans now tossed about with ease. But *Rehearsals for Living* makes clear that the truth and complexity of what it means to be an abolitionist or to reverse more than five hundred years of colonial domination exceeds the limits of a placard or a chant—or a survey or polemic by some leftist think tank. We have been, and will continue to be, flooded with big books and little books and reports and documentary films all showing us how capitalism, racism, prisons, patriarchy, walls, and war are killing the planet. But this book is different. How Maynard and Simpson came to understand the world we must abolish and the world we need to build is through *communing*—with each other, comrades, friends and family, and the movements to which they make themselves accountable. They dance together, sing together, meditate, worship, and study together through letters, by sharing, by making themselves *vulnerable* to one another and to all of us reading these pages. They won't stop dancing. They refuse to go to the quarry.

Maynard and Simpson are accomplished writers, intellectuals, and activists, but *Rehearsals for Living* is a work of profound humility that honours the ancestors, the land, the children, and the struggles that enabled every generation to survive. They braid the histories and collective memories of Black and Indigenous struggles to establish a basis for solidarity, to find answers, and to reveal and share valuable lessons for our movements. Braiding is an apt metaphor. In both Black and Indigenous cultures, braiding is both a communal and intimate act. Traditionally the work of women, braiding requires touch, patience, and deep listening, for it often occurs in communal spaces where stories are shared, lessons passed down, and elders bond with the young. The act of braiding involves gatherings of hair, each strand distinct and autonomous, held together in plaits wrapped and woven together in a protective embrace, creating a mighty force and a thing of beauty. These letters, the stories and lessons they impart, and the questions they generate are braided together, symbolizing what we must become and what we must do. Their decolonial abolition feminism calls us to resist, restore, reimagine, "rethink," "regroup," rebirth, rebuild, and, in the words of Dionne Brand, "to change the air."

While their letters reflect a particular moment of a global pandemic, like the Ghost Dancers and the stone workers, they are not bound by linear time or settler time. Maynard and Simpson came into movements that had declared states of emergency generations before the spread of COVID-19 or the Black rebellion of the spring and summer of 2020. We encounter Maynard and Simpson's correspondence not as a window onto an urgent, catastrophic moment but as meditations on transformative possibilities generated by the latest crises. They freely share historical knowledge, experience, and imaginings to mobilize what Ruth Wilson Gilmore calls an abolitionist critique: "to show how radical consciousness in action resolves into liberated life-ways, however provisional, present and past. Indeed, the radical tradition from which abolition geography draws meaning and method goes back in time-space not in order to abolish history, but rather to find alternatives to the despairing sense that so much change, in retrospect, seems only ever to have been displacement and redistribution of human sacrifice."

Abolition geography, Gilmore also observes, recognizes that "freedom is a place" and that we've been doing the work of place-making long before armed white men in ships came to take our people and our lands. Maynard and Simpson continually remind us that Indigenous people in this hemisphere and on the African continent had been building and sustaining complex societies, producing knowledge, and developing modes of governance and international relations for *thousands* of years before the era of colonialism, chattel slavery, and capitalism. *Thousands!* They were nations without states, governed by a culture that emphasized hospitality, care, grace, mercy, deep listening, "deep reciprocity," sharing, sovereignty, and a commitment to wellness, intimacy, joy, and love.

Maynard and Simpson both reclaim "nation" as a counter to the colonial/capitalist nation-state, decoupling these terms as an assertion of self-determination. Simpson speaks about the beaver nation, the squirrel nation, the Dene and Nishnaabeg nations. This definition of nation does not traffic in Western-style nationalism, which is inherently racist, exclusionary, and built on gendered hierarchies. Likewise, Maynard surveys the wreckage of postcolonial Black life, concluding that the nation-state has been a barrier to Black freedom. "Globally, the colonial nation-state, and the logics and carceral practices that it relies upon to function, have not served as an adequate container for Black liberation. Our citizenship is everywhere precarious and contingent, when it exists at all." They both imagine decolonized, liberated nations as queer, untethered from states, and grounded in a people's culture but not ossified and hierarchical. And, of course, land-based.

Freedom is a place. There is no liberation without land-based politics. "Land Back" is not a symbolic demand—nor is it utopian. Land Back is fundamental to end resource extraction, deforestation, industrial farming and the use of chemicals, and soil erosion, not to mention poverty and precarity. Restoring Indigenous sovereignty and returning the land will allow nations to create and maintain the institutions they need right now: free health care clinics, clean drinking water, healthy food, expanded midwifery services, and non-carceral systems of public safety capable of protecting Indigenous women, girls, queer, and two-spirit people from violence and abduction. They also fight for decolonized, antiracist education, demanding culturally relevant schools staffed by Native teachers, and creating their own Freedom Schools as a corrective to decades of boarding schools, foster care, apprenticeship laws, juvenile "reformatories," and a generally racist education system. The very structure of public education in Turtle Island is an ideological and pragmatic extension of the organizational logic of the prison, white supremacy, and settler colonialism—even in multicultural Canada.

Maynard and Simpson imagine an Indigenous and Black land-based politics that is responsive to and linked to movements resisting settler colonialism around the world. This work is both difficult and necessary. As Simpson acknowledged, "There is no justice in Land Back if it is not in concert with the destruction of racial capitalism, and if Black people remain landless. There is no justice in Land Back if we are silent with regard to the radical imaginings of Black futures and Black struggles for freedom, just as there is no justice if Black liberation is framed through the ongoing dispossession of Indigenous Peoples."

Land-based politics are also feminist politics, from North America to Palestine, to South Africa, to India, and beyond. Women have been on the front lines of fighting modern enclosure (land and resource privatization). They have waged militant campaigns against commercial logging, land grabs, pesticides, and the like, and have adopted subsistence agriculture to defend their communities from the impact of structural adjustment and dependence on global markets. The destruction of subsistence economies in rural areas has forced Black and Indigenous women into cities and across borders, into debt, low-wage labour, domestic service, childcare, and sex work. Women collectively resist the limited options available to them as they also fight to hold the land.

The struggle to hold the land, to block machines of annihilation, to grow food and feed one another—this is life in rehearsal. Robyn Maynard and Leanne Betasamosake Simpson are able to see past the catastrophe in order to make plans, but they are no mere dreamers. They understand that the work of building the new world is no luxury—and that our very survival depends on turning dreams of decolonization and abolition into action. They know this largely because of their children. Their letters wax intimately and lovingly about their kids and how to help them understand this world while protecting them from its worst ravages. And yet they both bear witness to their children's place-making practices in the stories they tell each other about running with them. These children run, not for their lives, not out of fear, not to stake out territory, but because they are free. They feel the earth beneath their feet, not as blood-stained enclosures but as their land. Perhaps they discovered the "portal, a gateway between one world and the next," that Arundhati Roy believed was opened up by the global pandemic. Or perhaps, as Maynard muses, "the portal has been there all along."

ACKNOWLEDGMENTS

We'd like to begin by thanking Jas Morgan for facilitating the initial conversation between the two of us so many years ago in Montreal. We didn't know it at the time, but this was a beginning. Thanks also to Rodney Diverlus, Sandy Hudson and Syrus Marcus Ware for publishing part of that conversation in *Until We Are Free: Reflections on Black Lives Matter in Canada*. Thanks to Kelsey Wrightson, executive director for the Dechinta Centre for Research and Learning, for supporting our solidarity gathering, to all of the participants at that gathering, and to the members of Yellowknives Dene First Nation for hosting us in their homelands.

Dionne Brand planted the seeds for this book. She watered them, put them in sunlight, and encouraged them. We are so grateful to her. We are also so appreciative of the conversation between Leanne, NourbeSe Philip, Andrea Fatona and Tania Willard as part of the Contingencies of Care virtual residency co-hosted by OCAD University, the Toronto Biennial of Art and BUSH Gallery in June 2020, and between the two of us and Zoé Samudzi at NAISA 2021, on many of the same topics as these letters.

Our very first readers of these letters, outside of one another, were crucial to the development of the manuscript. We're grateful for insightful feedback from Dionne Brand,

John Munro, Michelle Daigle, Glen Coulthard, Robert Nichols, Rachel Zellars, and to La Tanya Autry, who provided feedback on the section discussing "Temporary Spaces of Joy and Freedom." We are so appreciative of Naomi Murakawa and Lynn Henry's editorial brilliance. Thanks to Melanie Little whose careful attention during the copy-editing stage made the book tighter. All of these people made our contributions better. Their detailed and careful reading of the work was a lovely gift.

Ruth Wilson Gilmore graciously gave us permission to adapt her words "abolition is life in rehearsal" as a title, and her influence is in every line, as is the influence of Robin D. G. Kelley. We can't believe our words share space with theirs in this book. They are our heroes.

It would have been difficult to have the disciplined sense of possibility required to write this book in such a time without the movement of people the world over who have steadfastly committed to carving beautiful spaces of freedom over and against the brutality of these times. Especially these co-conspirators in abolitionist world-making: Andrea J. Ritchie, Sahra Soudi, Sarah Jama, Molly Swain, Karrie Auger, Rajean Hoilett, Souheil Benslimane, Danielle Smith, Beverly Bain, El Jones, Jessica Evans, Pascale Diverlus, Herman Bell, Leila Pourtavaf and Sheena Hoszko.

Extending enormous gratitude, too, to Dionne Brand, Glen Coulthard, Natalie Diaz, Nick Estes, John Munro, Katherine McKittrick, Andrea J. Ritchie, Harsha Walia, David Chariandy, Naomi Klein, and M. NourbeSe Philip for their generous blurbs. Thank you to Howardene Pindell for use of her art in the cover.

ACKNOWLEDGMENTS

Thanks to all of the folks at Haymarket and Knopf Canada who brought this book into the world—especially to Anthony Arnove, Lynn Henry, and Aricka Foreman.

NOTES

PART ONE

8 **if we are to avoid "untold suffering":** Damian Carrington, "Climate crisis: 11,000 scientists warn of 'untold suffering,'" *The Guardian*, November 5, 2019, https://www.theguardian .com/environment/2019/nov/05/climate-crisis-11000-scientists -warn-of-untold-suffering.

10 **the complete political, cultural, and social collapse:** Leanne Betasamosake Simpson, *Dancing On Our Turtle's Back: Stories of Nishnaabeg Re-Creation, Resurgence, and a New Emergence* (Winnipeg: Arbeiter Ring Publishing, 2011), 15.

10 **the two genocides at the heart of the Americas:** M. NourbeSe Philip, "Jammin' Still," in *Bla_K: Essays and Interviews* (Toronto: Book*hug Press, 2017), 36.

10 **In this burgeoning global logic:** Cedric J. Robinson, *Black Marxism: The Making of the Black Radical Tradition* (Chapel Hill, NC: University of North Carolina Press, 2000), 81.

11 **over 50 percent of the world's carbon emissions:** Bruno Oberlé, et al., *Global Resources Outlook 2019: Natural Resources for the Future We Want* (Nairobi: United Nations Environment Programme, 2019), https://www.resourcepanel.org/reports /global-resources-outlook.

12 **In 2018, they made a profit of:** "Barrick Reports 2018 Full Year and Fourth Quarter Results," Barrick, February 13, 2019, https://

www.barrick.com/English/news/news-details/2019/barrick
-reports-2018-full-year-and-fourth-quarter-results/default.aspx.

12   **were prepared to pay their new CEO**: Niall McGee, "Barrick
CEO Bristow stands to earn as much as $18-million if targets
are met," *Globe and Mail*, February 14, 2019, https://www
.theglobeandmail.com/business/article-barrick-ceo-bristow
-stands-to-earn-as-much-as-us18-million-if-targets/.

13   **The heavy metals and toxins produced at the site**: Catherine
Coumans, "Anger Boils over at North Mara Mine—Barrick/
Acacia Leave Human Rights Abuses Unaddressed—Field
Assessment Brief," MiningWatch Canada, July 2017, https://
miningwatch.ca/sites/default/files/2017_field_report_final_-
_anger_boils_over_at_north_mara_mine.pdf.

13   **will leach toxins into the lands and waters:** For background on
Belo Sun and possible environmental harms, see Raffael M.
Tófoli, et al., "Gold at What Cost? Another Megaproject
Threatens Biodiversity in the Amazon," *Perspectives in Ecology
and Conservation* 15, no. 2 (April 2017)129-31; for a legal
context facing Belo Sun and challenges undertaken against the
mine, see Jacob Lorinc, "A Canadian Company Wants to Build
Brazil's Largest Open-Pit Gold Mine: Now That Bolsonaro Is in
Power, It Just Might Succeed," *Toronto Star,* November 9, 2019,
https://www.thestar.com/business/2019/11/09/a-canadian
-company-wants-to-build-brazils-largest-open-pit-gold-mine
-now-that-bolsonaro-is-in-power-it-just-might-succeed.html.

13   **following the election of white-supremacist president Jair
Bolsonaro:** CBC News (@CBCNews), "Critics have lambasted
the former paratrooper for his homophobic, racist and misogynist statements, but his government could open new investment

opportunities," October 29, 2018, https://twitter.com/CBCNews
/status/1056712250113867776.

14   **Copper One is not yet dissuaded:** Brett Forester, "Barrière Lake
Algonquin triumph over Copper One Inc.," *Anishinabek News*,
April 10, 2017, http://anishinabeknews.ca/2017/04/10/barriere
-lake-algonquin-triumph-over-copper-one-inc/.

14   **more than one thousand mining companies based in Canada:**
Earthrights International, International Human Rights Program
(University of Toronto Faculty of Law), and MiningWatch
Canada, *Report to the U.N. Committee on the Elimination of
Racial Discrimination, 93rd session, July–August 2017*, pp. 2–3,
https://miningwatch.ca/sites/default/files/cerd_final_8.10.pdf.

15   **the hour of the barbarian is at hand:** Aimé Césaire, *Discourse
on Colonialism*, trans. Joan Pinkham (New York: Monthly
Review Press, 2001), 76.

16   **The IPCC reports bring to light what is to come:** Priyadarshi
Shukla et al., *Climate Change and Land: An IPCC special
report on climate change, desertification, land degradation,
sustainable land management, food security, and greenhouse
gas fluxes in terrestrial ecosystems,* Intergovernmental Panel
on Climate Change, August 2019.

16   **Nigerian activist and scholar Oladosu Adenike:** Jonathan
Watts, "'The crisis is already here': young strikers facing climate
apartheid," *The Guardian*, September 19, 2019, https://www.
theguardian.com/environment/2019/sep/19/the-crisis-is-already
-here-young-strikers-facing-climate-apartheid.

17   **the consciousness of our intended slaughter:** Audre Lorde,
"Learning from the Sixties," in *Sister Outsider: Essays and
Speeches* (Berkeley: Crossing Press, 1984/2007), 140.

19 **who is considered a full human:** She goes on to say that if this is the "we" from which we address the pending catastrophes, *"the proposals they're going to give for change are going to be devastating!"*—especially for the global poor. Sylvia Wynter, ed. Katherine McKittrick, "Unparalleled Catastrophe for Our Species? Or, to Give Humanness a Different Future: Conversations," in *Sylvia Wynter: On Being Human As Praxis* (Durham, NC: Duke University Press, 2015), 24. See also Kathryn Yusoff, *A Billion Black Anthropocenes or None* (Minneapolis: University of Minnesota Press, 2018).

20 **to supplement, expand, and work beyond the Anthropocene:** Donna Haraway, et al., "Anthropologists Are Talking—About the Anthropocene," *Ethnos* 81, no. 3: 535–564.

20 **the *racial Capitalocene:*** Françoise Vergès, "Racial Capitalocene," in *Futures of Black Radicalism*, eds. Gaye Theresa Johnson and Alex Lubin (New York: Verso, 2017), 72–82. See also Bedour Alagraa's "The Interminable Catastrophe."

20 **The *interminable catastrophe*:** Bedour Alagraa, "The Interminable Catastrophe," *Offshoot*, March 1, 2021, https://offshootjournal.org/the-interminable-catastrophe/.

21 **Vishwas Satgar refers to this as "imperial ecocide":** Vishwas Satgar, "The Anthropocene and Imperial Ecocide: Prospects for Just Transitions," in Satgar, ed., *The Climate Crisis: South African and Global Democratic Eco-socialist Alternatives* (Johannesburg: Wits University Press, 2018), 47–68.

21 **the inevitable consequences of slave labor and quick extraction:** Eric Williams, *Capitalism and Slavery* (Chapel Hill, NC: University of North Carolina Press, 1944/1994), 113.

21 **"decaying fast" due to soil exhaustion:** Ibid.

22 **As Thomas Jefferson wrote of the state of Virginia:** Eric Williams, *Capitalism and Slavery,* citing M.B. Hammond, *The Cotton Industry: An Essay in American Economic History,* (London: Swan Sonnenschein and Company, 1897).

22 **worked literally to death:** Cedric J. Robinson, *Black Marxism,* 200.

23 **Africans were considered "capable of no development or culture":** Georg W. F. Hegel, *The Philosophy of History* (Kitchener: Batoche Books, 2000), 116.

23 **set up *only* for colonial extraction:** Daron Acemoglu, Simon Johnson, and James A. Robinson, "The colonial origins of comparative development: An empirical investigation," *American Economic Review* 91, no.5 (2012): 1369–1401.

24 *So the real monster has arrived*: Leanne Betasamosake Simpson in conversation with Dionne Brand, "Temporary Spaces of Joy and Freedom," *Literary Review of Canada*, June 2018, http://reviewcanada.ca/magazine/2018/06/temporary-spaces-of-joy-and-freedom/.

26 **a program of complete disorder:** Frantz Fanon, *The Wretched of the Earth*, trans. Constance Farrington (New York: Grove Press, 1963), 36.

26 **racial and ecological violence are interwoven:** This is in reference to the words of BLM-UK protesters who stopped a flight leaving the London City Airport in 2016 to address Britain's disproportionate impact on global Black vulnerability to the climate crisis. See Matthew Weaver and Jamie Grierson, "Black Lives Matter protest stops flights at London City airport," *The Guardian*, September 6, 2016.

31 **a solidarity gathering that took place in March:** Kelsey Wrightson and Glen Coulthard were the other organizers, along with

Dechinta staff.

32 **one generative means of nourishing Black and Indigenous politics:** Zoé Samudzi and William C. Anderson, *As Black As Resistance: Finding the Conditions For Liberation* (Chico, CA: AK Press, 2018), 33.

32 **land and place-making:** Katherine McKittrick and Clyde Woods, eds., *Black Geographies and the Politics of Place* (Toronto: Between the Lines, 2007); Katherine McKittrick, *Demonic Grounds: Black Women and the Cartographies of Struggle* (Minneapolis: University of Minnesota Press, 2006).

33 **the possibilities to continue this work:** Present at the gathering were LeRoi Newbold and Nauoda Robinson, co-founders of Freedom School Toronto, and Tasha Spillet-Sumner, an organizer with Red Rising Freedom School in Winnipeg, MB.

33 **an honoured radical Black feminist methodology:** I thought of course of *Sister Love: The Letters of Audre Lorde and Pat Parker 1974–1989* (New York: A Midsummer Night's Press, 2018).

34 **The intersection was friendship:** Katherine McKittrick, *Dear Science and Other Stories* (Durham, NC: Duke University Press, 2021).

38 **there were only six critical care beds:** "Public health emergency declared in N.W.T.," CBC News, March 18, 2020, https://www.cbc.ca/news/canada/north/health-emergency-covid-nwt-1.5501801.

38 **The Assembly of Manitoba Chiefs was concerned:** Jorge Barrera, "Manitoba chiefs organization wants Cuban doctor aid on COVID-19," CBC News, March 27, 2020, https://www.cbc.ca/news/indigenous/coronavirus-manitoba-sco-wants-cuban-doctors-1.5511712.

38 **the Canadian health care system is shaped:** Mary Ellen

Turpel-Lafond, *In Plain Sight: Addressing Indigenous-specific Racism and Discrimination in B.C. Health Care,* Government of British Columbia, November 30, 2020, https://engage.gov .bc.ca/app/uploads/sites/613/2020/11/In-Plain-Sight-Summary -Report.pdf.

38   **the killing of Joyce Echaquan:** Leyland Cecco, "Canada: outcry after video shows hospital staff taunting dying Indigenous woman," *The Guardian*, September 30, 2020, https://www .theguardian.com/world/2020/sep/30/joyce-echaquan-canada -indigenous-woman-hospital.

38   **the death-making machine of white racism:** Lauren Boothby, "Man charged in Métis hunter killings denied bail," *Edmonton Journal*, April 2, 2020, https://edmontonjournal.com/news /crime/man-accused-of-killing-two-metis-hunters-denied-bail/.

38   **with threats to intentionally spread COVID-19:** Robson Fletcher, "Calgary police charge man over threat to spread COVID-19 to Indigenous people," CBC News, April 1, 2020, https://www.cbc.ca/news/canada/calgary/calgary-police-covid-19 -threats-charge-investigation-1.5517980.

38   **the women's shelter has adopted physical distancing measures:** "N.W.T. women's shelters receive over $300K as domestic violence rates surge," CBC News, August 6, 2020, https://www.cbc.ca/news /canada/north/nwt-women-shelter-covid-violence-1.5676436.

39   **women and children are more vulnerable:** European Public Service Union, "In our non gender equal world, COVID19 hits women harder," November 25, 2020, https://www.epsu.org /article/our-non-gender-equal-world-covid19-hits-women -harder-international-day-elimination-violence.

39   **blockaded the road to the Meliadine mine:** Kent Driscoll, "Nunavut community blocks access to gold mine over

COVID-19 fears," APTN News, March 19, 2020, https://
aptnnews.ca/2020/03/19/nunavut-community-blocks-access-to-
gold-mine-over-covid-19-fears/.

39 **continued to endanger Indigenous peoples:** Amanda Follett
Hosgood, "The Pipeline and the Pandemic: 'The Biggest Risk
We've Got Right Now,'" *The Tyee*, March 31, 2020, https://
thetyee.ca/News/2020/03/31/Pipeline-Vs-Pandemic/.

39 **while white, middle-class Canadians in the south:** Niigaan
Sinclair, "Industry puts First Nations at risk," *Winnipeg Free
Press*, April 4, 2020, https://www.winnipegfreepress.com/special
/coronavirus/industry-puts-first-nations-at-risk-569376002.html.

39 **transphobia and heteronormativity in the health care system:**
Jamie Jespersen, "Honouring Trans Lives, Historicising Trans
Death," *History Workshop*, November 20, 2020, https://www
.historyworkshop.org.uk/honouring-trans-lives-historicising
-trans-death/.

40 **People who call the Downtown Eastside (DTES) home:**
Christopher Cheung, "The 'Ticking Time Bomb' in the
Downtown Eastside," *The Tyee*, March 20, 2020, https://thetyee
.ca/News/2020/03/20/Downtown-Eastside-Ticking-Time-Tomb
-Coronavirus-COVID19/.

40 **basic supplies the city has refused to supply:** See https://www
.encampmentsupportnetwork.com/.

40 **The tent community at the DTES' Oppenheimer Park:** Cheung,
"'Ticking Time Bomb."

40 **the tired racist dichotomy:** Paula Ramon, "Virus poses cultural
threat to Brazil's Amazon people," CTV News, July 10, 2020,
https://www.ctvnews.ca/health/coronavirus/virus-poses-cultural
-threat-to-brazil-s-amazon-people-1.5018953.

40 **particularly vulnerable to the virus:** Miigwech to Robyn here

for pointing out that all peoples on the African continent are vulnerable from the afterlives of colonialism, not just Indigenous peoples, and pointing me to this article: Max Bearak and Danielle Paquette, "Africa's most vulnerable countries have few ventilators -- or none at all," *The Washington Post*, April 18, 2020, https://www.washingtonpost.com/world/africa/africa-coronavirus-ventilators/2020/04/17/903163a4-7f3e-11ea-84c2-0792d8591911_story.html

40 **conditions of the ongoing legacy of colonialism:** Terri Hansen, "How Covid-19 could destroy indigenous communities," BBC *Future*, July 29, 2020, https://www.bbc.com/future/article/20200727-how-covid-19-could-destroy-indigenous-communities.

41 **this crisis is adding poverty to poverty:** Ibid.

41 **similar problems with regard to Indigenous peoples:** ARISA (Advancing Rights in Southern Africa), *The Impact of COVID-19 on the Rights of Indigenous Peoples in Southern Africa* (report), 2020, https://freedomhouse.org/report/special-report/2020/covid-19-rights-indigenous-peoples-southern-africa.

41 **disproportionally impact the continent's Indigenous women:** Ibid.

41 **coping with the brink of environmental collapse:** Hansen, "How Covid-19 could destroy indigenous communities."

41 **gross inaction from the right-wing Bolsonaro government:** Philippe Charlier, "Is COVID-19 being used as a weapon against Indigenous Peoples in Brazil?" *The Lancet*, October 10, 2020, https://www.thelancet.com/journals/lancet/article/PIIS0140-6736(20)32068-7/fulltext.

42 **the ravages of capitalism and colonialism:** See Robin D. G. Kelley's "The Rest of Us," *American Quarterly* 69, no. 2 (2017): 267–276.

43 **COVID-19 will have a serious impact:** El Jones, "Black people

already struggle to breathe in Canada. Ignoring us during this
COVID-19 crisis will only make it worse," *Halifax Examiner*,
April 3, 2020, https://www.halifaxexaminer.ca/featured/black
-people-already-struggle-to-breathe-in-canada-ignoring-us
-during-this-covid-19-crisis-will-only-make-it-worse.

43 **their work on the front lines:** Ibid.

43 **We are invisibilized in the discourses of protection:** Ibid.

43 **increased police targeting:** Robyn Maynard and Andrea J. Ritchie,
"Black Communities Need Support, Not a Coronavirus Police
State," *Vice*, September 4, 2020, https://www.vice.com/en_ca
/article/z3bdmx/black-people-coronavirus-police-state.

44 **Imperialism and ongoing colonialism:** Yusoff, *A Billion Black
Anthropocenes or None*, xiii.

45 **A Michi Saagiig Nishnaabeg Chi'engikiiwang:** Doug Williams,
Elder, Curve Lake First Nation, Ontario, November 8, 2012.

45 **A Wendat Ouentaronk:** "Origin of the name of Toronto,"
City of Toronto Knowledge Base, https://www.toronto.ca/311
/knowledgebase/kb/docs/articles/311-toronto/information-and
-business-development/origin-of-the-name-of-toronto.html.

45 **the buried and forgotten creeks:** "Rouge River (Ontario),"
Wikipedia, last modified September 22, 2021, https://en
.wikipedia.org/wiki/Rouge_River_(Ontario).

45 **Cobechenonk Ziibi:** Donald B. Smith, "The Dispossession of
the Mississauga Indians: a Missing Chapter in the Early History
of Upper Canada," in *Historical Essays on Upper Canada:
New Perspectives*, eds. J. K. Johnson and Bruce G. Wilson
(Ottawa: Carleton University Press, 1989), 27.

45 **Waasayishkodenayosh:** "Wonscotonach Parklands: What We're
Hearing," The Don River Valley Park, March 20, 2019, https://
donrivervalleypark.ca/news/wonscotonach-parklands-what

-were-hearing/.

45 **Mazinige Ziibi:** Doug Williams, November 8, 2012.

47 **ultimately too overwhelmed with death:** See Kevin Plummer, "Historicist: The Murder of Wabakinine," *Torontoist*, May 30, 2015, https://torontoist.com/2015/05/historicist-the-murder-of -wabakinine/; and Donald B. Smith, "The Dispossession," as well as his *Sacred Feathers: the Reverend Peter Jones (Kahkewa-quonaby) and the Mississauga Indians* (Toronto: University of Toronto Press, 2013).

48 **hundreds of free Black people in Southwest Ontario:** Peggy Bristow, "'Whatever You Raise in the Ground You Can Sell It In Chatham': Black Women in Buxton and Chatham, 1850–65," in *We're Rooted Here And They Can't Pull Us Up: Essays in African Canadian Women's History*, eds. Bristow et al., (Toronto: University of Toronto Press, 1994), 69–143.

49 **three fatal police shootings of Indigenous people:** Sarah Berman, "Winnipeg Police Killed Three Indigenous People in 10 Days," *Vice*, April 22, 2020, https://www.vice.com/en/article/n7jazx /winnipeg-police-killed-three-indigenous-people-in-10-days.

49 **93 percent spike in overdose deaths:** Chantelle Bellrichard, "93% spike in First Nations overdose deaths recorded in B.C. during COVID-19," CBC News, July 6, 2020, https://www.cbc .ca/news/indigenous/bc-first-nations-overdose-deaths-1.5639098.

50 **Civil Twilight:** Previously published in the summer edition of the *West End Phoenix* (Toronto), under the title "Civil Twilight." Civil Twilight is a reference to a John K. Samson song of the same title, on the Weakerthans' album *Reunion Tour*.

PART TWO

58 **multiple ways to increase risks:** Daniela Curseu, et al., "Potential

Impact of Climate Change on Pandemic Influenza Risk," *Global Warming* (2010): 643–657. The main focus of this article is on pandemic influenza; see also "Coronavirus, Climate Change, and the Environment: A Conversation on COVID-19 with Dr. Aaron Bernstein, Director of Harvard Chan C-CHANGE," https://www.hsph.harvard.edu/c-change/subtopics/coronavirus -and-climate-change/.

59   **if we keep going on as we have been:** Octavia Butler qtd. in H. Jerome Jackson, "Sci-fi Tales from Octavia E. Butler" [1994], in *Conversations with Octavia Butler*, ed. Consuela Francis (Jackson: University Press of Mississippi, 2010), 44.

60   **the sociological aspects of our future lives:** Qtd. in Rosalie G. Harrison, "Sci-fi Visions: An Interview with Octavia E. Butler," in *Conversations with Octavia Butler*, 8.

60   **If this goes on:** Qtd. in H. Jerome Jackson, "Sci-fi Tales from Octavia E. Butler," in *Conversations with Octavia Butler*, 44.

62   **vulnerabilities of all kinds:** Ruth Wilson Gilmore, "Forgotten Places and the Seeds of Grassroots Planning," in *Engaging Contradictions: Theory, Politics and Methods of Activist Scholarship*, ed. Charles R. Hale (Berkeley and Los Angeles: University of California Press, 2008), 31–61.

66   **one-third of the prisoner population:** Valérie Ouellet and Joseph Loiero, "COVID-19 taking a toll in prisons, with high infection rates, CBC News analysis shows," CBC News, July 17, 2020, https://www.cbc.ca/news/canada/prisons-jails-inmates -covid-19-1.5652470.

69   **they have mattered for the wrong reason:** The event was "Black Grief: A Community Gathering for Black Lives," held on May 15, 2020, in Toronto. (See https://www.facebook.com/events /d41d8cd9/black-grief-a-community-gathering-for-black-lives

/174455457193807/.)

74 **thousands of those held in provincial jails:** Robyn Maynard and
Justin Piché, "No One Is Disposable: Depopulating Carceral Sites
During the COVID-19 Pandemic and Beyond," in *Sick of the
System: Why the COVID-19 Recovery Must Be Revolutionary*,
eds. Between the Lines Editorial Committee (Toronto: Between
the Lines, 2020), 105–115.

75 **make prisons dangerous at all times:** Burnside Prison Solidarity
in "Letters of Support from Coast to Coast for Detainees'
Hunger Strike," Solidarity Across Borders, April 1, 2020, https://
www.solidarityacrossborders.org/wp-content/uploads/From-the
-Burnside-prison-strikers-to-the-Laval-hunger-strikers.pdf.

76 **the possible impacts of hunger strike:** Editorial: "Critical
Care of Hunger Strikers," *The Lancet*, September 6, 2008,
https://www.thelancet.com/journals/lancet/article/PIIS0140
-6736(08)61313-6/fulltext.

79 ***This is an Honour Song: Twenty Years Since the Blockade*:** This
was co-edited with Kiera L. Ladner and published by ARP Books.

80 **there is no political will:** For a broader discussion, see Audra
Simpson, *Mohawk Interruptus: Political Life Across Borders of
Settler States* (Durham, NC: Duke University Press, 2014).

83 **the role of police and military violence:** Andrea J. Ritchie,
*Invisible No More: Police Violence Against Black Women and
Women of Color* (Boston: Beacon Press, 2017), 5–7.

84 **Raymond Lawrence had been shot and killed:** Shree Paradkar,
"The Yonge St. riot of 1992 . . . or was it an uprising?" *Toronto
Star*, May 5, 2017, https://www.thestar.com/news/gta/2017/05/05/
the-yonge-street-riot-of-1992-or-was-it-an-uprising-paradkar.html.

85 **organize and fight the nation-state for their lands:** Samudzi and
Anderson, *As Black as Resistance*, 21-22, and Robin D. G. Kelley,

"The Rest of Us."

86   **perpetuated by the mass kidnapping and genocidal trafficking:**
Samudzi and Anderson, *As Black as Resistance*, 23; see also
Sandra Harvey's "Unsettling Diasporas: Blackness and the Specter
of Indigeneity," *Postmodern Culture* 31, nos. 1 & 2 (2020–2021).

86   **Wolfe erased African Indigeneity:** Robin D. G. Kelley, "The Rest
of Us," 268.

87   **a sense of homespace:** Samudzi and Anderson, *As Black as
Resistance*, 24.

88   **to be in dialogue with each other:** You can watch the conversation, moderated by Andrea Fatoma, here: https://www.youtube
.com/watch?v=B3w_hwAhQd8.

88   **by reading each other's work:** M. NourbeSe Philip, "The Ga(s)p,"
in *Poetics and Precarity*, eds. Myung Mi Kim and Cristanne
Miller (Albany, NY: SUNY Press, 2018), 31.

88   **the final words of Eric Garner:** M. NourbeSe Philip, "The
G(a)sp," 40.

89   **What is *Sabe* in my own language?:** Contingencies of Care,
"Ga(s)p: Writing as Reparative Care [conversation between
M. NourbeSe Philip and Leanne Betasamosake Simpson],"
June 12, 2020, YouTube video, https://www.youtube.com
/watch?v=B3w_hwAhQd8.

90   **The legal decision *Gregson v. Gilbert* documented:** https://
torontoreviewofbooks.com/2014/04/in-conversation-with-m
-nourbese-philip/

92   **"The First Water is the Body":** Natalie Diaz, *Postcolonial Love
Poem* (Minneapolis: Graywolf Press, 2020), 46.

92   **The Great Lakes are my internal organs:** This is not my own
poetics: "[the] Great Lakes are my internal organs" is an
Anishinaabeg teaching that I've heard repeatedly from Elders

and Knowledge Holders over the past two decades.

93 **current manifestations of anti-Blackness, fungibility and colonialism:** Syrus Marcus Ware and Giselle Dias (Niigaanii Zhaawshko Giizhigokwe), "Revolution and Resurgence: Dismantling the Prison Industrial Complex Through Black and Indigenous Solidarity," in *Until We Are Free: Reflections on Black Lives Matters in Canada*, eds. Rodney Diverlus, Sandy Hudson, and Syrus Marcus Ware (Regina: University of Regina Press, 2020), 41.

94 **There is no justice in Land Back if we are silent:** Manu Karuka, "Black and Native Visions of Self-Determination," *Critical Ethnic Studies* 3, no. 2 (Fall 2017), 79.

94 **have led to incommensurability:** See Tiffany Lethabo King, Jenell Navarro, and Andrea Smith, *Otherwise Worlds: Against Settler Colonialism and Anti-Blackness* (Durham, NC: Duke University Press, 2020).

95 **treaties with the deer and beaver nations:** Simpson, *Dancing on Our Turtle's Back* and *As We Have Always Done: Indigenous Freedom Through Radical Resistance* (Minneapolis: University of Minnesota Press, 2017); see also Doug Williams, *Michi Saagiig Nishnaabeg: This is Our Territory* (Winnipeg: ARP Books, 2018); and Leanne Betasamosake Simpson, *A Short History of the Blockade: Giant Beavers, Diplomacy, and Regeneration in Nishnaabewin* (Edmonton: University of Alberta Press, 2021).

95 **to live in a way that brings forth more life:** I have written extensively about this in *Dancing on Our Turtle's Back* and *As We Have Always Done.*

95 **The global climate emergency:** Françoise Vergès, "Racial Capitalocene."

96 **who have always been doing this work:** Glen Coulthard,

"Once Were Maoists: Third World Currents in Fourth World Anti-Colonialism, Vancouver, 1967–1975," in *Routledge Handbook of Critical Indigenous Studies*, eds. Brendan Hokowhitu, et al. (New York: Routledge, 2020), 378–391.

96 **the fact that Black people exist today is not a miracle:** Cedric J. Robinson, *Black Marxism*, 171.

97 **the tragic killing of Abdirahman Abdi:** See http://www .justiceforabdirahman.ca/CommunityConference/.

98 **no charges would be laid:** Sandy Hudson, "Indigenous and Black Solidarity in Practice: #BLMTOTentCity," in *Until We Are Free*, 295.

PART THREE

106 **revolutionary Black-led but multiracial uprisings:** I wrote about this in "Police Abolition/Black Revolt," *TOPIA: Canadian Journal of Cultural Studies* 41 (Fall 2020), 70–78.

109 **in periods of mass unrest:** Cedric J. Robinson, "The First Attack is an Attack on the Culture," in *Cedric J. Robinson: On Racial Capitalism, Black Internationalism, and Cultures of Resistance*, ed. H. L. T. Quan (London: Pluto Press, 2019), 71

109 **In order for movements to be successful:** Robinson, "The First Attack," 73.

111 **the end of ICES and the CBSA:** ICES is an acronym for Integrated Customs Enforcement System and CBSA is an acronym for Canadian Border Services Agency.

111 **the opposite of a carceral society:** Beverly Bain, reflecting on my words and work in a public conversation on police abolition.

112 **LAEN:** LAEN is short for Latinx, Afro-Latin-America, Abya Yala Education Network.

113 **to fantasize that we would be reading:** Mariame Kaba, "Yes, we

mean literally abolish the police," *The New York Times,* June 12, 2020, https://www.nytimes.com/2020/06/12/opinion/sunday/floyd-abolish-defund-police.html.

115 **like getting a car but with no steering wheel:** Kikélola Roach (@RyeSJChair), "My Dad was one of the founding members of the Black Action Defense Committee . . ." (tweet), Twitter, July 24, 2020, https://twitter.com/RyeSJChair/status/1286847240720527360?s=20.

118 **hundreds of community members gathered at the border:** "Border authorities shut down Akwesasne crossing," CBC News, June 1, 2009, https://www.cbc.ca/news/canada/montreal/border-authorities-shut-down-akwesasne-crossing-1.776854.

119 **Indigenous resistance struggle has been foundational:** Leanne Betasamosake Simpson, "Oshkimaadiziig, The New People," in *Lighting the Eighth Fire: The Liberation, Resurgence, and Protection of Indigenous Nations,* ed. Leanne Betasamosake Simpson (Arp Books: Winnipeg, 2008), 13.

120 **a five-hundred-year-old struggle:** Ashanti Alston, qtd. in Robyn Maynard, *Anarchists in the Black Panther Party & the Black Liberation Army: Original Interviews from No One Is Illegal Radio* (Montréal: No One Is Illegal, 2010), 5.

123 **a majority of white New Yorkers:** David Sirota, "Polls Showed Many Americans Opposed to Civil Rights Protests in the 1960s. But That Changed," *Jacobin*, June 12, 2020, https://www.jacobinmag.com/2020/06/polls-george-floyd-protests-civil-rights-movement.

124 **we do not have to live this way:** Audre Lorde, in *I am your sister: Collected and Unpublished Writings of Audre Lorde*, eds. Rudolph P. Byrd et al. (Oxford: Oxford UP, 2009), 163.

128 **queering land-based education:** "Queering Land-Based
Education with Manulani Meyer and Melody McKiver"
(webinar), Dechinta Centre for Research and Learning Covid-19
Webinar Series, March 25, 2021, https://www.dechinta.ca/covid19.

128 **opportunity for unfolding coherence or awareness:** Ibid. See
also https://www.awakin.org/calls/341/dr-manulani-aluli-meyer
/.

129 **Kanaka Maoli practices:** Noelani Goodyear-Ka'ōpua,
"Ku'oko'a, Independence," in *The Value of Hawai'i 3*, eds.
Noelani Goodyear-Ka'ōpua et al. (Honolulu: University of
Hawai'i Press, 2020), 17–21.

129 **to awaken, amplify, intensify:** "Queering Indigenous Land-
Based Education" (webinar), Dechinta Centre for Research and
Learning Covid-19 Webinar Series, March 25, 2021, https://
www.dechinta.ca/covid19.

129 **Fred Moten and Stefano Harney Revisit** *The Undercommons*:
"'Give Your House Away, Constantly'—Fred Moten and
Stefano Harney Revisit *The Undercommons* In A Time of
Pandemic And Rebellion (part 2)" (podcast), July 11, 2020,
https://millennialsarekillingcapitalism.libsyn.com/give-away
-your-home-constantly-fred-moten-and-stefano-harney.

129 **Moten and Harney's insistence on centring Black intellectual
pursuit:** Ibid, 13:40–14:17.

130 **generate knowledge through an endless process of asking:** Ibid.

130 **He goes on to explain homelessness:** Ibid.

132 **The sap boils down to sugar:** Simpson, *As We Have Always
Done*, 145–175.

134 **his work about resistance in Palestine:** See, for example, Joe Sacco,
Footnotes in Gaza (New York City: Metropolitan Books, 2006).

134 **the Dene ethic and law:** Joe Sacco, *Paying the Land* (New York City: Metropolitan Books, 2020).

135 **So yes, we are homeless:** "'Give Your House Away, Constantly,'" 13:40–14:17.

137 **relationships based on bodily sovereignty:** Winona LaDuke, *All Our Relations: Native Struggles for Land and Life* (Cambridge, MA: South End Press, 1999), 4, 132.

138 **those very first treaties:** Simpson, *As We Have Always Done*, 9–10.

138 **a refusal of nation as a Westphalian nation-state:** See also Adom Getachew's *Worldmaking After Empire: The Rise and Fall of Self Determination* (Princeton: Princeton University Press, 2019).

138 **too contaminated and corrupted by states:** Dionne Brand, *Listening for Something . . . Adrienne Rich and Dionne Brand in Conversation* (National Film Board of Canada, 1996), 55 min. See https://www.nfb.ca/film/listening-for-something-adrienne-rich/.

139 **refuse the opposition of Blackness and Indigeneity:** See https://millennialsarekillingcapitalism.libsyn.com/give-away-your-home-constantly-fred-moten-and-stefano-harney; Sefanit Habtom and Megan Scribe, "To Breathe Together: Co-Conspirators for Decolonial Futures," Yellowhead Institute (web page), June 2, 2020, https://yellowheadinstitute.org/2020/06/02/to-breathe-together/; and Tiffany Lethabo King, *The Black Shoals: Offshore Formations of Black and Indigenous Studies* (Durham, NC: Duke University Press, 2019).

139 **the novel coronavirus exposes once again:** Dionne Brand, "On narrative, reckoning and the calculus of living and dying," *Toronto Star*, July 4, 2020, https://www.thestar.com/entertainment/books/2020/07/04/dionne-brand-on-narrative-reckoning-and-the-calculus-of-living-and-dying.html.

141 **thinkers like Hortense Spillers, Katherine McKittrick, and El**

Jones: Robert Nichols' Chapter 4 in *Theft as Property!* reminded me of this and was influential in this letter: Nichols, *Theft is Property! Dispossession and Critical Theory* (Durham, NC: Duke University Press, 2020).

141 **rejecting the kind of desecration:** Robert Nichols' edits and revisions of this chapter were crucial in the development of this paragraph.

145 **Indigenous thinkers like Sarah Hunt:** Sarah Hunt, "Violence, Law and the Everyday Politics of Recognition" (lecture, Native American and Indigenous Studies Association, Washington, DC, June 6, 2015).

146 **their New-World, diasporic plight marked a *theft of the body*:** Hortense J. Spillers, "Mama's Baby, Papa's Maybe: An American Grammar Book," *Diacritics* 17, no. 2 (1987), 64–81.

147 **Where life is precious:** Rachel Kushner, "Is Prison Necessary?: Ruth Wilson Gilmore Might Change Your Mind," *New York Times Magazine*, April 17, 2019, https://www.nytimes.com/2019/04/17/magazine/prison-abolition-ruth-wilson-gilmore.html.

148 **co-conspiratorial work with Native communities:** Samudzi and Anderson, *As Black As Resistance*, 31.

PART FOUR

153 **I've been arguing in my mind:** Editorial, "Let's save some outrage for treatment of Indigenous people," *Toronto Star*, June 12, 2020, https://www.thestar.com/opinion/editorials/2020/06/12/lets-save-some-outrage-for-treatment-of-indigenous-people.html.

157 **not a hundred policemen:** Dionne Brand, "100 musicians at Jane and Finch?" *Toronto Star*, June 4, 2007, https://www.theglobeandmail.com/arts/100-musicians-at-jane-and-finch/article686737/.

160 **something to wipe out:** "Revolutionary Hope: A Conversation Between James Baldwin and Audre Lorde," *The Culture* [originally published in *Essence*, 1984], http://theculture.forharriet.com/2014/03/revolutionary-hope-conversation-between.html. Emphasis added.

160 **the unrelenting and merciless brutality:** James Baldwin, "An Open Lettter to My Sister, Miss Angela Davis," *The New York Review,* November 19, 1970, https://www.nybooks.com/articles/1971/01/07/an-open-letter-to-my-sister-miss-angela-davis/.

164 **Black people's freedom:** Fanon, *The Wretched of the Earth*, 167.

165 **serve only the needs of national elite:** Ken Saro-Wiwa, *A Month and a Day & Letters* (Banbury, Oxfordshire: Ayebia Clarke Publishing Limited, 2005), 124.

165 **'Ogonis' being subject to environmental and cultural destruction:** Ibid., 123

166 **Undocumented Africans:** Thuso Khumalo, "South African Minister: Ban Migrant Workers From Informal Jobs," *Voice of America (VOA) News*, October 10, 2019, https://www.voanews.com/africa/south-african-minister-ban-migrant-workers-informal-jobs.

166 **non-status Haitians in Bahamas:** "Bahamas deports 112 Haitians," *Jamaica Observer*, October 12, 2019, http://www.jamaicaobserver.com/news/bahamas-deports-112-haitians_177011; Jason Beaubien, "After Dorian, The Bahamas Cracks Down On Undocumented Haitians," NPR: *All Things Considered*, October 5, 2019, https://www.npr.org/2019/10/05/767572869/after-dorian-the-bahamas-cracks-down-on-undocumented-haitians.

166 **Our citizenship is everywhere precarious:** I would also like to credit William C. Anderson, who crafts a compelling case for Black statelessness and compels us to become *ungovernable*: William C. Anderson, *The Nation on No Map: Black Anarchism and Abolition* (Chico: AK Press, 2021).

167 **it is not only colonialism that is the enemy:** Howard Adams, *Prison of Grass: Canada From a Native Point of View* (Saskatoon: Fifth House Publishers, 1975/1993), 186.

168 **the United States as a settler colony:** Kwame Ture and Charles V. Hamilton, *Black Power: The Politics of Liberation in America* (New York: Vintage Books, 1967/1992), 191.

168 **mass national liberation struggles:** Robin D. G. Kelley, *Freedom Dreams: The Black Radical Imagination* (Boston: Beacon Press, 2002).

168 **In this period of radical experimentation:** Adom Getachew, *Worldmaking After Empire: The Rise and Fall of Self-Determination* (Princeton: Princeton University Press, 2019).

170 **an end to all restrictive practices towards minorities:** Claudia Jones, qtd. [1958] in Carole Boyce Davies, *Left of Karl Marx: The Political Life of Black Communist Claudia Jones* (Durham, NC: Duke University Press, 2008), 69.

170 **toward a world that could be free:** Claudia Jones, "American Imperialism and the British West Indies," in *Claudia Jones: Beyond Containment*, ed. Carole Boyce Davies (Banbury: Ayebia Clarke Publishing Limited, 2011).

170 **Her vision for liberated Black territories:** Claudia Jones, "'I was deported because . . .': An Interview with Claudia Jones by George Brown," in Davies ed., *Claudia Jones: Beyond Containment*. Jones' political life and thought is detailed

extensively in Davies, *Left of Karl Marx*. See also Bill Schwarz, "'Claudia Jones and the West Indian Gazette': Reflections on the Emergence of Post-colonial Britain," *Twentieth Century British History* 14, no. 3 (2003): 264-285.

171 **he was a Black radical exiled:** Carole Boyce Davies, "Deportable Subjects: U.S. Immigration Laws and the Criminalizing of Communism," *South Atlantic Quarterly* 100, no. 4 (2001): 949–966.

171 **little more than the old imperialist state:** C. L. R. James, *A History of Pan-African Revolt* (Oakland, CA: PM Press, 2012), 118.

172 **a home controlled by black people:** Alexis Pauline Gumbs, "'But We Are Not the Same': Generating a Critical Poetics of Diaspora," in *Audre Lorde's Transnational Legacies*, eds. Stella Bolaki and Sabine Broeck (Amherst and Boston: University of Massachusetts Press, 2015), 168.

173 **to refuse the state that refuses you:** This is a riff on Harney and Moten, *The Undercommons: Fugitive Planning & Black Study* (Chico, CA: AK Press, 2013)—"the right to refuse what has been refused to you."

175 **we need to protect the territory:** Anne Spice, qtd. in Christi Belcourt, "Wet'suwet'en Strong," *Canadian Art*, February 19, 2020, https://canadianart.ca/features/wetsuweten-strong/.

175 **we are our own liberators:** Ojore Lutalo (interview), in Maynard, *Anarchists in the Black Panther Party & the Black Liberation Army*, 10. This is also the title a book of prison writings by Black political prisoner Jalil Muntaqim: see J. A. Muntaqim, *We Are Our Own Liberators: Selected Prison Writings* (Oakland, CA: PM Press, 2010).

175 **what grounds my solidarity with you and yours:** Lethabo King, *The Black Shoals*.

183 **accepted into Anishinaabeg society as normal:** Simpson, *As We Have Always Done*, 124.

183 **2SQ people like Ozawendib:** Ibid.

184 **our physical bodies and our constructions:** Audra Simpson, "The State is a Man: Theresa Spence, Loretta Saunders and the Gender of Settler Sovereignty," *Theory & Event* 19, no. 4 (2016).

184 **Euro-Canadian heteropatriarchal marriages:** Simpson, *As We Have Always Done*, 124.

186 **chief and councillors are enmeshed in a colonial administration:** Bob Joseph, *21 Things You May Not Know About the Indian Act: Helping Canadians Make Reconciliation with Indigenous Peoples a Reality* (Port Coquitlam, BC: Indigenous Relations Press, 2018).

187 **They were to defuse any political organizing:** Victor Satzewich, "Indian Agents and the 'Indian Problem' in Canada in 1946: Reconsidering the Theory of Coercive Tutelage," *Canadian Journal of Native Studies* XVII, no. 2 (1997): 227–257.

187 **The Indian Act was often enforced by police:** James Daschuk, *Clearing the Plains: Disease, Politics of Starvation, and the Loss of Aboriginal Life* (Regina: University of Regina Press, 2013), 57 of e-book.

188 **well documented and horrific account:** This paragraph is a generalized summary of a complicated and long history, and is based upon the work of Daschuk in *Clearing the Plains*.

188 **European infectious disease:** Daschuk, *Clearing the Plains*.

188 **Indigenous children were being kidnapped by the state:** I first heard the Hon. Justice Murray Sinclair, who was appointed chair of the Truth and Reconciliation Commission of Canada, refer to Indigenous children in residential schools as human shields during a talk at Queen's University on March 27, 2015.

189 **the murder of Colten Boushie:** Gina Starblanket and Dallas Hunt, *Storying Violence: Unravelling Colonial Narratives in the Stanley Trial* (Winnipeg: ARP Books, 2020).

190 **eleven Indigenous children have died:** Kenneth Jackson, "11 Indigenous children died in last four months connected to Ontario's child welfare system," APTN National News, July 22, 2020, https://www.aptnnews.ca/national-news/11-indigenous -children-died-in-last-four-months-connected-to-ontarios-child -welfare-system/#disqus_thread.

190 **the outcomes of the foster care system are horrific:** Katie Hyslop, "How Canada Created a Crisis in Indigenous Child Welfare," *The Tyee*, May 9, 2018, https://thetyee.ca/News/2018 /05/09/Canada-Crisis-Indignenous-Welfare/.

191 **surveilled and monitored through the church:** *Reclaiming Power and Place: Final Report of the National Inquiry Into Missing and Murdered Indigenous Women and Girls*, 2017, Vol. 1a, 253, https://www.mmiwg-ffada.ca/final-report/.

191 **the imposition of a strict gender binary:** Simpson, *As We Have Always Done*, 95–145.

191 **This "total control" was key:** *Reclaiming Power and Place* Vol. 1a, 253.

192 **It is work that white settlers willingly take on:** Starblanket and Hunt, *Storying Violence*.

192 **two Nishnaabeg brothers being attacked and assaulted:** Jorge Barrera, "'Illegal assault' on First Nations brothers by police caught on video was racist, lawsuit alleges," CBC News, July 24, 2020, https://www.cbc.ca/news/indigenous/first-nations-police -video-lawsuit-1.5661097.

193 **The "Calls for Justice" in the final section of the report:** *Reclaiming Power and Place: Final Report of the National*

Inquiry Into Missing and Murdered Indigenous Women and Girls, 2017, Vol. 1b, https://www.mmiwg-ffada.ca/final-report/.

195 **feminist-inflected internationalism:** Angela Davis, "An Interview on the Futures of Black Radicalism," in eds. Johnson and Lubin, *Futures of Black Radicalism*, 242.

195 **all living things are precious:** As Ruth Wilson Gilmore says, "Where life is precious, life *is* precious." See Kushner, "Is Prison Necessary?"

196 **regenerate Indigenous communities and mitigate the trauma of colonialism:** https://blacklivesmattertoronto.ca/defund-the-police/.

197 **It requires a radical divestment:** Saidiya Hartman, interview by Catherine Damman, *Artforum*, July 14, 2020, https://www.artforum.com/interviews/saidiya-hartman-83579.

198 **we have not been absorbed:** Manu Karuka, "Black and Native Visions of Self-Determination," *Critical Ethnic Studies* 3, no. 2 (Fall 2017): 79.

199 **undoing the system of colonialism in Canada:** Brand, "On narrative."

PART FIVE

204 **Europe's colonization of Africa:** Manthia Diawara and Ngugi-wa Thiong'o, *Sembène: The Making of African Cinema* (Third World Newsreel, 1994), 60 minutes.

205 **the state targets our communities:** Ingrid Waldron, *There's Something in the Water: Environmental Racism in Indigenous and Black Communities* (Halifax and Winnipeg: Fernwood Publishing, 2018).

205 **toward the destruction of the land:** I am including multinational corporations in this use of the word "colonizer," given

the role they play in facilitating neo-colonial, extractive, unidirectional economic relationships between the global north and the global south.

205 **Forcible concessions of land:** *Lagos Standard*, September 5, 100, 3. Available from Readex: African Newspapers: The British Library Collection, https://www.readex.com/products/african -newspapers-british-library-collection.

206 **technologies of forcible confinement:** Florence Bernault, "The Shadow of Rule: Colonial Power and Modern Punishment in Africa," in *Cultures of Confinement: A History of the Prison in Africa, Asia, and Latin America*, eds. Frank Dikotter and Ian Brown. (Ithaca: Cornell University Press, 2007).

206 **violence was tacitly and at times formally supported:** Yves Engler, "Canada's contribution to British colonial violence in Kenya," *rabble.ca*, September 16, 2015, https://rabble.ca/blogs /bloggers/yves-engler/2015/09/canadas-contribution-to-british -colonial-violence-kenya.

207 **Haitian police and prisons:** Kevin Walby and Jeffrey Monaghan, "'Haitian Paradox' or Dark Side of the Security-Development Nexus? Canada's Role in the Securitization of Haiti, 2004– 2009," *Alternatives: Global, Local, Political* 36, no. 4 (November 2011): 273–287.

207 **a *global* economy of racial and gendered subordination:** Jean-Philippe Robillard, "Quebec police officers engaged in sexual misconduct in Haiti," CBC News, April 6, 2016, https://www.cbc.ca/news/canada/montreal/quebec-haiti-police -sexual-misconduct-1.3523153.

207 **contain and confine much of the Haitian population:** Walby and Monaghan, "'Haitian Paradox.'"

208 **they wanted the land *and* the labor:** Robin D. G. Kelley, "The

Rest of Us."

208 **homogenized for transformation into capital:** In the post-1492 Americas, the property regime was totalizing in its scope, encompassing not only the fruits of the earth, but human flesh, with Black women's wombs sutured to the property regime, rendered factories of dispossession and reproduction. Nothing was off-limits. See Jennifer L. Morgan, "*Partus sequitur ventrem*: Law, Race, and Reproduction in Colonial Slavery," *Small Axe: A Caribbean Journal of Criticism* 22, no. 1 (March 2018): 1-17.

208 **non-exploitative relationships to the land:** Justin Hosbey and J. T. Roane insist that we centre the "insurgent knowledge" produced by Black communities at the forefront of environmental disaster, which must impact how "we conceive of futures outside of destruction." See Hosbey and Roane, Black Ecologies Initiative, https://ihr.asu.edu/black-ecologies. Their work on "Black Ecologies" is crucial to work on Black peoples' relationships to land and land protection globally, and I am indebted to their labour in forwarding this concept.

208 **The protection of ecosystems and the earth:** Ike Okonta and Oronto Douglas, *Where Vultures Feast: Shell, Human Rights, and Oil* (New York: Verso, 2003), 146.

208 **land as a marketable commodity:** Julius K. Nyerere, *Ujamaa: Essays on Socialism* (Dar es Salaam: Oxford UP, 1977), 7.

209 **Because imperialism is the arsonist:** Thomas Sankara, "Imperialism is the Arsonist of our Forests and Savannas" (speech transcript), February 26, 2018, https://anti-imperialism .org/2018/02/26/thomas-sankara-imperialism-is-the-arsonist -of-our-forests-and-savannas/. Thanks to Harsha Walia for introducing me to these words.

209 **fighting against both intolerable labour conditions:** Greg Marinovich, "How the women of Marikana are taking on the World Bank," *Al Jazeera*, July 4, 2015, https://www.aljazeera.com /news/2015/07/women-marikana-world-bank-150703100250209 .html.

209 *stay human:* Winona LaDuke, "How to Be Better Ancestors," Center for Humans and Nature, February 27, 2017, https:// www.humansandnature.org/how-to-be-better-ancestors.

209 **We are peoples of the lands:** I had originally, and mistakenly, attributed these words to Suzanne Césaire, having inscribed them into a notebook while taking copious notes from her assorted works in *The Great Camouflage*. To the best of my knowledge these words are my own, inspired by "The Malaise of a Civilization" in Suzanne Césaire, *The Great Camouflage: Writings of Dissent (1941–1945)*, trans. Keith L. Walker (Middletown, CT: Wesleyan University Press, 2012).

212 **He also used the public health State of Emergency:** Emma McIntosh, "Doug Ford government restores environmental protections it suspended amid COVID-19," *National Observer*, June 15, 2020, https://www.nationalobserver.com/2020/06/15 /news/doug-fords-government-restores-environmental- protections-it-suspended-amid-covid-19. On July 8, 2020, Bill 197—the provincial *COVID-19 Economic Recovery Act, 2020*— was introduced, and became law two weeks later. Not only did it do little for those most harmed by the pandemic—such as precaritized and unemployed workers—Indigenous groups, including Attawapiskat First Nation, denounced the bill because it involved changes to the Environmental Assessment Act that endangered, they argued, already weak protections for

the environment. See "Attawapiskat First Nation Denounces Ford's Undemocratic Environmental Risk: Statement on Bill 197 Changes to the Environmental Assessment Act," *Newswire*, July 30, 2020, https://www.newswire.ca/news-releases/ attawapiskat-first-nation-denounces-ford-s-undemocratic-environmental-risk-statement-on-bill-197-changes-to-the-environmental-assessment-act-850523046.html.

212 **the carceral state upholds the earth's devastation:** J. P. Antonacci, "Six Nations group occupying Caledonia construction site vows to stay despite court order," July 31 [updated August 12], 2020, https://www.thespec.com/news/hamilton-region/2020/07/31 /six-nations-group-occupying-caledonia-contruction-site-vows -to-stay-despite-court-order.html.

212 **the Prison Ecology Project:** Nation Inside, "Prison Ecology Project," https://nationinside.org/campaign/prison-ecology.

212 **prison expansion in Canada is increasingly marketed as "green":** Justin Piché, Shanisse Kleuskens, and Kevin Walby, "The Front and Back Stages of Carceral Expansion Marketing in Canada," *Contemporary Justice Review* 20, no. 1 (2017): 26–50.

212 **a new immigration detention centre being built:** Qtd. in Jon Milton, "This Is a Prison, No Matter What You Call It: Fighting the Construction of a New Migrant Detention Centre in Laval," *Briarpatch,* June 25, 2019, https://briarpatchmagazine .com/articles/view/this-is-a-prison-no-matter-what-you-call-it.

213 **the women's wing of Nova Scotia's largest jail:** "Inmate says conditions in Burnside jail 'absolutely horrid' during heat wave," CBC News, July 25, 2018, https://www.cbc.ca/news /canada/nova-scotia/jail-inmates-corrections-heatwave

-conditions-1.4761159.

213 **the injustices we face in prison:** "The prisoners at the Burnside jail are engaged in a non-violent protest; here is their statement" (transcribed by El Jones), *Halifax Examiner*, August 19, 2018, https://www.halifaxexaminer.ca/province-house/the -prisoners-at-the-burnside-jail-are-engaged-in-a-non-violent -protest-here-is-their-statement/.

216 **For the earth to live, capitalism must die:** I'm building here from the words of Indigenous revolutionary feminist group The Red Nation in "The Red Deal: Indigenous Action to Save Our Earth" ("For our Earth and relatives to live, capitalism and colonialism must die"), referencing Glen Coulthard in *Red Skin, White Masks* ("For Indigenous nations to live, capitalism must die"). The Red Nation, "The Red Deal: Indigenous Action to Save Our Earth," The Red Nation, April 2020; Coulthard (Minneapolis: University of Minnesota Press, 2014.)

217 **the importance of ephemeral expressions:** Thank you to La Tanya S. Autry for reading over previous versions of this section and providing feedback.

219 **rest as a form of resistance:** The Nap Ministry (website), https://thenapministry.wordpress.com/about/.

220 **historic documents around the commodification of black people:** "Atlanta-Based Organization Advocates For Rest As A Form Of Social Justice," NPR, *All Things Considered*, June 4, 2020 (transcript), https://www.npr.org/2020/06/04/869952476 /atlanta-based-organization-advocates-for-rest-as-a-form-of -social-justice.

221 **when i began this blog:** M. NourbeSe Philip, "Conditions of expanse: Algebraic equations of death" (blog post), *Jacket2*, July

16, 2020, http://jacket2.org/commentary/conditions-expanse. This is the last in a series of seven blog posts in Philip's series "Covidian catastrophes: deep, dark places of life" in *Jacket2*.

222 **The aim of the Residential School System was cultural genocide:** Will Sloan, "Plaque unveiling a step towards truth and reconciliation," Ryerson Today, July 10, 2018, https://www .ryerson.ca/news-events/news/2018/07/plaque-unveiling-a-step -towards-truth-and-reconcilliation/.

223 **"For the child taken, for the parent left behind":** Ibid.

223 **a satirical and exuberant rebuke:** "Look Closer: Kara Walker's *Fons Americanus*" (web page), TATE, https://www.tate.org.uk /art/artists/kara-walker-2674/kara-walkers-fons-americanus.

224 **the gorgeous actions of Black Lives Matter:** Kevin Ritchie, "Ryerson president responds to Black Lives Matter protest," *NOW Toronto*, July 21, 2020, https://nowtoronto.com/lifestyle /education/ryerson-president-responds-to-black-lives-matter -protest.

227 **Members of Not Another Black Life were up all night:** Angelyn Francis, "'No tenderness,' 'no listening.' Why supporters sat outside a police station overnight to greet Black trans woman Moka Dawkins after her arrest," *Toronto Star*, July 31 [updated August 1], 2020, https://www.thestar.com/news/gta/2020/07/31 /no-tenderness-no-listening-why-supporters-sat-outside-a -police-station-overnight-to-greet-black-trans-woman-moka -dawkins-after-her-arrest.html.

228 **that's been ingrained in them:** Moira Donovan, "Harvard research on Nova Scotia slavery ads aims to broaden under- standing of history," CBC News, Sept. 13, 2017, https://www .cbc.ca/news/canada/nova-scotia/harvard-research-slavery-ads

-newspapers-nova-scotia-1.4287485.

229 **the "seductions of assimilation":** Angela Davis, "An Interview on the Futures of Black Radicalism," interview by Gaye Theresa Johnson and Alex Lubin, in eds. Johnson and Lubin, *Futures of Black Radicalism*, 246.

229 **it's not possible to talk about abolition:** Robyn Maynard, *Policing Black Lives: State Violence in Canada from Slavery to the Present* (Halifax and Winnipeg: Fernwood Publishing, 2017), 233.

230 **83 percent of the COVID-19 cases:** Jessica Cheung, "Black people and other people of colour make up 83% of reported COVID-19 cases in Toronto," CBC News, posted July 30, 2020, https://www.cbc.ca/news/canada/toronto/toronto-covid-19-data-1.5669091.

232 **Circle breathing:** M. NourbeSe Philip, "The Ga(s)p," in eds. Kim and Miller, *Poetics and Precarity*, 40.

PART SIX

237 **The world is on fire, again:** Priya Krishnakumar and Swetha Kannan, "The Worst Fire Season Ever. Again," *Los Angeles Times,* September 15, 2020, https://www.latimes.com/projects/california-fires-damage-climate-change-analysis/.

237 **the University of California in San Francisco recently put out a guide:** UCSF Weill Institute for Neurosciences, "Coping with Wildfires and Climate Change Crises," https://psych.ucsf.edu/copingresources/wildfires.

238 **the cilia are also among the first to succumb:** Robert Webster Jr., "LiveSmart: COVID-19 and Its Impact on Lung Health," St. Peter's Health Partners (web page), April 10, 2020, https://news.sphp.com/wellness/livesmart-covid-19-and-its-impact-on

-lung-health/.

240 **outbreaks have ravaged North America's incarcerated populations:** Emma Newburger, "As blazes spread, Covid-19 in California prisons hits crucial inmate firefighting force," CNBC, August 21, 2020, https://www.cnbc.com/2020/08/21/california-fires-coronavirus-sidelines-prison-inmate-firefighters.html.

240 **limited California's ability:** Thomas Fuller, "Coronavirus Limits California's Efforts to Fight Fires With Prison Labor," *New York Times*, August 22, 2020, https://www.nytimes.com/2020/08/22/us/california-wildfires-prisoners.html.

240 **the brutal efficacy of the political choice:** Frank Carber, "As wildfires sweep through California, COVID-19 impacts the state's ability to rely on inmate fire crews," *Business Insider*, August 20, 2020, https://www.insider.com/california-facing-a-shortage-of-inmates-to-fight-wildfires-2020-8.

240 **"a tremendous resource":** Fuller, "Coronavirus."

241 **the sophisticated use of controlled burns:** Robin Wall Kimmerer and Frank K. Lake, "Maintaining the Mosaic: The Role of Indigenous Burning in Land Management," *Journal of Forestry* 99, no. 11 (November 2001): 36–41.

241 **It is the innocence which constitutes the crime:** James Baldwin, *The Fire Next Time* (New York: Vintage International, 1962/1993), 5–6.

242 **a gateway between one world and the next:** Arundhati Roy, "The pandemic is a portal," *Financial Times*, April 3, 2020, https://www.ft.com/content/10d8f5e8-74eb-11ea-95fe-fcd274e920ca.

242 **They are in constant motion:** Ann E. Tilley, et al., "Cilia Dysfunction in Lung Disease," *Annual Review of Physiology* 77 no. 1 (February 2015): 379–406.

242 **fifteen cycles every second:** F&P Healthcare, "Introduction to Mucociliary Transport Video Microscopy" (video), https://www.youtube.com/watch?v=HMdrhwEnY6M.

243 **I experienced her words like a line of bullets:** Toni Cade Bambara, *The Salt Eaters* (New York: Vintage Books, 1992), 1.

246 **to withdraw and be quiet within herself:** Paule Marshall, *Brown Girl, Brownstones* (Cheshire Stellar Books, 2013), 168–169.

248 **we are an unmitigated disaster:** Baldwin, *The Fire Next Time*, 89.

251 **History is a battle royal:** Saidiya Hartman, *Lose Your Mother: A Journey Along the Atlantic Slave Route* (New York: Farrar, Straus and Giroux, 2007), 192.

255 **a new Hanadagá:yas, or Town Destroyer:** Onondaga Nation, "US Presidents—Hanadagá•yas" (web page), https://www.onondaganation.org/history/us-presidents-hanadagayas/.

257 **The tentacles of racial capitalism:** Damman, Saidiya Hartman interview.

260 **my body and water and land are one in the same:** See the Women's Earth Alliance and the Native Youth Sexual Health Network's *Violence on the Land, Violence on our Bodies* report and toolkit at https://landbodydefense.wordpress.com/.

261 **Starting out as a single nucleus of desert dust:** Leanne Betasamosake Simpson, *Noopiming: The Cure For White Ladies* (Toronto: House of Anansi Press, 2020), 224–225.

261 **the delegation of Indigenous, Black and women of colour:** See their call for justice: "Justice for Palestine: A Call to Action from Indigenous and Women of Colour Feminists," https://www.jadaliyya.com/Details/24193.

261 **committed to the Boycott, Divestment and Sanctions (BDS) movement:** See also Angela Davis's analysis of the trip in "An

Interview on the Futures of Black Radicalism" in eds. Johnson and Lubin, *Futures of Black Radicalism*, 245–246.

262 **the monstrous destructiveness of settler colonialism's war:** Waziyatawin, "Malice Enough in their Hearts and Courage Enough in Ours: Reflections on US Indigenous and Palestinian Experiences under Occupation," *Settler Colonial Studies* 2, no. 1 (February 2013): 172.

262 **to link our struggles:** Steven Salaita, *Inter/Nationalism: Decolonizing Native America and Palestine* (Minneapolis: University of Minnesota Press, 2016).

262 **it is common to see Palestinian solidarity:** "Joint Solidarity Statement with 1492 LandBack Lane," *Spring*, August 11, 2020, https://springmag.ca/joint-solidarity-statement-with-1492 -landback-lane.

262 **the Wet'suwet'en mobilization:** Palestinian BDS National Committee (BNC), "Palestinians stand in solidarity with the Wet'suwet'en nation," February 13, 2020, https://bdsmovement. net/news/palestinians-stand-solidarity-wetsuweten-nation-and -land-defenders.

262 **Smaller grassroots organizations:** Families of Sisters in Spirit (FSIS), "Theland's Journey: Walk/Run for Children of Missing and Murdered Indigenous Women, Girls, Two-Spirits," https:// fsismmiw.wordpress.com/.

264 **give to others what has been gifted to you:** Niigaanwewidam Sinclair, "Miigwech in a Time of Crisis," *Winnipeg Free Press*, March 30, 2020, https://www.winnipegfreepress.com/special /coronavirus/miigwech-in-a-time-of-crisis-569229752.html.

264 **hope is a discipline, hope is a practice:** Mariame Kaba, "Hope Is A Discipline," interview by Brian Sonenstein and Kim Wilson,

Beyond Prisons episode 19 (podcast), *Stitcher*, https://www
.stitcher.com/show/beyond-prisons/episode/hope-is-a-discipline
-feat-mariame-kaba-53864185.

AFTERWOR(L)D

265 **Too bad for those who consider us mere dreamers:** Suzanne
Césaire, *The Great Camouflage*, 33.

266 **the Ghost Dance and the Wounded Knee massacre:** Much has
been written on Wovoka and the Ghost Dance movement, but
I'm especially persuaded by Mark Rifkin's reading as an
expression of Indigenous futurities and ways of being and
becoming that both decentres the massacre at Wounded Knee
and resists settler conceptions of time and space. See Mark
Rifkin, *Beyond Settler Time: Temporal Sovereignty and
Indigenous Self-Determination* (Durham, NC: Duke
University Press, 2017), 129–78.

267 **so intense is the belief:** "Think the End of the World is Coming,"
Chicago Daily Tribune, November 26, 1892.

271 **to find alternatives to the despairing sense:** Ruth Wilson
Gilmore, "Abolition Geography and the Problem of Innocence,"
in eds. Johnson and Lubin, *Futures of Black Radicalism*, 228.

271 **"freedom is a place":** Gilmore's concept of "freedom is a place"
was first articulated in print in Alexander B. Murphy, H. J. de
Blij, B. L. Turner II, Ruth Wilson Gilmore, and Derek Gregory,
"The Role of Geography in Public Debate," *Progress in Human
Geography* 29, no. 2 (2005): 178.

271 **for *thousands* of years before the era of colonialism:** This fact
is beyond dispute and should not require a footnote, and yet
most of my students balk when I make this very basic point. It

seems as though every few years there is a new book that puts to rest the prevailing myth that the world outside of Europe (and possibly China) was frozen in time, a reflection of John Locke and Thomas Hobbes's vivid imagination, and only the Europeans developed society, economies of scale, laws, and so on. The latest book, and arguably the best, is David Graeber and David Wengrow, *The Dawn of Everything: A New History of Humanity* (New York: Farrar, Straus and Giroux, 2021).

274 **opened up by the global pandemic:** Arundhati Roy, "The Pandemic Is a Portal," in *Azadi: Freedom. Fascism. Fiction.* (Chicago: Haymarket Books, 2020), 191.

INDEX

Métis in Space (podcast), 176
Métis Nation, 38, 187–88
Meyer, Manulani Aluli, 128–29, 139
Michi Saagiig Nishnaabeg (ON),
    46–48, 73, 231–32. *See also*
    Nishnaabeg peoples
migrants, 36, 68, 74–76, 105, 111,
    166. *See also* detention centres
miigwech (as concept), 263–64
Mi'kmaq Nation, 133–34
Milan, Kim Katrin, 97
mining. *See* extractive industries
Minneapolis, 109, 114
Minnis, Hubert, 166
mino-bimaadiziwin (continuous
    rebirth), 137, 257
Mire, Hawa Y., 97
missionaries, 183, 187, 189–90
MMIWG (National Inquiry into
    Missing and Murdered
    Indigenous Women and
    Girls), 191, 193–94
Modi, Narendra, 214
Mohawk Nation (Kanien'kehà:ka),
    79–80, 82, 94–95, 117, 133–34.
    See also Akwesasne; Oka crisis
Montreal (Tio'tia:ke)
    Blacks in, 31, 48, 63, 75, 114, 207
    policing in, 114, 123, 207
    protests in, 251–52
monuments, 103–4, 222–23, 224–25,
    250–52
Moore, Chantel, 49, 67
Morgan, Jas, 174–75
Moten, Fred, 129–30, 135–36, 139,
    141
Movement Defence Committee, 104
Movement for the Survival of the
    Ogoni People (MOSOP), 164
Mugabo, Delice, 228
Munk, Peter, 15
murder
    of Blacks, 48

    of Indigenous people, 13, 38,
      46–47, 189
    by police, 49, 67, 84, 97–98, 114–15
Museum of Contemporary Art
    Cleveland, 217–20
Mwase, George Simeon, 205

names and naming
    of institutions, 222, 223, 250–51
    of people, 47, 186
Namibia, 22, 41
Nanny Maroon, 252
Nap Ministry, 219–20
nation, 136, 138, 271. *See also*
    nation-states
nationalism, 169–72, 271
nationhood, 94–95, 136–37, 167
    in Africa, 164, 168
nation-states, 163
    Black-run, 164–65, 166
    vs. nations, 164, 171, 172–73
    and othered people, 156–57,
      158–61, 165–66, 172, 271–72
    refusal of, 33, 173–74
    rethinking, 161–62, 166
Native Alliance for Red Power
    (NARP), 96
Nelson, Charmaine, 227–28
Newbold, LeRoi, 112. *See also*
    Freedom School Toronto
New International Economic Order
    (Africa), 168
New York City, 123
Nichols, Robert, 140–41
Nigeria, 12, 16, 21–22, 164, 208
Nishnaabeg peoples, 85, 182. *See also*
    specific communities
    language of, 89–90
    and natural world, 179–80, 258–61
    in Ontario, 46–48, 73, 231–32
    way of life, 36–37, 179–81
Niumeitolu, Vaimoana, 217
Nkrumah, Kwame, 165–66

    224–25. *See also* X University

Sacco, Joe, 134
safety, 110–11, 123, 161
Salaita, Steven, 262
The Salt Eaters (Bambara), 237,
    242–43
Samburu people (East Africa), 84–85
Samudzi, Zoé, 84–85, 86–87, 94,
    147–48, 173
Sankara, Thomas, 209
San people (southern Africa), 84–85
Sansom, Jake, 38, 49
Saro-Wiwa, Ken, 164–65
Satgar, Vishwas, 21
Saunders, Mark, 124
schools. *See* education; residential
    schools; *specific schools*
science fiction, 151–52
self-determination, 136, 180, 197–98
Sembène, Ousmane, 203–4
settler colonies. *See* colonialism
sexism, 116, 185. *See also* women
sex workers, 40, 162, 166
Seychelles, 17
Shaheen-Hussain, Samir, 38
Shakur, Assata, 252
sharing, 95, 131–36, 167, 180
Sharpe, Christina, 259
Shooting Without Bullets, 218–19
Sikhala Sonke (South Africa), 209
Silva Forest Foundation, 209
Simpson, Ansley, 220–22
Simpson, Audra, 118, 173, 198
Simpson, Leanne Betasamosake
    as artist, 217–19
    in Kanehsatà:ke, 79–80
    letters to Robyn, 29–53, 79–99,
        128–48, 178–99, 217–33,
        255–64
    as mother, 51, 53, 273–74
Sipekne'katik First Nation (NS), 145

Sitting Bull, 223
Six Nations (ON), 120, 212
Sixties Scoop, 190
slave trade, 85, 86, 87, 146, 227–28
    impacts, 21–22, 23, 33, 93
Smoke, Ida, 50
social workers, 190, 191, 197
solidarity, 31–32, 120, 175–76
Solidarity Across Borders (Montreal),
    75
Somalia, 17
Somb'ke (Yellowknife), 38–39
South Africa, 23, 41, 166, 209
South America, 40. *See also* Brazil
sovereignty, 136, 165, 167, 272
Soyinka, Wole, 205
Spice, Anne, 174–75
Spillers, Hortense, 93, 141, 146
Spillet-Summer, Tasha, 218–19
Standing Rock Indian Reservation
    (US), 83
Stanley, Gerald, 189, 192
Star Trek, 151, 178
Stone Mountain (GA), 266–67
Strong, Amanda, 217
Sun Ra, 177

Tagaq, Tanya, 92
Tanzania, 12–13, 208
Tate Modern (London), 223–24
tent cities, 63–64, 98–99
Theft Is Property! (Nichols), 140–41
Thiong'o, Ngugi wa, 205
This Is an Honour Song (Simpson),
    79–80
Timmerman, John, 205
Tiny House Warriors, 39
Tolley, Bridget, 115
Tolley, Gladys, 115
Toronto, 14–16, 17–18, 45–48, 63–65
    Black Lives Matter in, 34, 68–69,
        97–98, 103–4, 112, 195, 224–25
    homelessness in, 40, 63–65